If a Pirate
I must be...

If a Pirate I must be...

THE TRUE STORY OF "BLACK BART," KING OF THE CARIBBEAN PIRATES

RICHARD SANDERS

Skyhorse Publishing

10 9 8 7 6 5 4 3 2 1

Picture credits:
Page 1 © British Library Board. All rights reserved.
Page 2 top © private collection/The Stapleton Collection/The Bridgeman Art Library
Page 2 – 3 bottom: artwork by Tony Bryan from NVG70, The Pirate Ship 1660 – 1730
© Osprey Publishing Ltd, www.ospreypublishing.com
Page 3 top, page 5 top, page 6 bottom: Mary Evans Picture Library
Page 4: The Buccaneers by Frederick Judd Waugh (1861 – 1940) © private collection/The Bridgeman Art Library
Page 6 bottom: artwork by Christian Friedrich Zincke, National Maritime Museum image no. PW3381
Page 8: © private collection/Peter Newark Pictures/The Bridgeman Art Library

Every effort has been made to trace the copyright holders of all material used in this book. In the case of any omission, please contact the publisher, who will make suitable acknowledgment in subsequent editions.
Text design by www.bluegumdesigners.com
Typeset by SX Composing DTP, Rayleigh, Essex
Maps created by Martin Lubikowski

Library of Congress Cataloging-in-Publication Data

Sanders, Richard.
    If a pirate I must be / Richard Sanders.
        p. cm.
    Includes index.
    ISBN-13: 978-1-60239-019-5 (alk. paper)
    ISBN-10: 1-60239-019-3 (alk. paper)
    1. Roberts, Bartholomew, 1682?-1722. 2. Pirates—Wales—Biography. 3. Pirates—Caribbean Area—History–18th century. I. Title.

G537.R74S36 2007
910.4'5—dc22
                                2007002418

Printed in the United States of America

CONTENTS

ACKNOWLEDGEMENTS

First and foremost I should like to thank my father for his help with French and Latin sources, for his advice and thoughts on the book and for instilling a love of history in me. I should also like to thank Phoebe Clapham and Natasha Martin, my two editors at Aurum, for their invaluable comments and suggestions; Celia Hayley at my agents, Lucas Alexander Whitley, for her help in the early stages of the project and Julian Alexander for his advice in the latter stages; the ever-helpful and efficient staff at the National Archive in Kew, as well as the staff at the British Library, the National Library of Wales, the National Archives of Scotland and the National Maritime Museum. Finally I would like to thank my wife Mary, without whose love and support this book would have been impossible, for reading and re-reading countless drafts, and my sons, Louis and Charlie, for indulging my endless pirate stories.

For Louis and Charlie, my own pirates

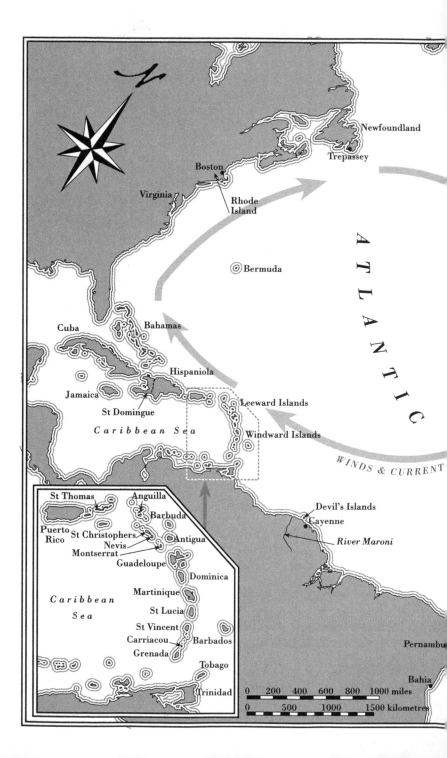

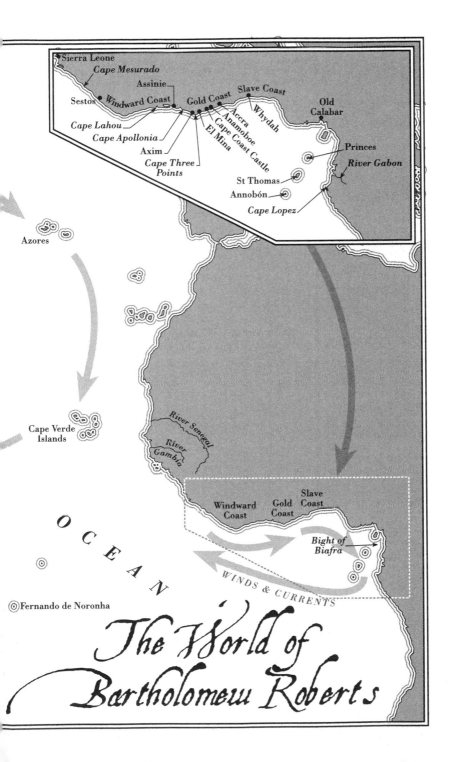

Sierra Leone
Cape Mesurado
Assinie
Windward Coast
Sestos
Gold Coast
Slave Coast
Old Calabar
Cape Lahou
Accra
Anamoboe
Cape Coast Castle
El Mina
Whydah
Cape Apollonia
Axim
Cape Three Points
Princes
River Gabon
St Thomas
Annobón
Cape Lopez

Azores

Cape Verde Islands

River Senegal
River Gambia

Windward Coast
Gold Coast
Slave Coast
Bight of Biafra

O C E A N

WINDS & CURRENTS

Fernando de Noronha

The World of Bartholomew Roberts

'In an honest service there is thin commons,

low wages, and hard labour; in this,

plenty and satiety, pleasure and ease,

liberty and power. No, a merry life and a

short one shall be my motto.'

Bartholomew Roberts

PROLOGUE

CAPTURE

Anamaboe, West Africa
6 June 1719

'HE ASKED WHICH OF THEM WOULD ENTER

WITH HIM AND TOLD THEM THAT HE WOULD

MAKE GENTLEMEN OF THEM ALL'

*T*HE MORNING OF 6 JUNE 1719 found Bartholomew Roberts still an honest sailor – a slaver rather than a pirate. Tall, dark and broad-shouldered, the thirty-seven-year-old Welshman was toiling on the deck of the *Princess*, a 140-ton ship from London, off Anamaboe on the Gold Coast of West Africa. It was hot and it was humid and he was tired, hungry and thirsty. Flies and malarial mosquitoes buzzed around his head, and his clothes steamed from the frequent tropical downpours. His one consolation was that the only people in the world whose lot was worse than his own were the shackled men and women he was hauling over the rail and on to his ship.

To the modern observer the scene Roberts beheld as he looked up and wiped the sweat from his eyes was a tropical paradise. The *Princess* was a solid, three-masted ship, around 85 feet from bow to stern and 20 feet across. Two other vessels bobbed on the waves nearby, the *Royal*

Hind, also of London, and a small sloop from Barbados called the *Morrice*. All three had their sails neatly furled and were riding at anchor. Around them buzzed a multitude of canoes endlessly shuttling merchandise and slaves to and from the shore. The African canoemen stood as they rowed, drums beating time, and the air rang to the sound of their singing.

Looking landwards Roberts could see a sandy, palm-fringed beach, about a mile and a half distant, and beyond that the mud huts of Anamaboe, a ramshackle town of a few thousand inhabitants. Nearby stood a small, dilapidated stone fort belonging to the British Royal African Company. Further inland was a cluster of five densely forested hills that served as a landmark for ships approaching the village from the west. Green parakeets with bright red heads and tails darted to and fro. It was a busy, industrious scene which would have warmed the hearts of the slave traders back in London, Bristol and Bordeaux. But for Roberts and everyone else there that day it was a scene of utter wretchedness.

The slaves, for the most part, had been brought from deep inland by African traders. Most had been captured in war, enslaved as punishment for crimes or sold into slavery by relatives — often their own parents — as a result of poverty. A minority, particularly children, had simply been kidnapped. Thousands died on the dreadful forced march to the coast. But the greatest trauma of all came at the moment of boarding the slaving vessels. Many had never seen the sea. And while slavery was a widespread, commonly understood — if brutal — feature of African life, sale to the white man aboard these enormous 'ships with wings' for transport across the seas was as traumatising and disorienting as abduction by aliens would be for us. It was a peculiarity of the slave trade that both Africans and Europeans believed the other to be cannibals. One slave later described how he stared in horror at the slavers with their 'horrible looks, red faces and long hair', convinced he was to be eaten.

The scene on the beaches was pitiful. The slaves were stripped naked and chained in twos to be hauled into the canoes by African boatmen. Many fell to the ground and clutched frantically at the sand. Others threw themselves out of the canoes to be drowned in the surf. 'We have . . . seen diverse of them eaten by the sharks, of which a prodigious number kept about the ships,' wrote a merchant captain in the 1690s. Once on board they often infuriated their captors by putting their head between their knees and simply dying. European captains were convinced they had mastered the art of holding their breath until they suffocated. More likely they were suffering from extreme shock. Others starved themselves to death in the belief that when they died they would return to their own country. The slavers broke their teeth and forced food down their throats. When this failed they mutilated the corpses, cutting off the head and scattering 'ye limbs about ye deck', the Africans believing only a whole body could return home.

History has little time for men like Bartholomew Roberts, their tormentors. But their brutality was in part a product of their own appalling conditions. Roberts knew that by the end of his voyage it was more likely he would be dead than one of the slaves. Studies later in the century showed that more than one in five of slaving crews died during the course of the three-legged journey between Europe, Africa and the West Indies, compared to one in eight of the slaves – although they, of course, were on board for only one leg of the journey.

Malaria, to which many Africans were immune, was the great killer. Seamen were painfully aware of mosquitoes – 'troublesome devils [which] would sting through clothes'. But the state of medical knowledge was primitive and no one had yet made the link between the insects and the disease. 'The fever generally begins with a violent pain and dizziness of the head,' wrote a Royal Navy surgeon, describing an outbreak off Africa in 1721. 'Nausea, vomiting and restlessness' followed. 'The patient . . . falls into excessive sweats . . . inextinguishable thirst and involuntary urinating.' Then came 'either delirium, convulsions or speechlessness . . . They commonly expired at four or five days.' The 'bloody flux', as dysentery was known, was also common, and sailors who went up the river estuaries often fell victim to 'river blindness'.

Surgeons were only carried on the larger slavers and had few treatments to offer other than bleeding. The common sailors had little time for them. 'The surgeons . . . are very careless of a poor man in his sickness,' wrote one sailor. They 'come to him and take him by the hand when they hear that he hath been sick two or three days, thinking that is soon enough, feeling his pulses when he is half dead'. Their medicines did 'as much good to him as a blow upon the pate with a stick'. Some captains ordered the doctors to prioritise the slaves who, after all, were worth money.

Roberts was third mate aboard the *Princess* – an officer, albeit a lowly one. He was a 'seasoned' sailor – that's to say he'd already survived a few trips to West Africa and had built up some immunity to the local diseases. But he and his shipmates knew that the period spent anchored off the African coast was the most dangerous part of the whole voyage for them. The rains were now beginning – great downpours, 'more like fountains than drops, and as hot as if warmed over a fire'. Their medical knowledge may have been rudimentary, but simple observation had taught them that this was when Europeans died in the greatest numbers. Roberts' commander, Captain Abraham Plumb, was desperate to fill the hold of the *Princess* with slaves and to get away. But the African traders at Anamaboe – 'desperate villains', so 'proud and haughty' that they demanded Europeans remove their hats to address them, according to one visitor – deliberately dragged out negotiations, forcing up the prices as both crew and cargo died aboard the ships.

The process of slave trading was slow, cumbersome and dangerous. There are almost no natural harbours in West Africa. The coast forms a long, straight line and slave ships were obliged to anchor off-shore in the 'road', as the sea in front of a port was called. They relied on the African canoes to transport them and their goods back and forth from the beach. 'There runs such a prodigious swell and surf that we venture drowning every time we go ashore and come off, the canoes frequently over-setting,' wrote one captain. Few Europeans were good enough swimmers to survive in these conditions, and sharks followed the canoes to land in the hope of a meal. A British surgeon described the following incident at Whydah, just down the coast from Anamaboe, in 1721:

> A canoe was going on shore from a merchant-ship with some goods, and in attempting to land, overset: a shark nigh hand, seized upon one of the men in the water, and by the swell of the sea, they were both cast on shore; notwithstanding which the shark never quitted his hold, but with the next ascent of the sea, carried him clear off.

And if the sharks and the mosquitoes spared them, there was a third peril that grew with every day Roberts and his shipmates stayed on the coast – slave revolt. Around one ship in ten experienced some sort of uprising, and they were most common when the slaves were still within sight of land. 'They fell in crowds on the English on the deck,' wrote one ship's captain, describing a revolt off Congo in 1699. The slaves 'stabbed one of the stoutest of the crew, who received fifteen or sixteen wounds with their knives before he expired. They next assaulted the boatswain, and cut the flesh round one of his legs to the bone, so that he could not move. Others cut the cook's throat to the windpipe and wounded three of the sailors, one of whom they threw overboard in that condition, from the forecastle, into the sea.'

This revolt, like most, was savagely suppressed. But even in open sea some slaves attempted to rebel. Unable to sail the ship, those that succeeded were generally condemned to drift to a slow death by starva-tion. But a few managed to navigate their way back to Africa and freedom. Roberts knew that if he died in mid-Atlantic his corpse would be slung overboard at night to conceal the crew's shrinking numbers, and growing vulnerability, from the slaves.

'I have never seen among my people such instances of brutal cruelty, and this not only shown towards us blacks but also to some of the whites themselves,' wrote one slave. Conditions aboard the slavers were appalling even by the standards of the merchant navy at that time. Water and food were always in short supply. Alexander Falconbridge, a ship's surgeon, described seeing a sailor rise at dawn to lick the dew from the roof of the chicken coop. On another voyage sailors were caught begging food from the slaves. Once the slaves were aboard the crew was generally obliged to sleep on the open deck with only a tarpaulin for cover. In poor weather, conditions quickly deteriorated for everyone on board. One sailor recalled watching 'steam coming through the gratings, like a furnace' from the slaves confined below. Nevertheless, it was not unknown for crewmen to open the hatches at night and lower themselves into this hell to escape the wind and the rain.

Slaving crews were generally drawn from the lowest class of seamen, and many were on board no more willingly than the slaves. 'The method at Liverpool [of getting sailors] is by the merchants' clerks going from public house to public house, giving them liquors to get them into a state of intoxication and, by that, getting them very often on board,' recalled one sailor. 'Another method is to get them in debt and then, if they don't choose to go aboard of such Guinea men then ready for sea, they are sent away to gaol by the publicans they may be indebted to.' Once off Africa, the men sometimes swam through shark-infested waters to Royal Navy vessels in order to escape – a rare example of voluntary impressment.

The captains regarded their men as 'the very dregs of the community', and treated them accordingly. The surgeon Falconbridge described one captain who forced a crew member to work for weeks with a heavy chain attached to a log wrapped around his neck for a minor misdemeanour.

He then flogged him till his back was raw and rubbed salt and cayenne pepper into the wounds. Afterwards 'a large Newfoundland dog was frequently set at him, which, thus encouraged, would not only tear his clothes, but wound him. At length, after several severe floggings, and other ill treatment, the poor fellow appeared to be totally insensible to beating, and careless of the event.'

An elderly seaman on the same ship had several of his teeth knocked out after complaining about his water allowance. 'Not content with this, while the poor old man was yet bleeding, one of the iron pump-bolts was fixed in his mouth, and kept there by a piece of rope-yarn round his head. Being unable to spit out the blood which flowed from the wound, the man was almost choked, and obliged to swallow it.'

When the ship finally docked in the West Indies a third victim of the same captain 'carried his shirt, stained with the blood which had flowed from his wounds, to one of the magistrates of the island and applied to him for redress'. But the slaves on the ship were bound for the magistrate's plantation and he was deaf to his pleas. The Royal African Company's own chief surgeon, conducting a survey of conditions aboard ships off West Africa in 1725, wrote that 'tyrannical oppression and want of necessities of life' were 'epidemical'.

Falconbridge, who was an abolitionist, was convinced brutality 'was the common practice of the officers in the Guinea trade'. It was in the nature of a trade which 'gradually brings a numbness on the heart and renders those who are engaged in it too indifferent to the sufferings of their fellow creatures', argued another campaigner. Captains had absolute power on board their ships. 'I am as absolute in my small dominions . . . as any potentate in Europe. If I say to one, come, he comes; if to another, go, he flies,' wrote one. All too often this power was combined with a sadistic temperament.

Brutality could serve a purpose. A large crew was necessary for security until the ship docked in the West Indies. But thereafter, with a cargo of sugar on board for the final leg of the journey back to Europe, many of the men were surplus to requirements. At that stage captains were often happy to see them desert, particularly if they were owed back pay. Others would sail away while part of their crew was ashore. These abandoned, emaciated seamen were a common sight on the docks of towns like Kingston in Jamaica where they lay side by side with the 'refuse slaves' who could find no buyers and were left to starve. Such was the example Bartholomew Roberts had been set by his social betters.

And there was one final peril that, again, was at its greatest while the ships were stationary off the African coast. It was this peril that, shortly after noon on 6 June, suddenly loomed before Bartholomew Roberts.

At some point between midday and one o'clock two large vessels approached Anamaboe from the west. Initially, as he paused work to peer at them through the shimmering heat haze, Roberts took them for slaving ships, and was irritated. It meant competition and would probably drag out his stay at Anamaboe. But they moved unusually swiftly through the water. And there seemed to be an extraordinary number of men on deck. They were also remarkably well armed. As they drew near he could pick out men crowding onto the forecastle, waving cutlasses and howling curses into the wind. Suddenly the lead vessel fired three guns and raised a black flag. They were pirates.

Their appearance sparked panic. The African canoes sped back to the shore. At the fort the tiny handful of emaciated soldiers frantically prepared to fire the guns. But the pirates knew they could take their time. They were well out of range, and could expect little resistance. The three slave ships were outnumbered and outgunned, and even if their captains wanted to resist, they knew it was rare for the starving, disease-ridden crews of slavers to fight to defend their masters' property. With the fire from the fort falling lamely short, all three quickly struck, or lowered, their colours, signalling surrender.

The pirates didn't even trouble to board them at first. Instead, the three ships were obliged to haul out their long boats and send delegations across. From the *Princess* a party of six was sent, headed by the second mate, John Stephenson. The pirate captain greeted them politely and quizzed them as to what the ship contained. Then boarding parties were dispatched and the looting began.

Aboard the *Princess* the liquor store was the first target. We can imagine what Roberts experienced over the next few hours through the description of Captain William Snelgrave, an English slaver whose ship had been plundered by this very same crew just a few weeks before.

> They hoisted upon deck a great many half hogsheads of claret, and French brandy, knocked their heads out, and dipped cans and bowls into them to drink out of. And in their wantonness threw full buckets of each sort upon one another. As soon as they had emptied what was on the deck they hoisted up more. And in the evening washed the decks with what remained in the casks. As to bottled liquor of many sorts, they made such havoc of it, that in a few days they had not one bottle left. For they would not give themselves the trouble of drawing the cork out, but . . . struck their necks off with a cutlass, by which means one in three was generally broke.

Most of the pirates were soon drunk. They turned their attention next to any loose valuables. From Roberts' commander, Captain Plumb, they took a £50 silver sword and a £4 silver watch. Then they ransacked the cabins of the senior officers, taking mainly items of clothing. Sartorial elegance was important to these men. Roberts and his shipmates had noticed immediately how well dressed the pirates were and their jewellery, embroidered silk vests and expensive white shirts rammed home a crude message to the impoverished seamen of the *Princess* – crime paid. Each of the boarding party was entitled to a new 'shift of clothes' from the prize. The effect was sometimes comical. 'I could not refrain laughing when I saw the fellows,' recalled one pirate victim in 1716, 'for they had, in rummaging my cabin, met with a leather powder bag and puff, with which they had powdered themselves from head to foot, walked the decks with their hats under their arms, minced their oaths, and affected all the airs of a beau with an awkwardness that would have forced a smile from a cynic.'

Next, the various specialists in the pirate crew came on board, one by one, and systematically stripped the ship of everything they needed. The cook helped himself to two casks of beef, the gunner looted the armoury and the carpenter looted his counterpart's tool box. On one ship seized by pirates in 1720 we are told that nothing 'was so much valued by the robbers as the doctor's chest, for they were all poxed to a great degree'. Cut off from access to ports or shipyards, pirates had to acquire everything they needed for their daily lives in this way. But the *Princess*'s cargo itself was left virtually untouched. Consisting of bulky trade items such as metal bars and textiles, it was of little use to them.

As the looting progressed a couple of Roberts' shipmates sensed an opportunity. The pirates had sent only a small party aboard. If they could overpower them and run the *Princess* under the protection of the guns of the fort they would be free. Taking advantage of the pirates' drunken state, they attacked, trusting their shipmates would leap to their aid. But the rest of the crew simply stood and watched, and they were quickly beaten into submission. Most, it seems, were less than enthusiastic about escaping. Indeed, for many, it was the pirates who represented salvation.

Many of the men now plundering their vessel had themselves served previously on slave ships. They saw themselves as the avengers of common seamen and it was the custom of the pirates to place captured captains on trial. They quizzed the crew on how they had been treated and if they felt a captain had been brutal and tyrannical he was punished, sometimes to the cheers of their men. A particular favourite was 'the sweat', described by a captain taken prisoner in 1724:

> Between decks they stick candles round the mizzen-mast, and about
> 25 men surround it with points of swords, penknives, forks and
> compasses in each of their hands: Culprit enters the circle; the violin
> plays a merry jig; and he must run for about ten minutes, while each
> man runs his instrument into his posteriors.

Captain Plumb of the *Princess* and the other two captains taken that day were lucky. There is no record of their being mistreated. But their encounter with the pirates cost them more than half of their men.

The pirate captain 'asked which of them would enter with him and told them that he would make gentleman of them all', the second mate, John Stephenson, later told the Admiralty. He met with an enthusiastic response. One of the first to join the pirate crew was John Eshwell, the *Princess*'s carpenter. He 'took an oath to be true to them', John Stephenson said, and seemed euphoric at his escape from the slaver, placing ribbons in his hat and putting on his best suit of clothes. He plundered Captain Plumb's cabin, and forced open Stephenson's sea chest, taking two hats 'of the value of ten shillings'.

A total of thirty-four other men followed him from the three ships. Some were coy. Not wanting to appear too enthusiastic in front of witnesses, they feigned reluctance. But the pirates were old hands at this game and were happy to oblige with a pantomime of force, beating them softly aboard with the flats of their cutlasses, winking as they swore and cursed. Most were as openly enthusiastic as Eshwell. For the pirates West Africa was one vast recruitment centre. A Royal Navy captain sailing these same waters a year later reported to the Admiralty that 'the men in general [were] ripe for piracy'. He left it for 'their lordships to judge . . . whether it be occasioned by the masters' ill usage or their own natural inclinations'.

But Bartholomew Roberts was not one of those who clamoured to take up the pirates' offer. The man who would become the greatest of all pirate captains was initially a reluctant recruit.

Officers were generally less willing to turn pirate than the common men. They had more to lose, less to gain. But mates like Roberts occupied a strange, ambiguous position in the power structure of the ship. Although officers by rank, they were closer to the crew in terms of class. They'd usually risen from being common sailors and were often more experienced seamen than their captain, which could make for a prickly relationship. Many were to be found among the leaders of mutinies and it would not have surprised anyone had Roberts accepted the pirate offer. It was another, more intangible factor, that inclined him against it – that of temperament.

Much of what we know about Roberts comes from a book entitled *A General History of the Robberies and Murders of the Most Notorious Pirates*, written in 1724 by Captain Charles Johnson. Johnson's identity is a mystery. But he had superb sources – including members of Roberts' crew – and there is some speculation he may even have been a pirate himself. He had an ambivalent attitude to his subject matter, veering continuously between admiration for their bravery and daring, and moral condemnation. His book is the bible of pirate historians and it devotes more space to Roberts than to any of his contemporaries. Johnson provides us with a vivid portrait of Roberts' personality. He makes clear that he was a sober, somewhat solitary man. He disliked alcohol – highly unusual among sailors – and preferred tea, which he drank constantly. And he had little taste for gratuitous violence. Above all, he was disciplined and intelligent. He couldn't have been more different from the pirate stereotype and, as he watched the pirates steadily drink themselves into a stupor as they looted the *Princess,* it's likely he felt a visceral revulsion against the apparent anarchy of pirate life.

But pirates were always desperately short of skilled officers. The middle-aged Welshman begged, pleaded and wept. But the pirate captain was adamant. Men 'he wanted [and] men he would have', he declared, 'for he intended to fight a piracy that gave no quarter'. Roberts was dragged aboard to join his more enthusiastic shipmates. As the sun set on 6 June 1719 he had swapped slaving for piracy.

1

THE BAPTIST AND THE PIRATE

'HE MADE A SHORT SPEECH, THE SUM OF

WHICH WAS A DECLARATION OF WAR AGAINST

THE WHOLE WORLD'

ARTHOLOMEW ROBERTS WAS BORN in the village of Casnewydd Bach, or Little Newcastle, in Pembrokeshire, in the damp, wind-swept south-western corner of Wales, in around 1682. It would be hard to imagine more of a backwater. A visitor in the early nineteenth century described it as 'a mean village, consisting of a few straggling houses, and a church of the very meanest fashion', and it was no more impressive in Roberts' day. The south of Pembrokeshire was agriculturally rich and English-speaking. But Roberts was raised in the poorer, more rugged, Welsh-speaking north.

The 1670 Hearth Tax assessment for Little Newcastle reveals a 'George Robert', who was either Roberts' father or grandfather. He had just one hearth, but it was made clear he was not a pauper, like many others in the village. A will by 'William Robert', certainly a relative and quite possibly Bartholomew's brother, written in Welsh in 1744, shows he had cash and cattle to dispose of – at least £45 and eight oxen, as well as a horse and saddle. He was described as a 'yeoman', indicating a farmer of some standing. But he was unable to write, signing only with a mark. Bartholomew himself was literate, but it's unlikely he'd had more than the most rudimentary education.

The family, then, was middle class, but in the context of a backward, rural society that was poor even by the standards of late seventeenth-century Britain. 'The vulgar here are most miserable and low as the rich are happy and high, both to an extreme,' wrote a visitor in 1684. Ireland lay just 50 miles across the St George's Channel and Pembrokeshire was subject to periodic waves of immigration, the Irish providing an impoverished, often resented bottom tier of the population.

The economy was dominated by cattle-rearing. George Owen, a local aristocrat, left a description of what may well have been Roberts' own childhood:

> I have by good account numbered 3,000 young people to be brought up continually in herding of cattle within this shire who are put to this idle education when they are first come to be ten or twelve years of age . . . They are forced to endure the heat of the sun in his greatest extremity, to parch and burn their faces, hands, legs, feet and breasts, in such sort as they seem more like tawny Moors than people of this land, and then the cold, frost, snow, hail, rain and wind. They are so tormented, having the skin of their legs, hands, face and feet all in chinks and chaps.

Roberts grew up with such a swarthy Welsh complexion that Captain Johnson described him as a 'black man'. Owen described the farming people of Pembrokeshire as 'very mean and simple, short of growth, broad and shrubbye, unacceptable in sight'. Roberts, described later in life as 'tall', 'large and stout', must have stood out as he grew to manhood.

By the 1740s at least some of the Robert family of Little Newcastle were fervent Baptists, playing a prominent role in the local chapel. It's likely Bartholomew Roberts was raised in the same faith and that this helped shape his disciplined, slightly puritanical personality. Little Newcastle had a Baptist meeting house as early as 1697 and we can be sure there was Baptist preaching in the area prior to this date during Bartholomew's childhood. He'd certainly have received little pastoral care from the established church. According to the Churchwarden's report of 1684 the parish church in Little Newcastle was very much 'out of repair' and there had 'not been one sermon preached within ye said parish church . . . within this three years last past'.

Bartholomew was not his real name. For a period in the middle part of his career as a pirate the records generally refer to him as 'John Roberts'. In the eighteenth century John was a common name among the Robert family of Little Newcastle and this was probably the name he was christened with. Pirates often adopted aliases and he may have taken the name 'Bartholomew' in honour of Bartholomew Sharp, a well known Buccaneer of the 1680s. One name he was never known by was 'Black Bart'. This was the title of a poem written in the twentieth century by the Welsh poet I.D. Hooson, which portrays Roberts, entirely inaccurately, as a British hero preying primarily on the Spanish. Over the years a strange confusion has arisen and this is now the name by which Roberts is referred to in all modern history books. Hooson was presumably picking up on Captain Johnson's description of Roberts' 'black' complexion. But this pantomime nickname was never applied to him in his own lifetime.

Roberts may have been driven from Little Newcastle by shortage of land. The late seventeenth century was a period of steady population growth and the English had abolished 'gavelkind' – the traditional Welsh practice of dividing up inheritances amongst all the sons in the family – in the Act of Union of 1535. Perhaps William Robert, the man who left behind the Welsh-language will, was the older brother and inherited the family farm. Or perhaps Roberts simply had a romantic, roving frame of mind and was eager to escape the drudgery of rural life. Pembrokeshire had a tradition of sending its sons to sea and it's likely that as a child Roberts was regaled with tales of piracy. In the latter part of the sixteenth century and the early part of the seventeenth south-western Britain was infested with pirates, particularly the Welsh coastline from Cardiff to Milford Haven. Small-scale, generally local, piracy was an extension of the wrecking and smuggling industries, preying on the everyday goods being shuttled to and from the tiny ports along the coast. It enjoyed widespread popular support and often had sponsors among the local gentry. John Callis, the most famous Welsh pirate of the time, often sold his ill-gotten gains in the village of Carew in Milford Haven, just a few miles south of Little Newcastle. Piracy in British waters was stamped out in the early seventeenth century. But tales of hidden coves and desperate cut-throats doubtless lingered in local folklore and helped fill the dark evenings of Roberts' youth.

Although Little Newcastle itself was an inland village there were plenty of opportunities for a young man wanting to make his living at sea. A few miles to the north lay the port of Fishguard which sent fishing vessels out into the Irish Sea. More likely he looked south to the town of Haverfordwest in the Milford Haven estuary. With a popu-lation of over 2,000 it was rapidly becoming one of the most important trading centres in Wales. From here fleets of small coastal vessels exported the product of South Wales's primitive but rapidly expand-ing coal industry. Most went to Bristol and from Bristol the whole world was open to a young man.

His date and place of birth aside, all we know about Roberts prior to his capture at Anamaboe is that at some point shortly before he had served as mate aboard a sloop out of Barbados. By then he would have already been an experienced deep-sea sailor and accustomed to a life of ceaseless, unremitting toil. His existence at sea was governed by the 'watch system', which required the crew to work in alternating, four-hour shifts. The late seventeenth-century mariner Edward Barlow left a vivid description of what this life of constant sleep deprivation meant.

> When we went to take our rest, we were not to lie still above four hours; and many times when it blew hard were not sure to lie one hour, yea, often we were called up before we had slept half an hour and forced to go up into the maintop or foretop to take in our topsails, half awake and half asleep, with one shoe on and the other off, not having time to put it on: always sleeping in our clothes for readiness; and in stormy weather when the ship rolled and tumbled as though some great millstone were rolling up one hill and down another, we had much ado to hold ourselves fast by the small ropes from falling by the board; and being gotten up into the tops, there we must haul and pull to make fast the sail, seeing nothing but air above us and water beneath us, and that so raging as though every wave would make a grave for us: and many times in nights so dark that we could not see one another, and blowing so hard that we could not hear one another speak, being close to one another.

It's unlikely Roberts had spent his entire career on merchant ships. For much of his life Britain had been at war against France, in the War of the Grand Alliance from 1689 to 1697 and the War of the Spanish Succession from 1702 to 1713. Both required a massive expansion in the manpower of the Royal Navy.

It was common for sailors to switch constantly between merchant ships and the Royal Navy. In times of peace there was little to choose between them. Wages were broadly similar. And while the workload was less on naval vessels, because of the larger crews needed on fighting ships, the discipline was harsher, if less erratic. But this changed dramatically in times of war. The massive influx of men into the Royal Navy, and consequent shortage of sailors, meant wages on merchant ships doubled. In the Royal Navy they remained static and the crew's share of any prize money was generally a pittance. 'Who would serve his King and Country and fight and be knock'd o' the head at 24 shillings per month that can have 50 shillings without that hazard?' asked Daniel Defoe, rhetorically, in 1697. Not surprisingly, men weren't exactly clamouring to do their patriotic duty, and the authorities were forced to resort to the press gang.

The press was difficult to enforce on land. Men would hide or resist, particularly in the colonies. In Port Royal, Jamaica, the mob was 'ready on all occasions, to knock any of the Officers of ye King's Ships on the Head, who shall attempt doing their Duty [of impressment] there', according to one official. But it was more effective at sea, and the press tenders often lurked in the Channel to seize men en masse from returning merchant ships, sending them straight back out to sea. 'It is a very bad thing for a poor seaman when he is pressed in this manner,' one sailor complained, 'for if he have a wife and children he is not suffered to go to see them, nor to go and look after his wages,'

It's inconceivable Roberts went through his career without at some point serving in the Royal Navy, either voluntarily or as a forced recruit. Most sailors first took to the sea between the ages of twelve and sixteen and Roberts may have served initially as a 'powder monkey', ferrying gunpowder between the powder room and the guns during the War of the Grand Alliance. Service in the Royal Navy would have given him many things – experience of working in large, disciplined, well-organised fighting vessels, a knowledge of the culture and operating methods of the Navy and perhaps an anger at the press and a resentment of brutal naval captains to go alongside his experiences in the merchant navy. Above all, it would have given him experience of combat.

It may be that he had also served on privateers. These were

freelancers who operated in times of war with 'letters of marque', or 'commissions', authorising them to attack enemy shipping. Discipline on privateers was slacker and the potential rewards for ordinary seamen in terms of prize money greater. Many were little more than pirates.

If Roberts' career had been dominated by war, it had been shaped too by the sudden arrival of peace. Following the end of the War of the Spanish Succession in 1713 the Royal Navy downsized from 49,860 men to 13,475 men in just two years. For a time this was partially compensated for by a post-war boom in trade. But by 1715 there was mass unemployment. Wages in the merchant navy were slashed in half and conditions of service deteriorated sharply.

Records from Admiralty courts capture the tension of the period. One sailor in 1715 threatened to cut his captain's ears off 'and challenged him to go on shore and fight him' during an argument about unpaid wages. Another, in 1721, told his captain he could 'kiss his arse' in response to an unpopular order. Such behaviour was generally brutally punished. A safer tactic was the 'round robin', a list of grievances signed by the entire crew in circular fashion so that no ringleaders could be identified. But these too were often ignored by captains who knew the scarcity of work left the men with little option but to knuckle under.

Many crews felt they had no option but open revolt. Of the fifty-eight mutinies recorded on merchant vessels in the first half of the eighteenth century, forty-eight took place between 1715 and 1737 and twenty-one between 1718 and 1723. Most took place off West Africa or in the Caribbean and they were often brutal affairs. In 1725, during a mutiny aboard the *George*, Michael Moor declared he 'would make the sun and moon shine through' the bodies of the captain and senior officers. 'Damn you, you Dogs, I'll hang you when you are dead,' he told them. Three of the officers were murdered and Moor placed a rope around the chief mate's neck and hoisted his corpse upon deck. This mutiny, like many others, ended in the crew taking to piracy. But in the period after 1713, for the most part, sailors were powerless before the arithmetic of the labour market and Roberts' own fate – a highly experienced and capable seaman reduced at the age of thirty-seven to serving as third mate in the least attractive branch of the merchant navy – was probably typical.

This, then, was the man who stood upon the deck of the pirate ship that sweltering afternoon at Anamaboe in June 1719. Born between the folds of the hills in South Wales he had seen the world. He'd watched the dolphins chase the flying fish along the coasts of Africa. He'd seen hurricanes sweeping across the Caribbean. In all likelihood he'd weathered the storms about the two great Capes and voyaged into the Indian and Pacific Oceans. He'd listened to the roar of the broadsides in the sea battles against the French. He'd seen life and he'd seen death. But he had little to show for it. He had no wife or children and no permanent home. His few possessions were gathered together in a sea chest down in the hold of the *Princess*. And, at thirty-seven, he knew his best years as a seaman were behind him. It was common for sailors to slip back down the career ladder as their physical strength declined and all he had to look forward to was an old age of increasing hardship and deprivation. Aware of his own abilities, he could be forgiven for being an angry and a bitter man. It was only his temperament that prevented him enthusiastically embracing the life of a pirate.

It's possible Roberts knew the pirate captain who had captured him. He was called Howel Davis and he came from Milford in

Pembrokeshire, a few miles to the south of Roberts' birthplace. He'd later lived in Bristol and, like Roberts, had served as a mate aboard the slavers.

Davis was a *bon viveur*, a lover of wine and women, a romantic and, in some ways, attractive figure, far closer to the pirate stereotype than Roberts himself. He became involved in piracy after his ship, the *Cadogan*, was seized off Africa by the pirate Edward England. Some of England's crew had previously served under the *Cadogan*'s skipper, Captain Skinner and, according to Captain Johnson's *General History of the Pirates*, they wreaked a brutal revenge. 'Ah, Captain Skinner! Is it you?' cried his old boatswain on seeing him. 'I am much in your debt, and now I shall pay you all in your own coin.' They tied him up, then pelted him with glass bottles, 'after which they whipped him about the deck, till they were weary, being deaf to all his prayers and entreaties'. Finally they shot him through the head.

The story may be exaggerated. Although generally reliable about Roberts, Johnson occasionally repeated wild rumour in his chapters on other pirate leaders and we should not accept every tale of pirate atrocity that has come down to us at face value. Davis himself – and later, Roberts – never treated captains with this degree of brutality, and, far from repelling him, Davis's encounter with England left him with a taste for a life of piracy. Shortly afterwards he made his way to the Caribbean, determined to enlist in a pirate crew.

The Caribbean had been the heartland of Atlantic piracy for 150 years. It was men like Francis Drake and John Hawkins who first exposed both the fabulous wealth and the vulnerability of the Spanish superpower. In the seventeenth century the gentlemen adventurers of the Elizabethan era were replaced by one of the strangest groups ever to grace the history of the Americas. They originated on the island of Hispaniola, today divided between Haiti and the Dominican Republic. The Spanish had abandoned their settlements in the impoverished north of Hispaniola in 1605 and it became a magnet for the flotsam and jetsam of the Caribbean – runaway slaves, escaped servants, mutinous soldiers and sailors; anyone with a reason to hide. They lived deep in the forests and survived by hunting pigs and the cattle which had been introduced by the Spanish, and had proliferated and run wild. They smoked the meat over an indigenous type of wooden barbecue known as a 'boucan', and so they became known as 'Buccaneers'.

Most were English or French Huguenots and they were united by an intense hatred of the Catholic Spanish. They called themselves the Brethren of the Coast and developed a unique society, democratic and egalitarian. They knew each other only by *noms de guerre,* each having undergone a baptism as they entered the tropics which they claimed freed them from all previous obligations. Their strangest practice was that of living in male couples. Together they would disappear into the forests for between six months and two years, emerging – unwashed, dressed in skins and covered in blood – only to sell meat and hides to passing ships.

Harried by the Spanish, by the 1630s many of the Buccaneers were already turning to piracy. They carried with them on to the high seas the democratic culture of the forests. Captains were elected and booty divided in common – a stark contrast to Drake and Hawkins. But, like Drake and Hawkins, these ragged bandits enjoyed the tacit support of the English, French and Dutch governments, who saw in them a cheap, risk-free way of prising open the Spanish monopoly in the New World.

Between 1655 and 1671 the Buccaneers sacked eighteen cities, four towns and more than thirty-five villages around the Caribbean, as well as capturing countless ships. In the last great raid of this period, on Panama in 1671, the Buccaneer leader Henry Morgan sailed at the head of a confederation of no fewer than thirty-eight ships and 2,000 men, English, French and Dutch. They needed 175 mules to carry their booty back to the coast.

But their success was their undoing. By the 1680s the Northern European powers had established formal colonies in the Americas and were more interested in trade than plunder. The Buccaneers had served their purpose and soon the British were hanging them with as much enthusiasm as the Spanish. When the great Buccaneer haven of Port Royal in Jamaica was destroyed by an earthquake in 1692 it marked the end of an era.

But this proved only the beginning of what has become known to history as the Golden Age of Piracy. Far from retiring into decent obscurity, over the next thirty years the bandits of the Caribbean extended their activities down to Brazil, across to West Africa, and into the Pacific and the Indian Oceans. These men shared the strange, democratic culture of the Buccaneers. But they were true outlaws, preying on the shipping of all nations, and hunted by the ships of all nations – 'the enemies of all mankind', as they were legally defined.

The two wars between 1689 and 1713 absorbed much surplus manpower. But each was followed by an explosion of piracy as navies downsized and the privateers were called in. After 1715 the Spanish compounded the problem by driving hundreds of logwood cutters out of the British settlement in the Bay of Campechy in Mexico. Another of those curious, all-male communities which dotted the early colonial Americas, the settlement was a haven for desperadoes of all kinds. Most instantly 'turned pirates and infested our seas', according to an exasperated British official.

As Howel Davis looked about for a pirate crew to join in the early part of 1718 his eyes turned towards the Bahamas, the chain of hundreds of tiny islands which lay to the north-east of Cuba. A labyrinth of narrow channels, shifting cays and submerged sandbanks, they had replaced Hispaniola and Jamaica as the main pirate haven in the Caribbean. Although they were formally a British colony, there had been no government there since they were sacked by the Spanish ten years before and by 1718 it was estimated there were up to a thousand pirates living there, 'all subjects of Great Britain and young, resolute wicked fellows'. The famous pirate Blackbeard, who would be killed off North America later that year, had initially been based here. There was even a sail-maker's widow who made a living stitching black flags, for which she was paid in brandy.

But when Howel Davis arrived looking for a crew to enlist in he found he was out of luck. Spurred into action by the frantic appeals of the British colonies in the region the government in London had finally decided to act against this nest of thieves.

The man they'd chosen for the job was a former privateer, Captain Woodes Rogers, who had led a famous expedition around the world between 1708 and 1711. Rogers was as tough as any of the men he'd been sent to confront. In a battle off the coast of Mexico in 1709 he'd lost part of his upper jaw to a musket ball but continued to issue orders by scratching with a quill pen on a piece of paper while spitting blood and teeth over the deck. Probably no one else could have succeeded in taming the pirates of the Bahamas, certainly not with the pitiful resources given him and the limited assistance he received from the Royal Navy. But Rogers was a man of tireless energy and determination.

He arrived at the ramshackle little town of Nassau on the main island of New Providence on 26 July 1718 with six ships and a company of soldiers. His policy was one of carrot and stick. With him he carried an Act of Grace from the King, offering a pardon to any pirate who surrendered before 5 September 1718. He was greeted by the sight of a ship blazing in the harbour and came under fire as some of the pirates hastily made their escape. But most were keen to accept the pardon. The majority had been privateers during the War of the Spanish Succession and they retained some of their old principles, a number of them refusing to attack English shipping. As Rogers came ashore they drew up their crews in two lines as a guard of honour, stretching from the port to the fort, and fired a salute over his head as he walked between them, by way of welcome.

Rogers was a shrewd judge of character and he quickly recruited a number of the leading captains to hunt down their former colleagues. Before the end of the year he was hanging pirates at Nassau. Mounting the gallows on 12 December 1718 one of them, Dennis Macarty, remarked bitterly that 'he knew the time when there were many brave fellows on the Island, who would not have suffered him to die like a Dog'. 'He exhorted the people, who were at the foot of the walls, to have compassion on him,' Johnson wrote, 'but however willing, they saw too much power over their heads to attempt anything in his favour.'

Rogers succeeded in temporarily reducing the level of piracy in the Caribbean. But within months many of those who had accepted the pardon were returning to their old profession, 'like the dog to the vomit'. Rogers had managed to deprive the pirates of a secure haven in the Bahamas, which was no mean achievement. But in the long term the effect was simply to disperse them. It's estimated there were soon over 2,000 pirates roaming the Atlantic, more than ever before.

Starved of supplies and geographically isolated from Britain's other Caribbean colonies, in September 1718 Rogers fitted out two sloops, the *Buck* and the *Mumvil Trader*, to buy goods and provisions from the Spanish colonies of Cuba and Hispaniola. This was illegal – officially Spanish colonies were allowed to trade only with the mother country – and the two ships were heavily armed. They were crewed with a combination of men brought across from Britain by Rogers and former pirates who'd taken up the pardon. Howel Davis, thwarted in his bid to join a pirate crew and now out of work, also found a berth.

A few days later, off the coast of Hispaniola, the *Buck*'s young surgeon, twenty-one-year-old Archibald Murray, was rudely awakened one morning by a blow from the flat of a cutlass. He looked up to see a number of the crew staring menacingly down at him. He leapt out of his hammock and ran to the captain's cabin, telling him 'he suspected that the crew had mutinied and they designed to have him in their power'. There were two pistols lying by the captain's bed and Murray picked them up. Handing one to the captain, he took up guard by the door. But when the mutineers barged in a few moments later the captain, slightly embarrassed, was forced to point out the guns were not actually loaded and the two men had no option but to surrender.

The mutineers – Davis among them – soon had both sloops under their command. They put the two captains and various other men who were reluctant to turn pirate aboard the *Mumvil Trader* and dispatched it to the Bahamas, although Murray himself, who was invaluable to them as a surgeon, was forced to stay. The remaining mutineers aboard the *Buck* then filled a large bowl of punch and convened a council of war. 'It was proposed to choose a commander,' Captain Johnson wrote. 'The election was soon over, for it fell upon Davis by a great majority . . . He made a short speech, the sum of which was a declaration of war against the whole world.' And so was born what would prove the most successful pirate crew in the history of the Caribbean.

Davis soon showed his ability as a commander. Spotting a French ship off Cuba a few days later, he ordered his men to attack. They were reluctant. The French vessel had 24 guns and around sixty men. The *Buck* was a mere sloop. Sloops were the standard vessel for small-time pirates operating in the Caribbean at this time. They varied greatly but were rarely more than 65 feet in length, 20 feet across, with a depth in the hold of around 9 feet. They had just one or, at most, two masts and rarely carried more than 12 guns. Packed with pirates they were sufficient to terrify most merchant men into submission. But the

Frenchman was better armed than most and Davis and his men were clearly outgunned. Davis decided to use cunning.

They'd taken a smaller French ship of 12 guns shortly before. He ordered the prisoners to put on white shirts and come up on the deck of this earlier prize and to hoist a dirty tarpaulin, which was the nearest thing they had to a black flag. Davis then boldly sailed the *Buck* alongside the larger French ship and raised his own black flag. The French captain, 'much surprised, called to Davis, telling him, they wondered at his impudence in venturing to come so near them', and ordered him to surrender. In reply, Davis ordered *him* to surrender, telling the Frenchman he was just waiting for his consort to come up before attacking, and warned him he would show no mercy if he resisted. At this point Davis's men aboard the first French prize fired a gun and the French captain, seeing the dirty tarpaulin and believing it to be a second pirate ship, struck his colours. Davis ordered him to come on board the *Buck* with twenty of his men and quickly clapped them in irons.

This set the tone for Davis's pirate career, which was marked as much by intelligence and cunning as brute force, qualities Roberts would later observe and imitate. Shortly afterwards the *Buck* headed across the Atlantic to St Nicholas in the Cape Verde Islands, owned by the Portuguese. There, posing as English privateers, they spent five weeks carousing with the local women before heading for the nearby Isle of May, where they took a number of prizes. By now the *Buck* was becoming crowded and Davis decided to 'trade up', switching to a ship from Liverpool that he'd taken, renaming it the *King James* and loading it with 26 guns. He then sailed for the coast of Africa, his crew now seventy strong. Arriving at Gambia he captured the small Royal African Company fort in the river there before heading down to Sierra Leone.

By now Davis's crew numbered 150 men and he was acting in concert with two other pirates he had encountered on the coast of

Africa – Jeremiah Cocklyn and a Frenchman called Captain La Bouche. At Sierra Leone the three pirate crews took thirteen prizes and it was here they came across William Snelgrave, captain of the slaver *Bird*, whose memoirs provide a vivid portrait of Davis and his crew just a few weeks before the capture of Roberts.

Snelgrave was originally taken by Jeremiah Cocklyn and received a beating from his men. It was a relief for him when he encountered Davis a few days later. He painted Davis as a sympathetic figure who claimed to be driven by a sense of injustice. Davis 'was ashamed to hear how I had been used by them', Snelgrave wrote, and said 'they should remember their reasons for going a pirating were to revenge themselves on base merchants, and cruel commanders of ships'. He suspected the 'ill-usage' Snelgrave had received was because he had ordered his crew to defend the ship, rather than surrendering. 'If he had had the good fortune to have taken me,' Davis told Snelgrave, 'and I had defended my ship against him, he should have doubly valued me for it.'

Snelgrave noted that all three of the pirate captains were Jacobites, backing the claim of the ousted Stuart dynasty to the throne of England over that of the Hanoverian King George I. Davis's ship was named after the would-be King James III and they even claimed, doubtless falsely, to have commissions from him. They regularly drank the Pretender's health and so were 'doubly on the side of the gallows, both as traitors and pirates', wrote Snelgrave. Other captives of Davis's crew also recalled them cursing King George, calling him a 'son of a whore' and a 'cuckoldy dog'. Jacobite politics were common among pirates at this time and were often used to lend a spurious legitimacy to their activities.

The three pirate crews left Sierra Leone at the end of April and headed east along the African coastline. When Bartholomew Roberts encountered Davis and his men a few weeks later at Anamaboe they were emerging from a period of turmoil. At the end of May Davis quarrelled with Cocklyn and La Bouche and the three crews agreed to separate. A couple of days later Davis came close to disaster off Cape Three Points at the western end of the Gold Coast. Spotting a large ship, he closed to engage what he thought was a harmless merchant vessel and found himself on the receiving end of a broadside which killed nine of his men. It turned out to be the *Marquis del Campo*, an East Indiaman from Ostend, with 30 guns and a crew of ninety. Davis returned fire, and a fierce fight followed, lasting from one in the afternoon until nine the next morning, when the Dutch finally surrendered. The pirates were still licking their wounds when they arrived at Anamaboe a few days later and it was the *Marquis del Campo* that was trailing in the *King James*'s wake when Roberts first caught sight of it.

With the capture of Roberts and the other thirty-four men on 6 June Davis was stronger than ever. As his men joyously plundered the liquor stores of the three ships that afternoon he was already considering trading up again. He set the Dutch crew of the *Marquis del Campo* free, but he kept their ship, intending to convert it for his own use later on, handing them the *Morrice* to return home. Then, as the sun set, he weighed anchor and headed east, riding a powerful coastal current, the *Marquis del Campo* now joined by Roberts' old ship, the *Princess,* and the *Royal Hind* in his growing flotilla of prizes.

BLADES OF FORTUNE

2

BIGHT OF BIAFRA
JUNE 1719

'NEVER DISPUTE THE WILL OF A PIRATE!'

artholomew Roberts remained a sullen, resentful presence aboard the *King James* for some time. He was not a prisoner. But he knew there was little chance of escape. A few days later Davis released the *Princess,* having plundered it of all he needed. As Roberts watched his old ship disappear over the horizon, he knew his chances of ever returning to his former life were disappearing with it. The pirates may have kept their distance from the tall, muscular Welshman as he stared moodily over the ship's rail. But they'd seen this before and they knew that the pleasures of pirate life had a way of wearing down even the most stubborn personality. Sure enough, it was not long before Roberts began to show the first stirrings of interest in the lives of the men around him.

He witnessed them take a prize for the first time on the very morning after his capture. A cry from the mast-top alerted the pirates to the presence of a sail on the horizon as dawn broke, just off Accra, and they gave chase. It proved to be another Dutch ship. The captain tried desperately to run ashore at the sight of Davis's black flag. But the pirates were too quick and they pulled alongside, firing a broadside. The Dutch struck their colours and called for quarter – or mercy – which was granted, it being a rule among Davis's men that quarter should always be given when asked for.

As at Anamaboe the pirates initially sent aboard a small boarding party to assess the prize. It turned out to be carrying a senior Dutch official and had £15,000 in cash aboard, an unusually rich haul. It's unlikely Roberts and the other new men from Anamaboe received a cut so soon after being captured. But the solitary Welshman watched with interest as the loot was divided among the rest of the crew. Each man received a share of close to £100. Just a day earlier Roberts had been on a salary of £2 a month.

From Accra the pirates headed out into open sea, bound for the Bight of Biafra, 500 miles to the east. They arrived at High Cameroon, close to the modern Nigeria/Cameroon border, around the middle of June and set about converting the *Marquis del Campo* for their own use, knocking down the bulkheads in the hold and clearing the decks of any unnecessary obstacles.

As the days passed Roberts paid close attention to the work going on around him and Davis's choice of vessels told him that he was among serious and ambitious pirates. Pirates tended to start out small scale, often beginning their careers in *periaguas*, a type of indigenous Caribbean canoe. They'd gradually work their way up as they seized larger and larger prizes. But in the Caribbean at this time only a minority operated in anything larger than sloops like the *Buck* that had been Davis's first vessel. Part of the purpose of coming to West Africa, with its large, ocean/going vessels, was to move up a league. The *King James* was a 'ship', a term which at this time was restricted to vessels with three or more masts and square rigs – rectangular sails that ran across the ship, rather than being fixed 'fore and aft' the mast as on a modern yacht. The *Marquis del Campo* was a larger version of the same thing. The pirates loaded it with 32 carriage guns and 27 swivel guns (small cannons fitted on stanchions) and renamed it the *Royal Rover.*

Roberts knew he was now part of a fighting force that was more than a match for any other ship they were likely to encounter on the African coast. And, like many other pirate captives before him, he was starting to realise that the apparent anarchy of pirate life concealed a surprising degree of organisation. He was soon made aware that Davis's crew was governed by a strict set of rules – rules that were startlingly democratic and egalitarian. Not only Davis but all other officers on board were elected. And Davis's authority was restricted to command in battle. All other decisions were put to a vote. At High Cameroon the pirates debated for some time whether to keep the *King James* and continue in two ships. It was only after a vote was taken that they agreed to abandon their old vessel.

During his period as a prisoner at Sierra Leone two months before William Snelgrave had been equally intrigued by the pirates' democratic power structures. He noted that officers on board were the same as on a man of war, with one exception – the quartermaster. This was a minor position in Royal Navy and merchant vessels but had been elevated to second-in-command among the pirates as a counterweight to the power of the captain. He 'has the general inspection of all affairs and often controls the captain's orders. This person is also to be the first man in boarding any ship they shall attack,' wrote Snelgrave. He was responsible for dividing up the loot on prizes they took, and also acted as a 'civil magistrate', arbitrating disputes and handing out punishments for minor offences. More serious offences were tried by a jury of twelve pirates.

For Roberts the physical environment of the ship emphasised its democratic nature. The removal of the bulkheads below deck was mainly to enable free movement in times of battle and mirrored the design of conventional warships. But Davis's men went further and also knocked down most of the cabin partitions in the rear of the ship. This broke down the great vertical class divide between officers in the rear and men in the f'o'csle that Roberts was accustomed to on merchant ships. At Sierra Leone, William Snelgrave had noted that 'everyone lay rough, as they called it, that is, on the deck, the captain himself not being allowed a bed'. Many pirates also cut down the raised quarterdeck at the rear of the ship and the f'o'csle at the front to make the deck 'flush', although this wasn't done on Davis's ships. Again, this was mainly a practical measure to remove obstacles in time of combat. But it also had the effect of levelling class distinctions since the quarterdeck was traditionally the preserve of the officers, the common sailors not being allowed to set foot on it.

There was none of the pomp and ceremony that accompanied power on a merchant ship. The 'Great Cabin' was preserved and set aside for the use of the captain, Captain Johnson wrote, 'but then every man, as the humour takes him, will use the plate and china, intrude into his apartments, swear at him, seize a part of his victuals and drink, if they like it, without his offering to find fault or contest it.' Invited to drink with his captors at Sierra Leone, Snelgrave found 'there was not in the cabin either chair, or anything else to sit upon, for they always kept a clear ship ready for an engagement. So a carpet was spread on the deck, upon which we sat down cross legged.'

The rules governing the ship were set out in a list of what were called 'articles', which Roberts, like every other new recruit, was obliged to sign within a few days of joining. These were drawn up by the crew as a whole and made fascinating reading for the new recruits. Davis's men pledged, according to a crew member, 'to stand by one another . . . to ye last drop of blood in ye piratical practice, and to share ye purchase according to ye custom of Blades of Fortune'.

The precise articles do not survive. But those of a number of other pirate crews do. They outlawed cowardice and desertion, established mechanisms for resolving disputes without bloodshed, and placed restrictions on gambling, which was often a source of discord among pirates. Some rules had an obvious practical purpose. Captain John Phillips' articles, drawn up in 1723, stipulated that no man 'shall snap his arms [pull the trigger of his musket], or smoke tobacco in the hold, without a cap to his pipe, or carry a lighted candle without a lanthorn' – a precaution against fire. Others were surprisingly chivalrous. 'If at any time we meet with a prudent woman, that man that offers to meddle with her, without her consent, to suffer present death,' read item nine of Phillips' articles.

Execution was usually by firing squad. Pirates at this time never made men walk the plank – one of the great pirate myths. The practice was introduced much later by Hispanic pirates off Cuba in the brief explosion of piracy that followed the end of the Napoleonic Wars, and was never used during the Golden Age. Most punishments were less extreme. They ranged from flogging (often 'Moses' law . . . forty stripes lacking one') to marooning on an island or some other desolate shore. Those guilty of minor misdemeanours might find themselves left on a large island with water and animals. Men guilty of more serious crimes were abandoned on a sandbar and were given a pistol and some shot so they could kill themselves if they chose to. Marooning was so common that pirates often referred to themselves as leading 'a marooning life' or even referred to themselves as 'marooners', the term capturing their sense of apartness from the rest of society.

Articles also laid out elaborate systems of injury insurance. This was a practice which dated at least back to the 1660s when the Buccaneer Alexander Exquemelin described a complex sliding scale:

For the loss of a right arm 600 pieces-of-eight [a Spanish gold coin, worth around four shillings and sixpence] or 6 slaves; for the loss of a left arm 500 pieces-of-eight, or 5 slaves; for a right leg 500 pieces-of-eight, or 5 slaves; for a left leg 400 pieces-of-eight, or 4 slaves; for an eye 100 pieces-of-eight, or 1 slave; for a finger of the hand the same reward as for the eye.

Captain George Lowther's articles, drawn up in 1721, were simpler:

He that shall have the misfortune to lose a limb, in time of engagement, shall have the sum of £150 and remain with the company as long as he shall think fit.

Invalids were given non-combatant jobs and, like Long John Silver in *Treasure Island,* many ended up as ships' cooks. Roberts probably saw a number of eye-patches and wooden legs among the men of Davis's crew, more than on a conventional ship where crippled men struggled to find work.

Above all, articles laid out the rules for the division of booty. Captain Lowther's were typical:

The captain is to have two full shares; the master is to have one share and a half; the doctor, mate, gunner, and boatswain, one share and a quarter.

The rest of the men received a single share. For Roberts, as he watched the loot being divided up following the capture of the Dutch ship at Accra, this egalitarianism was a stark contrast to the merchant ships he was used to, where captains earned four times more than ordinary seaman and, more importantly, owned a substantial share of the cargo. Pirates, of course, were not obliged to share any of their profits with owners back in Britain. Articles set out severe punishments for any pirate who withheld loot from the common pot.

For William Snelgrave at Sierra Leone one incident had high-lighted the unusual power structures aboard the three pirate ships that had captured him. He was sitting in his cabin on the *Bird* one day when the three captains – Davis, La Bouche and Cocklyn – came aboard. They'd been inspecting his books and had noticed he had three embroidered coats in the hold, part of his own private 'adventure of goods' – that is, goods he was trading on his own account. They asked him to produce them since 'they were going ashore amongst the negro ladies' and wished to dress up for their night on the town. Snelgrave had little option but to comply. There was a minor dispute when Cocklyn, 'who was a very short man', found the coat he'd chosen 'reached as low as his ankles'. But the other two pointed out that since 'the negro ladies . . . did not know the white men's fashions, it was no matter'. Cocklyn was placated and off they went.

When they returned the following morning there was uproar among the men. They had no problem with the three captains enjoying a night of debauchery. 'It is a rule among the pirates,' wrote Snelgrave, 'not to allow Women to be on board their Ships when in the harbour. . . . This being a good political rule to prevent disturbances amongst them, it is strictly observed.' By going ashore the captains had complied with this rule. It wasn't the women that were the problem. It was the coats.

'The Pirate Captains,' wrote Snelgrave, 'having taken these clothes without leave from the quartermasters, it gave great offence to all the crew, who alleged, "If they suffered such things, the captains would for the future assume a power, to take whatever they liked for themselves." So, upon their returning on board next morning, the coats were taken from them, and put into the common chest, to be sold at the mast' – in other words, to be auctioned among the whole crew. Snelgrave himself only narrowly escaped a beating from La Bouche's quartermaster for having supplied them.

This egalitarianism had been part of the culture of Caribbean pirates since Buccaneer times. But by 1719 the changing composition of pirate crews had given it a sharper edge. The earlier Buccaneers had been drawn from many walks of life. Henry Morgan, the most famous Buccaneer of all, was a soldier. Others were originally servants or planters who had only ever served at sea on Buccaneer vessels. Many of the later pirates in the Bahamas had originally been privateers. But the majority of these men retired following the royal pardon of 1718. After that pirate crews would be drawn almost exclusively from the ranks of the merchant navy and piracy would be coloured by the fierce class antagonisms aboard merchant ships – above all, the slavers.

Howel Davis saw himself as a Robin Hood figure, at war with an unjust social order, and he was not alone. According to Johnson, Captain Bellamy, who operated off the North American coast in 1717, harangued a merchant captain with the following speech:

> Damn ye, you are a sneaking puppy, and so are all those who will submit to be governed by laws which rich men have made for their own security, for the cowardly whelps have not the courage otherwise to defend what they get by their knavery . . . Damn them for a pack of crafty rascals, and you, who serve them, for a parcel of hen-hearted numskulls. They vilify us, the scoundrels do, when there is only this difference; they rob the poor under the cover of law, forsooth, and we plunder the rich under the protection of our own courage. Had you not better make one of us than sneak after the arseholes of such villains for employment?

When the captain declined to turn pirate Bellamy retorted:

There is no arguing with such snivelling puppies, who allow
superiors to kick them about deck at pleasure; and pin their faith
upon a pimp of a parson; a Squab who neither practices nor believes
what he puts upon the chuckle-headed fools he preaches to.

In 1720 the famous female pirate Mary Read defended the death
penalty for piracy on the unconventional grounds that, without it,
'every cowardly fellow would turn pirate . . . many of those who are
now cheating the widows and orphans, and oppressing their poor
neighbours . . . would then rob at sea and the ocean would be crowded
with rogues, like the land, and no merchant would venture out'.

Piracy had been transformed since the days of Francis Drake and
the gentlemen adventurers of the Elizabethan era. The men Roberts
now found himself among were almost exclusively lower class. If
anything they attacked Spanish shipping less than that of any other
nation, including their own, and they made no attempt to present
themselves as patriots. Theirs was a 'World Turned Upside Down' –
the title of a song in John Gay's play *Polly*, the sequel to *The Beggar's
Opera*, which was banned in 1729 for drawing a moral comparison
between pirates and the inner circle of Prime Minister Robert
Walpole.

Gay was not alone in using pirates as a vehicle for a political
critique. Captain Johnson pointed out that the careers of Blackbeard,
Edward England, Howel Davis and others coincided with the scandal
of the South Sea Bubble, when thousands of investors lost a fortune in
savings. 'Whatever robberies they had committed,' he commented,
'they might be pretty sure they were not the greatest villains then living
in the world.' Many modern historians have seen pirates as proto-
revolutionaries, consciously challenging the conventional values of
their day. And, as Roberts looked around him on the *Royal Rover*,
one of the most striking features of Davis's crew was that almost a third

of the men were black. This was common on pirate ships and has led some historians to portray them as pioneers of racial equality.

But, as the astute Welshman no doubt quickly observed, if all pirates were equal, some were more equal than others. This was true even among the whites. Davis's crew was divided into two groups – the 'Lords' and the 'Commons'. Drawn from the more experienced pirates, the Lords advised Davis on important questions. They received the same share of loot as the rest of the crew, but were granted certain privileges, such as the freedom to go ashore whenever they liked, and the right to talk directly to the captains of captured ships. This feature was unique to this particular crew. But in most pirate crews there was a pecking order, with the longest-serving pirates at the top, and the newest recruits at the bottom. Blacks came lower still. Pirates, like the ancient Athenians, were a slave-owning democracy.

The Africans Roberts observed working aboard Davis's ships did not sign the pirate articles, they took no share of the loot, and they were not permitted to bear arms. They 'were kept in an underling way', a witness said. As the Buccaneer Exquemelin's sliding scale for injury insurance suggests, most pirates saw blacks primarily as commodities. And this view was shared by the Admiralty, which almost always sold the blacks captured aboard pirate ships as slaves, rather than try them as pirates.

Davis's men were no more humane in their treatment of Africans than the brutal slave traders and plantation owners they preyed upon. A couple of weeks before Roberts was captured they seized a group of nine or ten local people in retaliation for the murder of some of their men ashore. They hanged them by their feet from the yard-arm. Then, inviting men from Cocklyn and La Bouche's vessels aboard to join in the sport, they used them as target practice, firing their muskets at them 'as if they set themselves apart to study cruelty', according to one report. For variation they slung the survivors into the sea and carried on shooting at them until they were all dead. Such were the men Roberts now found himself among. They were democratic and egalitarian through not abstract idealism but self-interest. Their rules were designed to protect their new-found liberties. But they were not a universal code of brotherhood.

But, if the presence of large numbers of blacks aboard did not spell liberty and equality, Roberts quickly realized that, for him, it meant something far more tangible – less work. The Africans in Davis's crew were 'trained up' and capable of doing 'the work of the ship', according to witnesses, indicating that some, at least, could go aloft and do the work of skilled sailors. This probably spared a proportion of the crew from the tyranny of the watch system. It's likely the privilege was closed to new recruits. But, for a man like Roberts who, in twenty years, had probably never enjoyed an unbroken night's sleep while at sea, the prospect represented an almost unimaginable luxury.

Beneath the talk of brotherhood and equality Roberts was also beginning to see other, more concrete, benefits to pirate life. It was certainly an easier, more comfortable existence than that aboard the slavers. But he soon realised that the true appeal, for many, was the raw power it placed in the hands of common men.

This was something William Snelgrave had observed at first hand in Sierra Leone. Cowering in his cabin one day while Davis's men looted his ship he became aware of a figure entering the room – one 'more sober than the rest', Snelgrave recalled. He helped himself to 'a good hat and wig . . . whereupon I told him . . . I hoped he would not deprive me of them, for they were of no service to him in so hot a country.' He was brutally cut short by a blow on the shoulder with the flat of the pirate's broadsword. The pirate grabbed him and hissed in his ear, 'I give you this caution, never to dispute the will of a pirate, for supposing I had cleft your skull asunder for your impudence, what would you have got by it but destruction?'

The pirate's name was Walter Kennedy and he would loom large in Bartholomew Roberts' life over the next few months. The exchange captures the arrogance of a large, powerful pirate crew at this moment in April 1719 with the entire West African coast at their mercy. For a merchant captain like Snelgrave, accustomed to wielding absolute power, it was terrifying. But for a low-ranking seaman like Roberts, accustomed to a life of impotence and humiliation, the impact was very different. The promise of unlimited alcohol may have held little appeal to his sober, disciplined personality. But power did.

By the time the *Royal Rover* pulled away from High Cameroon towards the end of June 1719 the seductive magic of pirate life was already starting to have its effect on the austere Welshman.

3

LEADER-
SHIP

PRINCES ISLAND
JULY 1719

'IT IS MY ADVICE THAT, WHILE SOBER, WE

PITCH UPON A MAN OF COURAGE . . . WHO BY

HIS COUNCIL AND BRAVERY SEEMS BEST ABLE

TO DEFEND THIS COMMONWEALTH'

S THE PIRATES PONDERED THEIR next move they knew there was not a single warship within 2,000 miles. The West African merchants had repeatedly petitioned the government for protection, most recently in February of that year, only to be told the Admiralty could not spare the ships. If they wished Davis and his men had a free run. But the coast was already in a state of alarm. 'There is an account that the pirates have done so much mischief on the coast of Guinea by plundering and destroying of ships that the company's forts are crowded with seamen, who will be glad to go on board ships without wages, that will give them passage for England,' reported the *Weekly Journal* in London. They knew there would be fewer and fewer ships putting to sea and another rampage along the coast would bring diminishing returns. They also faced competition from Cocklyn and La Bouche who were still in the region. They decided to seek fresh pastures – but not yet. First they would need to stock up for a long voyage and to do this they headed to Princes Island in the Bight of Biafra. It was a fateful decision.

On the mainland of Africa, European authority extended no further than the dilapidated forts clinging to the coastline. But the three islands of St Thomas, Princes and Annobón, nestling in the great bend of Africa, were fully fledged Portuguese colonies. They tended to be the final port of call for ships after they left the coast and before they headed across the Atlantic. Princes was the second largest of the three and rivalled the main island, St Thomas, as a trading centre. It offered an abundance of fruit and fresh meat and slavers were able to top up on supplies of yams, maize, rice, millet, beans and plantains, used to feed the slaves during the middle crossing. For sailors weary with the end-lessly crashing surf of the West African coast there was also the luxury of a bay.

The main town of St Antonio, where the pirates arrived at the start of July 1719, was a familiar sight to a slaver like Roberts. A neat, trim little settlement, it consisted of around 300 houses, built of clapboard with lattice windows and long balconies, laid out in two broad streets. There were two churches and a small fort on the right of the bay. All around stood high mountains, covered in dense jungle. The trees came right down to the waterside and, as the pirates entered the bay, they could hear the incessant screeching of brightly coloured parrots. 'Blue . . . with fine scarlet tails', they could 'talk and whistle distinctly, sooner than any others', according to a French visitor, and were much coveted by passing seamen – both slavers and pirates. The locals trapped and sold them. Like Long John Silver in *Treasure Island*, a number of the men in Davis's crew probably kept parrots as pets, perched perma-nently on their shoulders. The woods around St. Antonio also swarmed 'with apes and monkeys . . . full of tricks, and pleasant gestures and motions'. These too the locals caught and sold, despite their nauseous smell, receiving in return 'haberdashery wares, or old linen rags, or sailors' clothes, especially old hats'. An English surgeon who visited Princes Island in 1721, was also offered the bark of a local tree which he was told had the 'peculiar property of enlarging the Virile Member'. He was sceptical about whether this was 'in the power of any vegetable' but admitted he had seen 'sights of this kind among the negroes very extraordinary'.

As everywhere in West Africa, at least when slaving vessels were present, the waters swarmed with enormous sharks. 'I have several times observed', wrote one slaver, 'how quick they ran at any of the dead slaves we threw overboard, and made but one mouthful of a young boy that was so cast overboard.'

Visitors had little time for the locals. 'The Portuguese are unbounded in their lusts . . . They have most of them venereal taints,' wrote one. The bulk of the island's population of 3,000 were slaves, many imported from Brazil – a 'malignant, treacherous race', in the words of another visitor. Neither blacks nor whites were 'very com-mendable, either for honesty or good temper', he continued, and both would take 'the opportunity of stealing a foreigner's hat off his head, not only in the dusk of evening, but in the day time'. Everyone went armed and the small garrison comprised mainly of former prisoners from Portugal who had had their sentence of death commuted to service in the colonies.

It was the sort of place where the *Royal Rover* was unlikely to be asked too many questions so long as it brought business. But Davis knew he had to be careful. As they approached St. Antonio a sloop came out to enquire who they were. Davis told them his was a King's ship, characteristically embellishing the lie with the sly claim they were 'in quest of pirates, and that he had received intelligence there were some upon that coast'. The ruse was easy to pull off. Neither officers nor men wore uniforms aboard Navy vessels at this time and Davis had doubtless taken care to have all the appropriate flags, and ordered his men to dress down so as to pass as common seamen. The authorities believed him and the *Royal Rover* was piloted into the harbour. Davis completed the performance by firing a salute to the fort and ordering his men to hoist out the ship's boat, man-of-war fashion, and row him ashore.

He was met at the quayside by a guard of honour and swaggered up to the governor's residence with great pomp, playing his part with such verve that the governor agreed to supply him with everything he needed. A few days later the pirates were even able to plunder a French ship which came into the bay, Davis fobbing the governor off with the story that it had been trading with pirates, and that he had found several pirate goods on board.

Roberts and the rest of the crew now set about cleaning, or *careening*, the hull of their new ship. Toiling in the sweltering heat, they heaved the guns out of the hold and, using winches, lowered them over the side into the long boat, which ferried them ashore. All other stores and provisions were taken out and the ship was hauled up on to the beach and, using blocks and tackles, laid gently on its side. This placed enormous stress on the superstructure and the Admiralty generally preferred Royal Navy captains to wait until they were back in dry dock in England before cleaning. But pirates had little option. In tropical waters barnacles and seaweed quickly gathered and ships were also often attacked by the dreaded *teredo* worm, a soft-shelled mollusc equipped with fine saw teeth which laid a million eggs a year and could quickly honeycomb the hull of a ship on a long voyage. For men who depended on speed for their lives and livelihood, it was vital to clean and carry out repairs as often as possible. They vigorously set to work with scrapers, applying flame to the more stubborn accretions, while the carpenter and his mate replaced any rotten timbers. The hull was then caulked with a combination of tallow, oil and brimstone to prevent it leaking, before being heaved upright and turned over so the whole process could be repeated on the other side. It was dirty, exhausting work. But, as in the most things, the slaves bore much of the burden and the pirates were left free to enjoy themselves.

It was 'the custom of the pirates' to spend 'their time in a riotous manner of living' while careening, according to Johnson, and the alcohol was soon flowing freely. It had now been three months since his night of debauchery with the 'negro ladies' of Sierra Leone and Howel Davis was soon casting his roving eye ashore. Accompanied by fourteen of his men he 'walked up the country towards a village where the governor and the other chief men of the island kept their wives, intending, as we may suppose, to supply their husbands' places', wrote Johnson. But the women fled before they got there and, frustrated, Davis and his men were forced to return to the ship. The pirates got away with this escapade because no one in the inland village realised who they were. But their sheer extravagance soon gave them away.

'The people . . . discovered what they were by their lavishness, in purchasing fresh provisions with goods,' wrote Davis's former prisoner William Snelgrave, who visited Princes shortly afterwards, and was given an account of their visit by two Capuchin friars who lived there. The governor was soon perfectly well aware of the identity of his guests but 'he winked at it, on account of the great gains he and others . . . made by them'. But, as the pirates became more brazen, his advisors warned him he was courting disaster should the court in Lisbon get wind of his complicity. He therefore 'plotted to destroy Davis and his crew, in order to colour over what he had so basely permitted in allowing them a free trade'. For all the pirates' extravagance, there was also a dispute about payment for a batch of supplies, which Davis apparently told the governor the King of England would pay for. The governor, it seems, preferred ready cash.

One night, while the governor was still debating how to be rid of his unwelcome guests, a slave slipped over the side of Davis's ship into the warm waters of the bay and, somehow evading the sharks, swam ashore. He brought news that the pirates were plotting to lure the governor and his leading men aboard and hold them hostage for a £40,000 ransom. This forced his hand. The next day, when Davis came ashore to escort him aboard the *Royal Rover* for 'an entertainment', the governor prepared an ambush.

Davis had with him his first surgeon, his trumpeter and ten to twelve others. Arriving at the governor's residence they were informed by his major-domo that he was at his country house but would be back soon. They were invited to make themselves at home. But they were uneasy. Outside in the street the surgeon noticed that an armed crowd had gathered. 'I am sure we shall see no Governor today,' he murmured to Davis. They decided to return to their boat. But as they left the major-domo called on the crowd to fire at them. The surgeon and two more were killed on the spot. The trumpeter was hit in the arm, and, seeing Snelgrave's two Capuchin friars, ran towards them in the hope they would protect him. They took him in their arms to save him but one of the crowd cold-bloodedly shot him dead. Davis had been hit four times, including a shot through the bowels, but he staggered on towards the beach. A fifth shot brought him down. With his dying breath he managed to draw his pistols and fire at his pursuers, 'like a game cock, giving a dying blow, that he might not fall unrevenged', wrote Captain Johnson. According to Snelgrave, 'The Portuguese, being amazed at his great strength and courage, cut his throat that they might be sure of him.'

Most of the men with Davis were killed. Only Walter Kennedy, the man who had struck Snelgrave at Sierra Leone, and one other escaped, leaping into the sea from the top of a cliff. They were picked up by the ship's boat, which Davis had left on the beach with its crew, who had rowed to safety when they heard gunfire. When they arrived back at the ship and explained what had happened there was uproar.

Davis had been an able and popular leader and a man of great charm and charisma. The pirates' immediate thought was of revenge. But before embarking on any military action they would need to choose a new leader. And so, characteristically, they responded to disaster by filling a bowl of punch and calling a meeting.

Many of the most senior members of the crew had been killed with Davis. But if the governor hoped he had decapitated the pirates he was wrong. As the pirates crowded around below decks in the dimly lit steerage – their customary meeting place – there were still a number of 'Lords' among them, experienced men who had been with the crew since the original mutiny aboard the *Buck* at Hispaniola.

Walter Kennedy was one of them. He was just twenty-four but already a hardened pirate. Born at Pelican Stairs in the sailors' district of Wapping in East London, he was of Irish descent. He'd been apprenticed to his father as an anchorsmith but when his father died he abandoned the trade. He'd worked as a pickpocket and a housebreaker before following his roving inclination to sea. He served in his teens aboard men-of-war during the wars with France and fell in love with the stories of pirates he heard from his fellow seamen. 'Being told what lords the pirates in America were, and that they had gotten several whole islands under their own command, he coveted to be one of those petty princes,' according to a contemporary account of his life. He shipped aboard the *Buck* from London with Woodes Rogers in the spring of 1718 for the Bahamas. Arriving there he found many of the former pirates had been reduced to goat-herding. But one detail fascinated him. He noticed that they tied rich brocades from a looted ship between the horns of each animal to distinguish one herd from another. 'This, notwithstanding the miserable condition which in other respects these wretches were in, mightily excited the inclination Kennedy had to following their occupation.'

Captain Johnson described him as a 'bold, daring fellow, but very wicked and profligate'. At the Isle of May in the Cape Verde Islands in February 1719 he had been among a group of men who tortured the chief mate of one ship to get him to reveal the whereabouts of hidden money. They 'beat and wounded him in a barbarous manner', the mate later told Admiralty officials. They 'then put a rope about his neck and drew him up under the main top and kept him hanging there about a minute and let him down again and then put a rope around his head and tied it across his ears and twisted it until he was almost blind and insensible'. This torture, known as 'woolding', had been a pirate favourite since Buccaneer days.

Kennedy was not the only candidate for the captaincy of the *Royal Rover*. There was Thomas Anstis from Bridgewater in Somerset, illiterate, but a man who had quickly emerged as one of the dominant, and most ambitious, characters in the crew. There was Valentine Ashplant, a twenty-nine-year-old from the Minories in East London, a volatile and explosive personality, but a highly experienced seaman who had previously served as master on a brigantine (a two-masted vessel slightly larger than a sloop.) And then there was David Simpson, a thirty-three-year-old from North Berwick in Scotland, known ironically as 'Little David' because of his vast size, a harsh, brutal man who had the capacity to terrify many of his rivals into submission. But the crew chose none of these men. The man they chose was Bartholomew Roberts.

It's the most astonishing twist in Roberts' entire story. Originally a reluctant recruit, he had been just six weeks among them. Captain Johnson said he was chosen because he 'exceeded his fellows' in 'knowledge and boldness (pistol proof as they call it)' and could 'make those fear who do not love him', the key requirements of a pirate leader. He puts a slightly unlikely speech into the mouth of John Dennis, one of the senior pirates:

It is my advice that, while we are sober, we pitch upon a man of courage and skilled in navigation, one who, by his council and bravery, seems best able to defend this commonwealth, and ward us from the dangers and tempests of an unstable element, and the fatal consequences of anarchy: and such a one I take Roberts to be.

The speech, said Captain Johnson, was loudly applauded and the choice was approved by both Lords and Commons.

We have just one other explanation, but it's perhaps more informative. It was given a couple of years later by Walter Kennedy, who said, 'Roberts was chose not so much for his strength and courage (though he was large and stout, and most desperate) as for his cunning and knowledge of the seas, and quick guess at the bulk and force of any ship they came nigh.' Kennedy's and Captain Johnson's explanations both point to an unmistakeable conclusion – that Roberts was already well known to the pirates at the time he was captured. He can have done little since – they'd taken only two ships and neither had required a fight. It's significant that, at Anamaboe, the pirates had forcibly taken him, a thirty-seven-year-old third mate, while they left John Stephenson, the twenty-nine-year-old second mate. Roberts was clearly a familiar figure in the West African and Caribbean trades and the pirates already knew him to possess the qualities they looked for in a leader. He must also have had extensive experience in combat. Nothing else could explain so extraordinary a promotion.

For some in the crew Roberts' lack of experience as a pirate may have been a virtue. Pirate life was a process of constant negotiation, and occasionally conflict, between the captain, eager to increase his power, and the crew, fiercely jealous of their liberties. It may be senior members of the crew saw Davis's death as an opportunity to rein in the power of the captain by appointing a comparatively weak candidate. It may also be that Roberts was a useful compromise candidate between powerful, competing blocs. But if they had chosen Roberts because they thought he could be manipulated and controlled they had misjudged their man. In time he would become a pirate leader like no other.

As for Roberts, his election as leader completed his gradual seduction by the pirate way of life. 'Being daily regaled with music, drinking and the gaiety and diversions of his companions, [his] depraved propensities were quickly edged and strengthened, to the extinguishing of fear and conscience,' wrote Captain Johnson – an explanation that sounds a little simplistic. Nothing else we know about Roberts suggests he found drinking attractive. Roberts himself claimed, according to Johnson, that he was motivated by a desire 'to get rid of the disagreeable superiority of some masters he was acquainted with, and the love of novelty and change'. But it was his election as captain that was the key moment. 'He changed his principles, as many besides him have done,' wrote Johnson, because of 'preferment'. It was power that was the attraction. Roberts accepted command with the memorable words: 'I have dipped my hands in muddy water, and if a pirate I must be, 'tis better being a commander than a common man.'*

Pirate life was highly theatrical and Roberts' election was probably marked by an inauguration ceremony similar to that described by Johnson for pirate captains in the Indian Ocean at the start of the eighteenth century:

> They carry him a sword in a very solemn manner, make him some
> compliments, and desire he will take upon him the command, as he
> is the most capable among them . . . On his accepting the office, he
> is led into the cabin of state, and placed at a table, where only one
> chair is set at the upper end, and one at the lower end of the table for

---

*Captain Johnson followed the peculiar eighteenthcentury practice of using italics to indicate a direct quote, but then writing in reported speech. I have returned this quote to direct speech.

the company's quartermaster. The captain and he being placed, the latter succinctly tells him that the company having experience of his conduct and courage, do him the honour to elect him for their head . . . Then the quartermaster takes up the sword . . . puts it into his hand and says, 'This is the commission under which you are to act, may you prove fortunate to yourself and us.' The guns are then fired, shot and all; he is saluted with three cheers; and the ceremony is ended with an invitation from the captain to such as he thinks fit to have dine with him, and a large bowl of punch is ordered to every mess.

Once this was over, other men were elected to fill the places of the officers killed with Davis. Then, finally, they could get down to the business of revenge.

Walter Kennedy was chosen to lead a group of about thirty in an attack upon the fort at St Antonio. They brought the *Royal Rover* in as close as possible to provide covering fire and, with cannon balls flying over their heads, Kennedy and his men charged the ramparts. The explosions set the monkeys and the parrots in the forest behind frantically chattering and screeching and, amidst the smoke and confusion, the pirates managed to break through the main entrance – only to find the fort deserted. The Portuguese soldiers had deserted their posts and fled to the town.

The pirates threw the guns into the sea and set fire to the fort. Many now wanted to burn St Antonio itself. But here for the first time

Roberts exerted his authority. The town was protected by a long expanse of shallow water and was out of range of the *Royal Rover's* guns. It was also surrounded by thick forests which would provide cover for the defenders. The pirates would inevitably sustain casualties for little gain, Roberts argued. This sensible advice prevailed. But still, they loaded around a dozen cannon on to a smaller boat and gave themselves the partial satisfaction of destroying several houses. Then, with night falling, they set two Portuguese ships alight and sailed out of the harbour by the light of the flames. It was less than three weeks since they'd first arrived.

Roberts quickly drew a dividing line between his own captaincy and that of Davis by having the crew agree a new set of articles. Described by Johnson, who got his information from members of Roberts' crew, they show the influence of his disciplined and slightly puritanical personality.

ARTICLE I. Every man has a vote in affairs of moment; has equal title to the fresh provisions or strong liquors at any time seized, and may use them at pleasure unless a scarcity make it necessary, for the good of all, to vote a retrenchment.

ARTICLE II. Every man shall be called fairly in turn, by list, on board of prizes, because (over and above their proper share) they were on these occasions allowed a shift of clothes. But if they defrauded the company to the value of one dollar in plate, jewels or money, marooning was their punishment. If the robbery was only betwixt one another they contented themselves with slitting the ears and nose of him that was guilty, and set him on shore, not in an uninhabited place but somewhere where he was sure to encounter hardships.

ARTICLE III. No person to game at cards or dice for money.

ARTICLE IV. The lights and candles should be put out at eight at night. If any of the crew after that hour still remained inclined for drinking they were to do it on the open deck.

ARTICLE V. To keep their piece, pistols and cutlass clean and fit for service.

ARTICLE VI. No boy or woman to be allowed amongst them. If any man were found seducing any of the latter sex and carried her to sea disguised he was to suffer death.

ARTICLE VII. To desert the ship, or their quarters in battle, was punished with death or marooning.

ARTICLE VIII. No striking one another on board, but every man's quarrels to be ended on shore at sword and pistol . . . The Quarter-Master of the ship, when the parties will not come to any reconciliation, accompanies them on shore with what assistance he thinks proper, and turns the disputants back to back, at so many paces distance. At the word of command, they turn and fire immediately . . . If both miss, they come to their cutlasses, and then he is declared victor who draws the first blood.

ARTICLE IX. No man to talk of breaking up their way of living till each had shared a £1,000. If in order to do this any man should lose a limb or become a cripple in their service he was to have 800 pieces of eight out of the public stock and for lesser hurts proportionately.

ARTICLE X. The captain and the quartermaster to receive two shares of a prize, the master, boatswain and gunner, one share and a half, and other officers one and one quarter.

ARTICLE XI. The musicians to have rest on the Sabbath Day but the other six days and nights none without special favour.

The outright ban on gambling was unique – other pirate articles simply attempted to limit it. The punishment of death for bringing a woman on board was unusually draconian. And Johnson believed that Article IV, requiring candles to be put out by eight at night, was intended by Roberts to check the crew's 'debauches'. Article XI offers a rare example of pirates observing the Sabbath.

With his revenge complete, and the new machinery of government in place, Roberts soon had his first prize – a Dutch ship seized just south of Princes Island on 25 July 1719. But we know more about his second, the *Experiment* of London, taken two days later close to Cape Lopez in modern Gabon. The ship's commander, Thomas Grant, was later interviewed by Admiralty officials, and his account provides further evidence of how unstable and unpredictable an element Walter Kennedy represented as Roberts struggled to establish his authority among the crew in the early months.

As usual, the ship surrendered at the first sight of the black flag and Grant was summoned aboard the *Royal Rover*. He and Kennedy had met before and Kennedy bore a grudge. 'Damn you, I know you and will sacrifice you,' Kennedy shouted, according to the Admiralty transcript. 'With his fist [Kennedy] struck the informant [Grant] with great violence upon his mouth which occasioned his nose and mouth to bleed. The informant believes that the said Kennedy would then have murdered him if some of the crew had not ordered the informant out of the way.'

Kennedy was later seen running about the *Royal Rover* looking for Grant 'with a naked cutlass in his hand', and he was lucky to escape further injury. The pirates plundered the *Experiment* of 50 ounces of gold, sixteen moidores (a gold Portuguese coin worth one pound seven shillings), ten guineas and a number of other 'movables of value' that Grant had in his cabin. Kennedy then persuaded his shipmates to burn the ship, leaving the crew with little choice but to join the pirates. Grant would be a prisoner for almost four months.

They cruised for a few more days without sighting a sail and then headed for Annobón, the smallest of the three Portuguese islands, just south of the equator. There they finished provisioning their ship, which had been interrupted at Princes Island. There were almost no Europeans on Annobón and Roberts dispensed with any pretence of being a man-of-war or privateer, simply forcing the governor to hand over supplies. The pirates were still planning to leave Africa and, with the ship fully stocked for an ocean crossing, the time had now come to decide on their next destination. This was always a subject of lengthy debate and, as the pirates crowded around in the steerage, two options were put forward – the East Indies and Brazil.

Both offered the possibility of rich pickings. The Indian Ocean had been a popular destination with pirates ever since the capture of the *Ganj-i-Sawai* by the pirate Henry Avery off the mouth of the Red Sea in 1695. The *Ganj-i-Sawai* belonged to the Mughal Emperor Aurangzeb and was carrying wealthy pilgrims bound for Mecca. It was packed with gold, silver and jewels and yielded shares of £1,000 each for the 150-man crew, a fortune for men who had earned thirty shillings a month as ordinary seamen. There were also a number of ladies of the imperial court aboard with their serving women. Avery always denied they were mistreated. But a member of his crew later admitted 'the most horrid barbarities' were committed and sources suggest the crew embarked on an orgy of rape and plunder which lasted several days.

Avery's success sparked a gold rush. The island of Madagascar became the base for the pirates flocking to the region and was soon the subject of numerous myths and legends. Captain Johnson wrote of a French pirate called Captain Mission who flew a white flag emblazoned with the words 'For God and Liberty!' and set up a utopian, egalitarian community called Libertalia where men of all nations and colours lived in peace and harmony. Sadly, this is the only entirely fictitious chapter in Johnson's *General History of the Pirates*. There was more of Mr Kurtz and the *Heart of Darkness* to some of the real pirate kings who established themselves deep in the jungles of Madagascar. According to one visitor, James Plantain, who ruled at Ranter Bay, 'took a great many wives and servants, whom he kept in great subjection; and after the English manner called them Moll, Kate, Sue or Peggy. These women were dressed in richest silks, and some of them had diamond necklaces.' But the story of Captain Mission captures the mythical status Madagascar had acquired as a pirate haven by the early eighteenth century. And whether the pirates there were debauched despots or utopian idealists, the island exerted a powerful pull on the imaginations of pirates and seamen alike as they gossiped in the f'o'csles and taverns of the Atlantic world.

But by the second decade of the century it was in decline. Many of the pirate settlements on the island had been over-run by natives. And, pressured by their trading partners in the east, the European East India Companies had taken steps to stamp out piracy in the region. When Woodes Rogers, later Governor of the Bahamas, visited Madagascar in 1711 he reported that 'those miserable wretches, who had made such a noise in the world, were now dwindled to between 60 and 70, most of them very poor and despicable, even to the natives, among whom they are married'. Roberts and his men were also aware that their former comrades Cocklyn and La Bouche were headed in that direction and would provide stiff competition.

It turned out Madagascar was on the brink of a brief renaissance as a pirate haven. In April 1721 La Bouche seized the Portuguese East Indiaman *Nostra Senhora de Cabo* at Réunion. It proved to be one of the richest prizes in the history of piracy, carrying a fortune in diamonds. It enabled him to briefly retire, although he was later hanged by the French authorities.

But Brazil was an attractive alternative. Portugal's only colony in the Americas, it had become wealthy initially through the cultivation of sugar, which it pioneered in the New World. When sugar prices collapsed towards the end of the seventeenth century it was saved by the discovery of gold in the province of Minas Gerais in the early 1690s. By 1709, 30,000 people had flocked to the region and its rivers teemed with African slaves, sifting and panning in the river beds for their white masters. By 1719 Brazil was the largest gold producer in the world, dispatching 27 tons a year to Lisbon – and that was just the amount declared to the royal tax collectors. The bulk of it ended up in London, traded by the Portuguese in exchange for manufactured goods.

Gold was in the process of transforming Brazil from an archipelago of isolated coastal settlements into a sub-continent. Combined with the earlier sugar boom it had spawned a society that was rich but backward and decadent. The main city of Bahia, now Salvador do Bahia, was reputed to have a church for every day of the year. It was equally rich in mulatta – mixed-race – prostitutes. Brazilians were notorious for their dependence on slaves, who heavily outnumbered the white population and were imported to Bahia at a rate of 11,000 a year. 'The rich people', wrote a French visitor at this time, 'would be ashamed to make use of the Legs which nature has given us to walk . . . [They] lazily cause themselves to be carried in beds of fine cotton, hanging by the ends to a pole, which two blacks carry on their heads or shoulders.'

All of which spelt rich pickings to the pirates and, when the vote was taken, it was Brazil they decided to head for. At the start of August

1719 they set their sails, picked up the south-east trade winds and headed out into the Atlantic, 'resolved', in the words of Walter Kennedy, 'to make their fortunes at once, or to be all killed'.

4

TRIUMPH AND DISASTER

SOUTH AMERICA
AUGUST–DECEMBER 1719

'ELATED WITH THEIR BOOTY, THEY HAD

NOTHING NOW TO THINK OF BUT SOME SAFE

RETREAT, WHERE THEY MIGHT GIVE THEM-

SELVES UP TO ALL THE PLEASURES THAT

LUXURY AND WANTONNESS COULD BESTOW'

HE *ROYAL ROVER* WAS close to the port of Pernambuco (modern Recife) on the eastern tip of Brazil when the look out's cry of 'sail ahoy!' punctured the sleepy tropical calm. The men ran to the edge of the ship, straining their eyes on the horizon. But their joy soon turned to apprehension. No sooner had the sail loomed into view than another appeared, then another, and another. Within a couple of hours Roberts, the novice pirate commander, found himself confronted with no fewer than thirty-eight ships – the entire Brazilian treasure fleet. To attack was clearly insanity. But, for Roberts, to sail away also carried grave risks.

By now they had been off the coast of Brazil for almost two months. The trip to South America had begun well. From Annobón they had sped across the Atlantic in just twenty-eight days, making landfall on Fernando de Noronha, a pin-prick of an island 200 miles off the Brazilian coast. But here their luck turned. They had planned to 'wood and water' in preparation for their assault on the Portuguese mainland.

But when they arrived it was early September, the start of the dry season, and the pirates found the island barren and destitute. There was little food and they were able to fill only nine butts of water, equivalent to 675 gallons. They 'boot-topped' the *Royal Rover* – a type of partial careening, which involved shifting guns and other heavy items to one side to tilt the ship and enable a scrubbing of the hull just below the waterline. Then they set sail, heading south-west towards the main Portuguese settlements.

They had never planned a frontal assault on the treasure fleet. But they were certainly after gold and they made initially for Bahia, several hundred miles south of Pernambuco, through which most of Brazil's gold flowed. The fleet sailed from here. But so did individual Brazilian ships, which traded directly with West Africa, exchanging gold, brandy and third-grade tobacco for slaves. And there were rich crumbs to be picked up in the coastal trade.

They sailed close enough that they could see the steep cliff that was Bahia's distinctive feature, rising sharply from the port, up which a complex series of pullies and winches constantly transported goods to the upper town. Churches and monasteries jostled on the skyline and they could see numerous ships in the harbour. But for two weeks none emerged. Then they seized a small fishing vessel with two Indians in it. The Indians had dramatic news – the treasure fleet was due to sail any day.

Fearful of confronting it directly, the pirates pulled out to sea. When the fleet set sail they followed it northwards at a discreet distance, hoping to pick off stragglers. But when it suddenly loomed into view off Pernambuco, Brazil's second city, it had come to a halt, waiting for ships to join it for the journey to Lisbon. It was also awaiting an escort of two 70-gun men-of-war.

As Roberts stood on the deck gazing at the fleet he knew he was confronting a decisive moment in his leadership. They were now well into October and almost three months had passed since they took their last prize, the *Experiment*, off the coast of Africa. In that time they'd travelled more than 4,000 miles. For a crew accustomed to success and warily eyeing its new captain to see what luck he would bring it was a long barren period.

With his quarry about to head out into the Atlantic, Roberts felt further delay was impossible. And, although technically the decision to attack or not was a collective one, it would be difficult for the pirates to go into battle if the man expected to lead them was reluctant. A pirate captain who showed little appetite for a fight could not expect to last long. Roberts opted for boldness – but he would also use cunning.

He ordered his men to conceal themselves. Then, under cover of French colours, he sailed up to one of the smallest ships in the fleet. He had a Portuguese pirate in his crew and, as he drew close, he ordered this man, quietly, to order the captain to come aboard, threatening to attack if he refused.

Taken by surprise, the Portuguese captain surrendered and came on board. According to Johnson, 'Roberts saluted him after a friendly manner, telling him, that they were gentlemen of fortune, but that their business with him was only to be informed which was the richest ship in that fleet, and if he directed them right, he should be restored to his ship without molestation. Otherwise, he must expect immediate death.'

Faced with these options the Portuguese captain complied and pointed them towards the *Sagrada Familia*, a powerful vessel with 40 guns and 150 men belonging to the vice-admiral of the fleet. Roberts' *Royal Rover* at this point had around 200 men but only 32 guns. Nevertheless, he headed straight for the ship, which sat slightly apart from the rest of the fleet. Again, he attempted a subterfuge. He ordered the captured Portuguese captain to invite the *Sagrada Familia*'s captain on board. The *Sagrada Familia*'s captain agreed but it was soon clear he was not fooled. In Johnson's words, 'By the bustle that immediately followed the pirates perceived they were discovered and that this was only a deceitful answer to gain time to put their ship in a posture of defence.'

For the first time Roberts would have to lead his men in the storm, ing of a ship. He was facing a vessel more powerful than his own, in the midst of a large, hostile fleet, with two Portuguese men-of-war anchored nearby. And he was about to find that his Royal Navy experience only partly prepared him for the pirates' unique way of fighting.

Pirates were street fighters. While the aim of conventional warships was the annihilation of the enemy, the aim of pirates was to capture prizes intact. Although their ships bristled with guns, they were reluctant to use them and rarely engaged in the artillery duels at distance which characterised conventional warfare at sea. Instead they sought to fight at close range and relied heavily on small arms, weapons that would kill men but preserve their vessel.

Pirates were one of the first groups to develop a 'gun culture'. They went into battle festooned with pistols. Roberts wore four, dangling on the end of a silk sling hung over his shoulders. And, as Article XI of his articles showed, they also duelled with pistols. This was highly unusual at the time and considered rather ungentlemanly, most duels still being fought with swords alone. It suggests they had developed a degree of marksmanship, unlike conventional sailors who only used pistols at close range. Even more important were muskets. Living by hunting on the island of Hispaniola the early Buccaneers were famous for their shooting skills, and developed an unusual gun, five or six feet long, designed to maximise distance and accuracy. It was a talent they passed on to pirates of the Golden Age, and 'Buccaneer guns' were readily available to men like Roberts in the holds of captured slavers, where they were carried as trade goods.

We have only a brief description of the battle that followed. But we can piece together the likely course of events from other accounts of pirate attacks. As the *Royal Rover* closed on the *Sagrada Familia* Roberts' sharpshooters raced up the rigging to the 'fighting tops' – the platforms high up on each of the three masts. From there they poured a torrent of fire into the enemy, targeting above all the helmsman and any officers on the quarter deck. At the same time Roberts primed his cannon and sprayed the Portuguese ship with grape shot.

As the *Sagrada Familia* reeled from this opening barrage Roberts' men crowded towards the edge of the ship preparing to board, brandishing their cutlasses and yelling insults. A frontal assault of this type was costly in terms of casualties and the Royal Navy avoided it whenever possible. But it was unavoidable if a ship and its cargo were to be captured intact – and pirates were masters of the art. As the ships passed they 'lashed' the Portuguese vessel, throwing grappling hooks across and pulling tight on the ropes to draw the two ships together. They were now eyeball to eyeball with the enemy. Confronting them was a grim-faced line of men clutching pikes – fearsome weapons, eight feet long, topped with four-inch spikes – ready to thrust them into the bellies of the first borders as they leapt across. To counter this, the pirates had with them large quantities of primitive grenades and other 'fireworks' which they now hurled among the *Sagrada Familia*'s defenders. The effect was horrific. Shrapnel tore into flesh and some of the explosives spewed smoke and noxious smells to add to the terror and confusion.

As the pikemen scattered the pirates leapt across the divide, clutching their cutlasses in their teeth to free their hands. They were led by either the boatswain or the quartermaster, Roberts remaining behind on the deck of the *Royal Rover* to direct operations. They fired their pistols at any defenders still standing. Then, as the Portuguese regrouped, they took their cutlasses in their hands and moved forward.

Broad and heavy, cutlasses were the classic pirate weapon. They were despised as crude meat cleavers by officers on conventional warships, who preferred the more dashing rapier. But for lopping off parts of your opponents' anatomy there were no weapons to match them and in this sort of vicious, hand-to-hand combat they were invaluable.

The death of Blackbeard after boarding a Royal Navy sloop in the Chesapeake Bay in 1718 captures the sheer gore of these encounters. 'The sea was tinctured with blood around the vessel,' wrote Captain Johnson. 'Blackbeard received a shot into his body . . . yet he stood his ground and fought with great fury till he received five and twenty wounds.' He fell after a blow from a broad sword 'cut off his head, laying it flat on his shoulder.' Blackbeard was unlucky in encountering a disciplined and determined naval crew. Few merchant ships could withstand the fury of a pirate assault, and the *Sagrada Familia* was no exception, despite being better armed than most. 'The dispute was hot and warm,' wrote Johnson, 'wherein many of the Portuguese fell, and two only of the pirates.' Within half an hour the battle was over.

Roberts' crew had little time to enjoy the victory. The *Royal Rover* was in the 'utmost danger', Walter Kennedy later recalled, 'well nigh surrounded by the whole Portuguese fleet' with two 70-gun warships bearing down on it. Flight was the obvious option. But that would mean abandoning the prize. Instead Roberts turned the *Royal Rover* directly towards the lead warship and prepared once more for battle.

The odds were now overwhelmingly against them and, rather than be captured, the pirates were preparing to go down in a blaze of glory. They were saved by 'the cowardice of the Portuguese', according to Kennedy. Confronted by the *Royal Rover* the lead warship 'ignominiously declined' to do battle. It 'tarried', waiting for the second warship. By the time it arrived the *Royal Rover* had made its escape, taking the *Sagrada Familia* with it. The Portuguese pursued them northwards. But 'they had as good sent a cow after a hare', the pirate carpenter Richard Luntly later wrote.

It was a stunning victory. But it was only as they examined their booty that the full scale of what they had achieved dawned on the pirates. The Portuguese ship contained 40,000 gold moidores, equivalent to £54,000 in money of the day. In addition there were 'chains and trinkets of considerable value, particularly a cross set with diamonds designed for the King of Portugal' as well as sugar, skins, tobacco and some timber. A contemporary press report put the total value of the prize at £150,000. This may have been an exaggeration. But even if we assume a lower figure of £100,000 it amounted to shares of almost £500 per man – more than an ordinary seaman could expect to earn in a lifetime.

Roberts showed compassion towards his vanquished foe. Like Howel Davis five months before with the crew of the *Marquis del Campo*, he spared the survivors aboard the *Sagrada Familia*, despite the fact they had resisted. So slow were the Portuguese men-of-war to pursue him that Roberts had time to load most of them into the smaller Portuguese prize, which was left behind. The remainder he took with him as he headed north.

'Elated with their booty,' Johnson wrote, 'they had nothing now to think of but some safe retreat, where they might give themselves up to all the pleasures that luxury and wantonness could bestow.' They voted to head for the port of Cayenne in French Guiana on the north-eastern coast of South America, taking the *Sagrada Familia* with them so they might plunder it at leisure.

It was a journey of 1600 miles. But the winds and currents were with them and it was a pleasant voyage. We can picture the men as they lounged on deck in the shade of awnings hung from the rigging, watching the jungle-fringed coastline of north-eastern Brazil scud by. They smoked, they drank punch – the passion of all pirates – and ordered their musicians to play for them, dancing jigs and reels on the hatchways in the cool of the evening. Most chose to sleep in the open, enjoying the fine weather – a pleasant alternative to the fetid air below decks where the pirates normally slung their hammocks between the guns. They fell asleep gazing up into the tropical night, listening to the waves breaking on the bow and the sails billowing in the wind, giddy with their unlikely victory.

For Roberts the change in his circumstances was breathtaking. He'd gone from being an ageing, lowly officer on a mid-sized slaver to the unquestioned commander of the largest, most powerful, and now richest pirate crew in the Atlantic. And it had happened virtually overnight. His own share of the loot from the *Sagrada Familia* was around £1,000. He must have remembered with a wry smile his initial reluctance to join Howel Davis's crew. The victory at Pernambuco was very much his victory. He'd shown himself a good student of Howel Davis in his use of cunning and subterfuge. But he'd combined this with an astonishing boldness and courage. It was a combination that would become his trademark and in time make Bartholomew Roberts the greatest of all pirate captains.

The *Royal Rover* and the *Sagrada Familia* arrived at Cayenne in the middle of November 1719. It was a stark contrast with the grandeur of Bahia. There was a small fort and a Jesuit mission – but little else. The streets were unpaved and the houses mostly made of wood. An earth rampart ran around the town.

Europeans had originally been drawn to this part of South America by the publication in 1596 of Sir Walter Raleigh's *The Discovery of the Large, Rich and Beautiful Empire of Guiana.*

Raleigh claimed the jungles of the interior were rich in gold. But the tales proved to be false and by the early 1700s French Guiana was already acquiring a reputation as a 'green hell' and a 'white man's grave'. Built between two rivers as they flowed into the sea, Cayenne was effectively an island and the land was low and marshy. It was 'an uncomfortable place to live', a French visitor had written a few years before, 'because of the long rainy season every year, the scorching close air night and day, which dispirits a man, and the heavy showers and vapours, exhaled from the swampy grounds, which . . . occasion diseases in men and beasts'. November was renowned as the most unhealthy month of the year.

In 1719 there were no more than a few hundred whites in the town and it was the only European settlement of any size in the whole colony. Sugar plantations, which dominated much of the Caribbean, had failed to take off and the Indian population was more significant than that of African slaves – always a sign of economic backwardness at this time. Of the small number of whites who had settled there many were former Buccaneers. Despairing of ever making a profit from it, the French later turned French Guiana into the notorious penal colony immortalised in the film *Papillon*.

Located over 800 miles from the nearest European settlements in the Caribbean, for the pirates Cayenne was an ideal backwater. It must have been obvious to the authorities who their visitors were. If the sight of the *Sagrada Familia* bobbing in the bay wasn't enough, they off-loaded a number of prisoners here, including Captain Grant of the *Experiment*, who had been with them since his capture off Africa at the end of July. But it wasn't every day a ship full of gold fell into your lap. Roberts made a gift of the diamond-studded cross which they had seized at Pernambuco to the governor, Claude Guillouet d'Orvilliers. Thereafter the pirates 'found the civilest reception imaginable, not only from the governor and factory, but their wives, who exchanged wares and drove a considerable trade with them', wrote Captain Johnson. Pirates always spent money like water and the people of Cayenne were more than happy to take advantage.

Spreading out among the ramshackle taverns and brothels, the pirates could now get down to a serious orgy of drinking and debauchery. This was the fourth time in less than a year this crew had come ashore to indulge its carnal appetites. On the previous three occasions – at St Nicholas in the Cape Verde Islands in January, at Sierra Leone in April and at Princes Island in July – it had been their captain, Howel Davis, who led the way. But Roberts was less enthu-siastic. He had no interest in wine and, his men quickly realised, very little in women. It may well be that, as they set off for their nights on the town, some of the crew cast knowing looks at the tall, dark thirty-seven-year-old bachelor who preferred to remain behind on the ship.

Within the context of pirate culture they may not have regarded their captain's behaviour as particularly odd. The early Buccaneers preferred each other's company to that of women, and a tradition of violent misogyny had continued among the pirates of the Caribbean into Roberts' day – a misogyny that probably concealed a degree of hearty homosexuality.

The Buccaneers referred to their partner as their *matelot* and their practice of living in male couples was known as *matelotage*. 'It is the general and solemn custom amongst them all to seek out . . . a comrade or companion, whom we may call partner . . . with whom they join the whole stock of what they possess,' wrote the Buccaneer Alexander Exquemelin, who arrived in the Buccaneer haven of Tortuga on Hispaniola in 1666. Together they would 'go into the woods to hunt for wild-bulls and cows. They commonly remain there the space of a whole twelve month or two years, without returning home.'

The contemporary historian Jean-Baptiste Du Tertre, also writing in the 1660s, made it clear that *matelotage* was more than a purely economic arrangement. *Matelots* would sometimes continue to live together, he wrote, even after one of them had married, 'but the jealousy which arises, and the problems resulting either from the indiscretion of the matelot or the imprudence of the woman compelled the governors to ban this arrangement'.

Du Tertre recorded that *matelotage* was common throughout the early French Antilles, not just among Buccaneers, as a response to the chronic shortage of women. 'There are two types of families in the islands. The first consist of married persons and the others of boys who live together,' he wrote. The early emigrants to both the English and French islands were almost all men. At this time there were relatively few slaves and Indians to rape and prostitute, since the slave trade in the Caribbean only took off in the second half of the seventeenth century, and, where they had not been annihilated, the Indians were fierce and hostile.

Once a more formal French colonial administration was estab-lished in western Hispaniola (later Haiti) in the 1660s the authorities imported large numbers of prostitutes from France for 'sale' to the locals in what might be seen as a conscious bid to heterosexualise the wild Buccaneers. Other islands also encouraged female migration and by Roberts' time a balance had been achieved between the sexes in the West Indies. But pirates of the Golden Age, to a greater extent even than the Buccaneers before them, lived a life largely cut off from con-ventional shore-based communities and from access to women. The frequency with which Roberts' crew managed to seek out pirate-friendly brothels during 1719 was unusual. They, like most pirate crews, spent the vast bulk of their time cooped up in a small wooden ship with only 200 other dandily dressed, testosterone-filled young pirates for company.

There was just one crew in this period that included women – that of Jack Rackham, better known as Calico Jack, who had two female pirates on his ship; Anne Bonny and Mary Read. Bonny was Rackham's lover and both she and Mary Read had originally gone to sea disguised as men seeking adventure. They were bold and fearless. According to Johnson, when finally they were captured they fought to the end, Read calling to the pirates cowering in the hold 'to come up and fight like men . . . Finding they did not stir [she] fired her arms down the hold amongst them, killing one and wounding others.' After Rackham was sentenced to hang in November 1720 Bonny, visiting him for the last time, told him 'she was sorry to see him there, but if he had fought like a Man, he need not have been hanged like a Dog'. Both she and Read escaped the gallows because they were pregnant (Bonny by Rackham, Read by another member of the crew).

For most pirates Rackham's short career and ignominious end merely confirmed their prejudice against having women on board. A recent study shows just 4 per cent of pirates were married and, in its isolation from the world of conventional domesticity, pirate culture was, in many ways, an extreme version of the sailors' culture from which it grew.

Sailors, too, were viewed as alien and apart by the rest of society. They were notoriously irreligious and rarely owned property, preferring to spend their money in wild drunken sprees. They were more likely to be married than pirates and they did not have the same taboo about having women on their ships. Even so, the majority were bachelors, and becoming pirates completed a process of separation from the norms and values of the rest of society. In their place pirates developed an almost mystical sense of brotherhood, a culture which was highly theatrical and full of ritual.

They formed pacts with the Devil and pledged to blow up their ships and 'all go to Hell together' rather than be captured. When challenged to identify themselves they said simply that they were 'from the seas'. And they swore friendship to each other by drinking a cocktail of sea water and gunpowder – a custom visitors to Madagascar in the early 1720s found the local people had adopted. They also discovered that one of the few English sentences the Madagascans had learned from the pirates was the intriguing 'God Damn ye John, me love you'.

There is an emotional intensity to pirate life that seeps through the dry, contemporary accounts. Captain Johnson tells the story of a pirate turned privateer who drowned rather than abandon his closest friend on a sinking vessel. And a contemporary French historian left the following curious description of Buccaneers preparing for battle: 'They never engaged in combat without embracing each other as a sign of reconciliation. At such times one might see them thumping their chests, as if they wanted to arouse some remorse in their hearts, something they had become scarcely capable of.' You sense it was a bitter and tangled emotional world these men inhabited.

Item VI of Roberts' Articles banned the men from bringing women on to the ship, on pain of death. This was, in part, because they would be a source of tension. But it's telling that boys were also barred. Given the circumstances of the pirates' lives it would be surprising if there were no homosexual undercurrents on the *Royal Rover*. It may well be that the sexual ambiguity Johnny Depp brings to the lead role in *Pirates of the Caribbean* is one of the more accurate elements of the film, and that Roberts' men noticed something similar in their solitary new commander. It probably disturbed them less than his aversion to wine.

Roberts watched, detached and distant, as his men indulged themselves in Cayenne. A ship full of gold and a port full of whores – whatever activities they indulged in during the long periods between shore leave, for most pirates this was as good as it got. But, paradoxically, it was immediately after the capture of a rich prize that a pirate crew was at its most vulnerable. It was then that divisions emerged – between those who felt the time had come to retire and enjoy their riches and those who wished to continue. Trouble was soon brewing aboard the *Royal Rover*.

At Cayenne the pirates seized a sloop from Rhode Island called the *Princess* captained by Edward Cane. Roberts now had grandiose ambitions. He decided to keep the *Princess* as a support vessel, or consort. He loaded it with ten cannon and several swivel guns, and renamed it the *Good Fortune*. He also planned to trade up, swapping the *Royal Rover*, which was leaky, for the larger and more powerful *Sagrada Familia*. The two ships would then raid shipping off Barbados for a few weeks, building up supplies and recruiting addi-tional men, before heading to the East Indies. But then, one evening in a tavern in Cayenne, a group of Roberts' men were overheard plotting mutiny.

There were about forty involved in the conspiracy – a dangerous combination of forced men and more hardened pirates who felt they had pushed their luck for long enough. Their plan was to seize the *Good Fortune* and then make their escape. Roberts acted swiftly and decisively. The conspirators were clapped in irons and the three pirate ships – the *Royal Rover*, the *Good Fortune* and the *Sagrada Familia* – immediately set sail from Cayenne.

Roberts wanted a location where he could confront the conspiracy free from distractions and hand out whatever punishments were deemed fit. He headed west for a group of bleak, deserted islands, known to the pirates as 'The Triangle', 30 miles to the west. Protected by high cliffs and swirling currents, they were more commonly known as the Devil's Islands and would later be the location for the most notorious of the French penal settlements. Few ships attempted to land there, but Captain Cane, who was still being held captive, was familiar with the waters and was able to act as their pilot.

The case was clear cut and a number of the men were immediately flogged. Many of the pirates wanted sterner punishments. 'Some of them was for shooting us,' the carpenter Richard Luntly, who was among the accused, later recalled, 'others not, and so they consented to put us away upon a desolate island.' Luntly named the island where they were to be marooned as Esphealy, which was probably Eripice, the Indian name for one of the Devil's Islands. But before this could happen they were saved by what must have seemed to the accused men a miraculous intervention, and what, for Roberts, was a catastrophe.

Captain Cane of the *Princess* was the first in a long series of merchant captains who was suspiciously cooperative in his dealings with Roberts. This was partly born of fear. But there were many other reasons for men in his situation to collaborate. If they decided not to punish a captain, pirates could be very generous. One captain, captured by pirates in the Cape Verde Islands in 1722, recalled that that they kept a store of 'linen, silk, spare hats, shoes, stockings, gold lace, and abundance of other goods' to distribute as gifts to captains they either knew or 'took a present liking to'.

It was gratifying to pirates' egos and their sense of their own power to be able to distribute largesse in this way. But there were also practical reasons for developing relationships with merchant captains. Pirates often found themselves laden down with bulky items they could make no use of. Merchant captains had access to ports and markets. It didn't take a genius to work out that they might be able to reach a mutually beneficial arrangement. It's suspicious how often Bartholomew Roberts ran into the same captain more than once, and at times the exchange of goods was so extensive it felt more like trade than plunder. The authorities were always suspicious of captains seized by pirates and insisted on inspecting the holds of their ships, forcing them to hand over half of anything they had been given – even if their original cargo had been stolen. But there were substantial opportunities for profit for any captain who could slip into a quiet cove to unload. By this time the vast bulk of ships and their cargoes were also insured, which opened up further opportunities for fraud.

Captain Cane was unusually helpful. 'He complimented them at an odd rate,' Johnson wrote, 'telling them they were welcome to his sloop and cargo, and wished that the vessel had been larger and the loading richer for their sakes.' Having piloted them to Devil's Islands, he informed them that he had set out from Rhode Island in company with a brigantine, laden with provisions for the South American coast, which was due to arrive any day. It was at this moment, in the midst of the pirates' deliberations over the punishment of the conspirators at Devil's Islands, that the brigantine loomed into view.

Roberts now revealed the flip side of the boldness which had served him so well at Pernambuco – an impulsiveness that could border on recklessness. Reluctant to entrust the mission to anyone else, he leapt into Cane's sloop, now the *Good Fortune,* and set off in pursuit with forty to fifty men. Walter Kennedy, who by now had been elected Lieutenant, took command of those left behind. In his haste Roberts failed to check what supplies the sloop had on board. They quickly lost sight of the brigantine. Worse, contrary winds and currents swept them far to the west. After eight days they found themselves around 100 miles from Devil's Islands and chronically short of food and water. They came to anchor and lowered a group of men in the long boat to row back and summon the others to their assistance. But this too proved to be rash. The following day the *Good Fortune* ran out of water and they realised they had no means of supplying themselves – despite the fact they were within sight of land – until either the boat or one of the other ships returned. With the sun blazing down they were soon raging with thirst. Eventually they were forced to tear up the floor of the cabin to build a raft to paddle ashore and fetch water.

When finally the long boat returned it brought catastrophic news. The islands were empty. Kennedy and the entire crew had deserted with both ships and all of the gold. Roberts cursed and raved. But many of his men cast sour glances at him. To tear off in pursuit of a minor prize, leaving behind a fortune in treasure at a time when the crew was riven with dissension, was insanity. At a stroke all the prestige and authority he'd gained by the victory at Pernambuco was undone. They were now back in the same situation as Howel Davis immediately following the original mutiny aboard the *Buck* at Hispaniola just over a year before – a small crew in a sloop. They passed a resolution that never again would they allow an Irishman in their ranks. But it was feeble revenge on the man who was now speeding northwards with their gold.

Kennedy had perhaps 140 men under his command – including the forty conspirators whose attempted mutiny at Cayenne had now been quietly forgotten. He kept the *Royal Rover*, handing the *Sagrada Familia* to Captain Cane as reward for his cooperation. It took some time to bring the company to any decision, Johnson wrote. 'Some of them were for pursuing the old game, but the greater part of them seemed to have inclinations to turn from these evil courses, and get home privately ... Therefore they agreed to break up, and every man to shift for himself.'

Kennedy and his men split up gradually over the course of the next month, during which time they took at least three ships. The first was a snow (a two-masted vessel, slightly larger than a sloop) called the *Sea Nymph* from New York which they seized just west of Barbados on 15 December. They took beef, pork, butter, flour and biscuits from it, and gave the captain tobacco, sugar, around ten slaves and even some guns in return. When they released him a few days later twenty of the pirates went with him, Kennedy telling the captain they were forced men that he was freeing. It was a description the authorities on Barbados, where they were landed a few days later, were apparently happy to accept.

The second was the *West River Merchant,* bound for Virginia from London, a particularly easy prize since its captain, Luke Knott, was a Quaker and carried no arms aboard. When they released him eight of the pirates went with him, slipping ashore in Virginia in small boats before Knott docked. The last was the *Eagle,* another New York vessel bound for Barbados. It was after seizing this that the remainder of the crew divided. Kennedy kept the *Eagle* for himself and headed across the Atlantic towards Britain with around fifty men. A similar number – around half of them black – stayed with the *Royal Rover* and headed for the Danish colony of St Thomas just east of Puerto Rico, a notorious pirate haven. En route they dropped off six of their number on the small British island of Anguilla, north of Antigua.

Having broken up into small groups, the deserters intended to melt quietly away. But melting quietly away was something pirates were peculiarly bad at. The fate of the eight men who slipped ashore in Virginia on Captain Knott's ship was typical. 'As soon as they came ashore their first care was to find out a Tavern, and ease themselves of some of their Golden Luggage,' the *Weekly Journal* in London reported. 'They quickly found a place to their minds, where, for some time they profusely treated all that came into their company.' They took a shine to some of the servant girls and paid their masters £30 each to release them. 'This extravagant way of living,' the *Weekly Journal* continued, 'soon discovered that they were not passengers from London, as they pretended, but rather pirates. Accordingly they were seized and committed.'

At the time they seized Knott's ship the pirates still had with them a handful of prisoners from the *Sagrada Familia.* These were freed into Knott's hands, and they now gave evidence against the captured pirates in Virginia. The authorities managed to recover 'two thousand pounds sterling in silver and gold' from the pirates, as well as 'three Negro men and a boy', who were described as part of the pirates' booty. Of the eight arrested, six were defiant. They 'appeared the most profligate wretches I ever heard of', complained Alexander Spotswood, the governor of Virginia. 'They behaved with the greatest impudence at the bar. They were no sooner taken from it than they vented their imprecations on their Judges and all concerned in the prosecution, and vowed if they were again at liberty they would spare none alive that should fall in to their hands.' On the gallows, according to the *Weekly Journal*, 'one of them called for a bottle of wine and taking a glass of it, drank damnation to the Governor and confusion to the colony, which the rest pledged'. The remaining two pirates showed what Spotswood called 'a just abhorrence for their past crimes' and were pardoned. Of those executed Spotswood 'thought it necessary for the greater terror to hang up four of them in chains'. This meant their bodies were covered in tar and then placed in iron gibbets and left to rot at prominent places along the coast as a warning to other pirates.

Captain Knott provided a rare example of a ship's master who not only swiftly informed the authorities of their presence but also handed over the substantial quantities of sugar, tobacco and gold that the pirates had given him. He even forced his crew to give back individual gifts they'd received. Governor Spotswood was keen that Knott's honesty be rewarded. 'When masters of ships are so honest as to discover and yield up what is thus given them in lieu of their own privates losses, I cannot but recommend them to his Majesty's favour that some consideration may be had of their suffering and damages,' he wrote to London. After due consideration the government awarded Knott £230 'as our gift and bounty', making it clear this should not be seen as a precedent. The goods Knott handed over were worth £800. He'd also been forced to abandon his career in the merchant navy in the face of threats from the pirates to 'torture him to death if ever he should fall into their hands'. It seems unlikely other merchant captains saw the government's 'bounty' as any great incentive to honesty in the future.

The men who went to St Thomas attempted to sell the *Royal Rover* to the Danish governor. Negotiations were proceeding when a detachment of British soldiers arrived, hunting down deserters, and the men were forced to flee, leaving behind substantial quantities of sugar, tobacco, iron and gunpowder on board the ship, as well as 'fifteen negroes'. The pirates managed to escape. But the six men they had left on Anguilla were quickly captured, the authorities giving short shrift to their claim to be shipwrecked mariners. They were taken to Nevis, found guilty and hanged. One of them was black, which suggests that some, at least, of the Africans among Roberts' crew were not regarded as slaves, at least by the authorities.

Kennedy and the group in the *Eagle* washed up on the west coast of Scotland a few weeks later. Illiterate and unable to navigate, he had been aiming for Ireland but missed and had been 'tossed about by hard storms of wind for several days', according to Johnson. Coming ashore, they 'alarmed the country wherever they came, drinking and roaring at such a rate that the people shut themselves up in their houses in some places, not daring to venture out among so many mad fellows. In other villages they treated the whole town, squandering their money away . . . This expensive manner of living procured two of their drunken stragglers to be knocked on the head, they being found murdered in the road, and their money taken from them.'

As they neared Edinburgh the main group, comprising seventeen men, was arrested. The authorities weren't quite sure initially what to charge them with. But two of the men turned evidence against their colleagues and they were brought to trial for piracy at the Scottish High Court of the Admiralty in November 1720. Ten were found guilty, of whom nine swung on the gallows in the freezing winds of Leith sands for crimes they had committed far away in the tropical waters of Brazil and West Africa. Archibald Murray, the surgeon forced to serve with the pirates following the mutiny on the *Buck*, was a key witness, as were a number of officers from ships seized by Howel Davis at the start of 1719. Seven men were acquitted, the court accepting their claim that they were forced men.

The trial record is an invaluable source for Roberts' early career and for Howel Davis's captaincy. It describes the mutiny on the *Buck,* the sojourn at Sierra Leone, the rampage down the African coast, the events at Princes Island and the pirates' actions off Brazil and in the Caribbean. But there is one glaring omission. Nowhere in the entire eighty-two pages of handwritten notes is there a single reference to their desertion of Roberts at Devil's Islands.

There was no reason why the captured pirates would want to cover this up. They were claiming to have been forced men. The fact they had deserted Roberts could only count in their favour. Indeed, they attempted to portray the separation of the crew after the seizure of the *Eagle* as a desertion by themselves of the more hardened pirates who remained aboard the *Royal Rover* – a claim the court dismissed as an 'affected story'.

There is just one brief reference to their departure from Devil's Islands. Summarising events prior to the defendants' arrest, the prose-cution said that when Roberts failed to return from his pursuit of the brigantine he was suspected of having 'perished at sea'. The carpenter Richard Luntly, who was one of those found guilty, gave a similar account in a lengthy 'Last Speech and Dying Words' written just two days before he was executed. When Roberts didn't come back that night, Luntly claimed, the quartermaster fitted out both the *Royal Rover* and the *Sagrada Familia* to go and find him. Only when this proved unsuccessful did they leave for Barbados.

There is just one other account. It was given to the authorities in Barbados by John Watson, one of the forced men put aboard the *Sea Nymph,* and is the most detailed. After Roberts set off in the *Good Fortune* a group of pirates climbed to a high point to watch the chase, he said. They were able to see the brigantine. But then they 'heard a noise as of a great gun' and saw 'a great smoke'. The *Good Fortune* never emerged from beneath the cliffs of the island. Assuming it was blown up and all the men lost, they left the islands just two days later.

Is it possible Roberts and his men had entirely misunderstood events at Devil's Island, that they were never betrayed and that Kennedy and the others genuinely believed them to be dead? It's more complicated than this. There were deep divisions among the men that left Devil's Island. The group that eventually remained on the *Royal Rover* was less eager to abandon a life of piracy and was hostile to Kennedy. So contemptuous and mistrustful of him were they that they considered throwing him overboard rather than allowing him to leave for Britain in the *Eagle*, fearing he would betray them when he got home. He was only allowed to go after swearing solemn oaths of fidelity.

Roberts also had differences with Kennedy. The Irishman was one of the most fervent Jacobites in the crew. Passengers aboard the *Sea Nymph,* seized by Kennedy off Barbados, recalled him cursing King George and saying, 'We have 32 sail of ships and will endeavour to place James III upon the throne.' With Kennedy gone, this empty Jacobite bragging was no longer reported by captives among Roberts' crew, and Roberts also abandoned the practice of giving his ships Jacobite names. It may well be he was hostile to Kennedy's Jacobite politics – the result perhaps of a Baptist upbringing, or simply the anti-Irish prejudices of his youth – and this soured relations between them.

Roberts did not place Kennedy in charge of the men left behind on Devil's Islands. He took charge automatically because he was the most senior officer among them. When Roberts didn't return immediately, Kennedy – anxious to break up the crew and to divide the treasure from the *Sagrada Familia* among a smaller number – probably pressed for a hasty departure, allying himself with powerful factions in the crew. Two days seems a very short time to have waited for Roberts.

And it's likely the story of an explosion recounted by Watson was a deception, since we know the *Good Fortune* did not blow up and there was no one else on the islands. Once out at sea the loyalist faction was outnumbered and isolated and eventually had to submit to the will of Kennedy and his supporters. All this Kennedy was able to achieve without ever explicitly presenting it as a desertion.

Captain Johnson had excellent sources and was convinced Kennedy betrayed Roberts. And Roberts himself never wavered in this belief – despite the fact that he later captured Captain Cane for a second time and quizzed him about events on Devil's Islands. He also met at least one of the men from the *Royal Rover* faction again, greeting him amicably and allowing him to rejoin the crew.

Walter Kennedy himself did not face trial in Edinburgh. Having led his men to disaster in the Scottish Highlands he and a number of others quietly slipped away from the main group, although not before he'd had all his gold stolen by the Highlanders, he later claimed. Kennedy made his way to Ireland and from there to London, where he opened a brothel in Deptford.

The deserters had benefited little from their betrayal. Twenty-one had been hanged and many of the others had lost their gold. Back on the *Good Fortune,* bobbing on the waves off Surinam, Bartholomew Roberts paid for his rash decisions at Devil's Islands. When we next hear of the sloop and its depleted crew a few weeks later its captain is named as Thomas Anstis, the aggressive West Countryman passed over for the captaincy at Princes Island. Roberts had been deposed.

5

IN THE WILDER-NESS

WEST INDIES
DECEMBER 1719–MAY 1720

'THE TAKING OF PIRATES . . . IS BUT A DRY BUSINESS, UNLESS THEY CATCH 'EM BY EXTRAORDINARY GOOD FORTUNE WITH A PRIZE FRESH IN THEIR MOUTHS'

THE SWITCH IN COMMAND was achieved without violence. Pirates 'often displaced Captains,' Walter Kennedy later explained, 'having a sort of commonwealth among them, but very rarely suffered any violence to be offered them, but held a respect for any one who had been their commander'. But it must have been a bitter pill for Roberts to swallow after his triumph at Pernambuco. Having tasted power, a man of his drive and ambition was not going to resign himself to a place in the shadows and he watched eagerly for any chance to regain his position. He would not have long to wait. The events at Devil's Islands proved to be the start of a difficult few months for the crew of the *Good Fortune* and Anstis quickly revealed his limitations as a commander.

Like Kennedy and his men a few weeks before, the *Good Fortune* headed for the Windward and Leeward Islands in the eastern Caribbean. Stretched in a chain at regular 20- to 30-mile intervals from the Virgin Islands to Trinidad, the archipelago formed one of the most beautiful waterways in the world – a series of vivid green emeralds, rising to densely forested volcanic peaks, each set in a frame of golden beaches, scattered across a sparkling blue sea. Set slightly apart from the rest, to the east, was the island of Barbados, the richest and most densely populated of the British colonies in the area. Barbados was often the first stop for ships coming from Europe, North America and Africa and the pirates, in desperate need of provisions, knew it would yield a plentiful supply of prizes.

Pirate tactics were simple and exploited the limitations of navigation in this age. The captains of merchant ships were able to calculate their latitude – or north–south position – by measuring the angle of the shadow cast by the sun at midday. This was a comparatively simple technique that had been known since ancient times. But there was no method for calculating longitude – a ship's east – west position. Parliament had offered a £20,000 prize to anyone who could solve the riddle in 1714, but it was not until the second half of the eighteenth century that a practical method was found. In the meantime captains simply hit the line of latitude required as soon as possible and then sailed due east or west, depending on their destination. Ships sailing for Barbados hit the line of 13 degrees north and then sailed west. All the men of the *Good Fortune* had to do was park themselves a few miles due east of the island and wait for ships to sail into their net.

The first to appear was the *Essex,* a two-masted schooner from Salem in New England, a welcome present on Christmas Day 1719. The pirates kept it for seven days, plundering it of pork, beer, bread, fish, butter, apples, cider, geese, fowls, running rigging, carpenter's tools and large quantities of clothing. Two of the crew were forced to join the pirates. The captain reported the *Good Fortune* to have eight guns and forty men.

They then headed briefly for Tobago, a few miles to the south.

They seized a small French sloop that was hunting for turtles in the area, liberating, on a whim, two boys, an Indian and a mulatto, who were serving aboard as slaves or servants. Then, on 10 January 1720 they attacked a sloop called the *Phillipa* from Barbados. The boarding party approached it in a long boat and the *Phillipa*'s captain, Daniel Graves, 'sick and lame with the gout' at the time, ordered his men 'to fire at them and kill them'. At this the pirates identified themselves as 'Englishmen and marooners' and threatened to murder every man aboard if they did not surrender. The crew wisely complied and the *Phillipa* was plundered of two cannons, 15 small arms, two pairs of pistols, a 60-gallon cask of rum, a hogshead of bread, some sugar and, once more, large quantities of clothes. The pirates also took three white sailors and 'six negro men', one of whom was identified as 'Kent a ship carpenter'. Captain Graves received only a rope and a couple of small sails in return.

They were back in the latitude of Barbados by 12 February when they took a ship called the *Benjamin*, en route from New York. They took bread, bacon and pork, giving the captain four barrels of old flour, a piece of old sail and 'three live hogs' in return. Their lack of generosity contrasted with Kennedy's following his desertion at Devil's Islands and reflected their straitened circumstances. On releasing the *Benjamin* three days later they threatened to kill the captain if he did not divert to the Leeward Islands – a threat he ignored, sailing in to Barbados the following day and giving a full description of the *Good Fortune* to the authorities. He told them the pirates had six guns and seventy men.

Over the next few days the *Good Fortune* took at least three more vessels off Barbados, including a sloop called the *Joseph*, whose captain they gifted a set of surgeon's instruments. But Anstis was pushing his luck. By 1720 a pirate could not stay bobbing on the waves indefinitely in one of the Caribbean's busiest shipping channels. This was no backwater and, unlike West Africa and Brazil, there was a substantial Royal Navy presence in the region.

This was a comparatively recent innovation. Until the mid-seventeenth century it had not been regarded as the Royal Navy's duty to defend merchant shipping and the Navy's ships had generally kept to home waters in peace time. But by the early eighteenth century there was a general recognition that Britain's wealth and power depended on her ability to trade – and Britain's possessions in the New World were the jewel in the crown of the country's burgeoning mercantile empire.

When the *Good Fortune* arrived off Barbados in the winter of 1719–20, the Navy had eleven ships on station in the Caribbean and North American mainland colonies, carrying a combined total of 288 guns and 1,485 men. The bulk of these were in the West Indies. And although most of the firepower was concentrated in Jamaica, far to the west, there were three vessels on station in the Eastern Caribbean: HMS *Rose* (with 20 guns and 115 men) and HMS *Shark* (14 guns and 80 men), both stationed in the Leeward Islands, and HMS *Milford* (30 guns and 155 men), stationed in Barbados. This was a substantial force and HMS *Milford* alone was more than powerful enough to blow the *Good Fortune* out of the water.

But the Royal Navy in the Caribbean was always weaker in reality than it appeared on paper. Captains were hobbled by a series of petty, penny-pinching rules from the Admiralty. They were obliged to return to England to take in provisions because supplies in the West Indies were more expensive. They were forbidden from hiring houses on shore to treat their sick men. Worst of all, in the years immediately after the arrival of peace in 1713, they had been forbidden from careening for fear it would damage the ships. This fatally slowed them. By 1720 some of the more absurd restrictions had been removed. But Navy ships remained fish out of water in the Caribbean compared to their pirate adversaries, who were superbly adapted to the tropical environment.

Sickness and disease were a major problem. It's estimated between 12 and 15 per cent of all European emigrants to the West Indies died within a year of arriving, and figures for the Royal Navy were, if anything, worse. As late as the 1780s one in seven seamen in the region could expect to die during the course of a calendar year. The main killers were malaria, yellow fever and dysentery, but dropsy, leprosy, yaws (a type of syphilis) and hookworm all took their toll. Pirates do not seem to have died in quite the same numbers. They were generally 'seasoned' men who had already spent time in the tropics and acquired a level of immunity. And their greater leisure and more ample provisions meant they were probably healthier, despite the extraordinary quantity of alcohol they drank.

The risk of death from disease made the Caribbean an unpopular posting and captains compensated for it in other ways. 'By dear experience we know [they] love trading better than fighting,' noted the *New England Courant* bitterly in 1722. Royal Navy captains were notorious for indulging in a whole range of moneymaking schemes to the detriment of their duties. In June 1718 Governor Nicholas Lawes of Jamaica wrote to the Council of Trade and Plantations complaining that piracy was rife around the island. 'This in great measure I impute to the neglect of the Commanders of HM ships of war,' he fulminated. The *Ludlow Castle,* he claimed, had sailed for the Spanish colonies within six days of arriving 'full of merchandise, without giving me the least notice thereof . . . and I am still altogether a stranger when that ship is to return. The *Winchelsea* has not been here since my arrival. I am given to understand she is likewise a trading on the Spanish coast. And the *Diamond* sailed about ten days ago full of goods (as I am informed) for the coast of New Spain.'

By the following January the situation had not improved and the seas around Jamaica was still infested by pirates. 'I must leave it to the commanders of HM ships to give an account on what service they have been employed ever since my arrival here,' Lawes concluded. 'All I shall say is had they been stationed in guarding our coast and cruising in proper places it might probably have prevented the mischief that has happened to us.' Their activities not only left the island defenceless but also provided unfair competition to legitimate traders since the Navy captains had a free labour force at their disposal. Jamaican seamen 'have not bread for want of employment, which is the chief occasion of so many of them going a pirating', Lawes complained.

Antagonism between colonial governors and Navy captains was endemic. Governor Alexander Spotswood in Virginia and Governor Walter Hamilton in the Leeward Islands, both tireless enemies of piracy, were exasperated by the lethargy of the captains on their station. And Governor Woodes Rogers in the Bahamas even challenged Captain Hildesley of the *Flamborough* to a duel at one point, although it was never fought. In theory governors had considerable authority over Navy captains, if not absolute control. In practice the captains were contemptuous of civilian officials and reluctant to obey their orders. The fact that few of the small-scale pirates in the Caribbean carried much gold or other valuables on board meant there was little incentive to track them down. As one contemporary pointed out, 'the taking of pirates . . . is but a dry business, unless they catch 'em by extraordinary good fortune with a prize fresh in their mouths'.

Between 1715 and 1720 the Royal Navy achieved just one significant success against the pirates – the defeat of Blackbeard off North Carolina in November 1718 by Captain Maynard in the *Jane*. Originally from Bristol, Blackbeard, whose real name was Edward Teach, had terrorised the Caribbean and North American coast for two years. A former privateer during the War of the Spanish Succession, he got his name from his long, thick beard, which he tied in ringlets and to which he attached burning matches when he went into battle, giving him a demonic appearance. Although better known, he was far less successful than Roberts would be and owes his fame to the fact that he actively cultivated a terrifying image and was later the subject of a successful play. Even his defeat was achieved largely at the prompting of Governor Spotswood of Virginia. Other than that the pirates were able to operate with extraordinary freedom. As Captain Johnson acidly commented;

> 'Tis strange that a few pirates should ravage the seas for years without ever being light upon by any of our ships of war, when, in the mean time, they [the pirates] shall take fleets of ships. It looks as if one was much more diligent in their affairs than the other.

When the *Good Fortune* arrived in the Windward and Leeward Islands in the winter of 1719–20 the Navy was distracted by the outbreak of the short-lived War of the Quadruple Alliance against Spain. All three local ships were away from their station, *Milford* and *Shark* on convoy duty while *Rose* had been stranded in Jamaica by an outbreak of sickness among the crew.

However, Barbados was not defenceless. By chance there were two other Royal Navy ships in Bridgetown – HMS *Squirrel* and HMS *Rye,* both normally based in North America. *Squirrel* was there to con-voy a fleet of merchantmen north. *Rye* had been driven south to avoid floating ice as the rivers of Virginia thawed following an unusually cold winter. Between them they carried 40 guns and 215 men, easily enough to overwhelm the *Good Fortune* which, at that moment, was bobbing on the waves a few miles to the east. For all its ineptness the Navy had a golden opportunity to stamp out this particular pirate crew before it could gather strength again. But the men of the *Good Fortune* were saved as the result of a bizarre decision by the authorities in Barbados.

Around 12 February Governor Robert Lowther summoned Captain Smart of HMS *Squirrel* and Captain Whorwood of HMS

Rye to see him. When they arrived he arrested them both and slung them into jail. A few days before they had seized a vessel called the *Pearl* that had previously been in use as a pirate ship under the command of Edward England. Lowther insisted that, since it had been taken in his jurisdiction, it should be handed over to him. Whorwood and Smart refused. These tugs-of-war over prizes was common. Captain Smart had been involved in a similar dispute with the governor of New England a year before – a dispute which also ended in his being thrown in jail after he fought a duel with the governor's secretary. Captain Whorwood of HMS *Rye* had also quarrelled repeatedly with Governor Spotswood in Virginia.

Whatever the rights or wrongs of this particular case, Governor Lowther was cutting off his nose to spite his face. He was not one of the more able governors in the region and was removed from his post later in the year, in part because of his actions at this time. Captain Smart managed to break out of jail after just a few hours, returned to his ship and immediately left the island. But Whorwood remained in prison for twenty-two days. During this time a procession of merchant captains arrived with tales of being robbed in their passage to the island by Anstis and his men. The merchants of Barbados begged Lowther to release Whorwood and offered to pay his bail, but Lowther was adamant.

Eventually, in desperation, the merchants decided to mount their own expedition against the *Good Fortune*. Governor Lowther agreed to grant them a twenty-day commission and they fitted out two vessels – the *Somerset Galley*, from Bristol, under the twenty-eight-year-old Captain Owen Rogers, and the *Phillipa*, the same sloop that had been captured by the pirates at Tobago a month previously, under the gouty Captain Daniel Graves. The *Somerset Galley* alone, with 16 guns and 130 men, was more than a match for the pirates, and the *Phillipa* carried an additional six guns and 60 men.

The two ships set sail from Bridgetown on Sunday 21 February 1720. The crews were recruited locally and the Barbados council saw fit to record pen portraits of each of the men – a precaution in case they absconded and turned pirate themselves, which wasn't unknown in these situations. Most of the descriptions were fairly simple – 'a tall thin man', 'a short thick man', 'a young fair man', 'a short, pox-broken man'. But forty-year-old John July from Cornwall, we are told, was a 'lusty jolly man', and twenty-four-year-old George Tucker from England was a 'pretty well set seaman, brown complexion'. Captain Rogers was 'short and thick'. Many were described as 'black' or 'brown', although for the most part, as with Captain Johnson's description of Roberts as a 'black man', this simply meant they had a dark, swarthy complexion rather than that they were Africans. The majority were in their twenties, like the pirates they were being sent to hunt.

After four days at sea they encountered a small French trader. The French captain informed them he'd been seized by the *Good Fortune* a few days before and that they had cut down his mizzen (rear) mast and a third of his main mast for their own use. The pirates had taken a small sloop from Virginia shortly before, he told them, and were now using it as a consort. He estimated they numbered about eighty, of whom twenty were in the new sloop. They had ten guns, all in their main sloop, and were now slightly to the north, in the latitude of Antigua, cruising 'up and down for a ship'.

The following morning, 26 February, Rogers and Graves spotted the *Good Fortune* and its consort, bearing down fast on them from the east with the wind behind them. 'The biggest sloop fired a shot at us, and then another, and when she came in musket shot she fired another,' wrote Captain Rogers in his log. Both of the pirate sloops then hoisted black flags 'with death's head & co.' and, drawing close, ordered Rogers to surrender. When he failed to respond they poured a broad-side into the *Somerset Galley* accompanied by 'a continual fire of small arms'. Rogers and his men 'lay still in expectation they would board us', presumably hoping to surprise them with their superior numbers (Captain Maynard had defeated Blackbeard using a similar ruse). But instead, perhaps sensing a trick, the pirates veered away. Rogers now ordered his men to open fire and cannon balls and grapeshot tore through the *Good Fortune*. Rogers saw three men, including the pirate drummer, killed instantly. Two others, who were in the long boat being towed behind the *Good Fortune*, were also killed and the remaining three men in the boat were cut adrift. A cannon ball ripped a gaping hole in the *Good Fortune*'s hull and the pirates' carpenter was forced to lower himself over the side in the midst of the battle to repair it, 'hundreds of bullets flying round him'. He succeeded in stopping the leak but two men who went with him were washed away.

Now was the moment to move in for the kill. The pirates' smaller consort had sped away to the south the moment the *Somerset Galley* opened fire, never to be heard of again. The *Good Fortune* was at their mercy. Rogers' men crowded to the edge of the ship with their pistols and cutlasses ready to board. But as they closed the *Phillipa,* which until now had played no part in the battle, suddenly came between the two vessels. It was all Rogers could do to stop his men firing across the decks of the *Phillipa* into the pirate vessel. Rogers called out to Captain Graves 'begging and praying that he would board the pirate, but he never made any assault, or fired a gun until the pirate was out of gunshot'.

The pirates sped away and were observed throwing bread chests overboard and even sawing down their gunwales (the upper planking along the sides of the ship) to lighten the load. The *Somerset Galley* was able to make little progress in pursuit of them – 'our running rigging &c being all shot about our ears', wrote Rogers. He screamed at Captain Graves in the *Phillipa,* which had not suffered damage, to give chase. But Graves was slow to set his sails and never pulled in his long boat which, towed behind, slowed him down. Around four in the afternoon he tarried to allow the *Somerset Galley* to draw level and asked how long they should continue the pursuit. 'Till night,' bellowed the exasperated Captain Rogers, but around 7 p.m. they were forced to give up the chase. Six days later, on 3 March, they limped back into Barbados amid bitter recriminations.

Captain Graves claimed his helmsman had made a mistake, which was why he'd ended up between the *Somerset Galley* and the pirate sloop, and that he'd been unable to catch the pirate because he didn't have enough sails on board. It's impossible to know whether he deliberately sabotaged the mission. He'd spent time, of course, with this very pirate crew a month before and it's possible he'd developed some sort of relationship with them. But he may simply have been incompetent.

The pirates gave three cheers and fired 'a volley and a broadside' in celebration as they watched their pursuers turn away. It had been a close call and would have been far worse if it had been HMS *Rye* and HMS *Squirrel* pursuing them. But this was the lowest point yet for them. Rogers claimed he'd killed around thirty-five of the pirates. This was probably an exaggeration. Even so, the *Good Fortune* was badly damaged and the crew had suffered a number of casualties. And they'd lost their consort. The slow recovery of the last couple of months had been undone and they were now in a worse position than when they left Devil's Islands. At this moment it looked as if the *Good Fortune* would be little more than a footnote in pirate history, part of the broader story of the break up of Howel Davis's crew.

Roberts saw it differently. He must have taken a grim satisfaction from the debacle. The near disaster had dented Anstis's authority and he knew this was his chance to regain command. It may even have been Roberts, with his sharp eye for 'the bulk and force of any ship', who guessed the true strength of the *Somerset Galley* and warned them against boarding it at the last moment. Shortly afterwards he was reinstated as captain.

The crew of the *Good Fortune* then disappeared from the radar of the authorities for the next three months, the only time this happened during the whole of Roberts' pirate career. It was a time of rest and gradual recuperation spent skulking in the backwaters of the Caribbean. They were back down to around forty men and lived from hand to mouth. But it was during this period that Roberts forged the core of what would soon, once more, be the most powerful pirate crew in the Atlantic. He restored their resolve and self-confidence. And from now on there would be no doubt that this was his crew, rather than the remnant of Howel Davis's.

They repaired the *Good Fortune* on some unrecorded beach or cay. Then they made their way to the island of Dominica – squeezed between the French colonies of Martinique and Guadeloupe, but officially ceded to the Carib Indians – to take in water and buy provisions from the small French community there. There they came across thirteen English smugglers, who had been dumped by a French coast guard vessel. One of them – Joseph Mansfield – was a former highwayman and a deserter from HMS *Rose*. All thirteen were happy to join the pirates and they were to prove enthusiastic recruits.

They needed to careen but Roberts knew they were vulnerable at Dominica because of the proximity of the French islands. Instead, they headed south for the Grenadines, the string of tiny islets between St Vincent and Grenada in the southern Windward Islands. There was no formal colonial government here and the islands were inhabited mainly by Indians and the occasional community of 'maroons': escaped slaves, many of whom had made their way across from Barbados and lived in small, self-governing communities. A maze of sandbanks and narrow channels, the islands were accessible only to smaller vessels and to those who knew the waters well. The pirates made their way to the tiny island of Carriacou. There they hauled the *Good Fortune* into a lagoon and prepared to clean it.

Travellers of the eighteenth century took little pleasure in tropical landscapes. The golden sands, the turquoise seas, the nodding palms — they held no appeal, perhaps because they were so associated with death and disease. But to modern eyes Bartholomew Roberts' career consisted of a tour of tropical paradises, and Carriacou was as beautiful as any of the islands he visited. Just a few miles across, it was ringed with white, sandy beaches and the countryside was a riot of brightly coloured, tropical flowers. The name means 'land surrounded by reefs' in the Carib language and the warm waters teemed with fish. After the stress and fear of Pernambuco, Devil's Islands and Barbados, Roberts' men were able to relax in the shade of the palms. Many pirate crews at this time never grew beyond fifty men and never left the Caribbean, and it's easy to see why. Freedom and an easy life, that was their motivation. But Roberts was different. He wanted to cut a figure in the world, to inspire awe and respect. He sought wealth, fame and power and, ultimately, a comfortable retirement. For all the disappointments of the last few months, he was still filled with restless energy and ambition. He knew they'd come close to disaster at Barbados and that they were vulnerable, not just to men-of-war, but to any large, armed sloop that local traders fitted out to hunt them down. He wanted more men, he wanted a larger ship, and he wanted them fast. There was a faction in the crew that also wanted to move on, if only for the want of wine and women on Carriacou. They careened unusually quickly, staying little more than a week. Their haste saved their lives.

At Dominica the local French community had somehow discovered the pirates' destination as they left. They informed the Governor of Martinique and he fitted out two sloops to pursue them. Navigating the narrow channels of the Grenadines they quickly closed in on the lagoon at Carriacou. But they arrived to find the island empty. They'd missed the *Good Fortune* by a matter of hours.

6

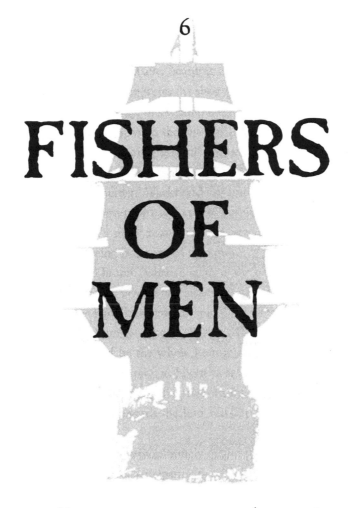

FISHERS OF MEN

NEWFOUNDLAND AND THE ATLANTIC
JUNE–SEPTEMBER 1720

'THERE WAS NOTHING HEARD AMONG THE

PIRATES ALL THE WHILE, BUT CURSING,

SWEARING, DAMNING AND BLASPHEMING TO

THE GREATEST DEGREE IMAGINABLE'

N 21 JUNE 1720 THE *Good Fortune,* with Roberts in command, sailed into the fishing harbour of Trepassey on the southern shore of Newfoundland with its guns blazing, drums beating and trumpets blaring, a black flag with 'death's head and cutlass' flying at the mast-head. There were twenty-two ships and somewhere between 150 and 250 small fishing boats, or shallops, in the bay. Between them they carried 1200 men and 40 guns but they surrendered without a shot fired, the men and their officers fleeing ashore for safety.

The *Good Fortune* still carried just 12 guns and around 60 men. But with the harbour secure the pirates were able to embark on an orgy of destruction. Captain Johnson lamented:

It is impossible to recount the . . . havoc they made here, burning and sinking all the shipping . . . destroying the fisheries and stages of the poor planters without remorse or compunction: for nothing is so

deplorable as power in mean and ignorant hands. It makes men wanton and giddy, unconcerned at the misfortunes they are imposing on
their fellow creatures, and keeps them smiling at the mischiefs that
bring themselves no advantage. They are like mad men that cast fire-
brands, arrows and death and say, are we not in sport?

Johnson was exaggerating slightly, relying on a sensationalist report
in the *Boston Newsletter*. From eyewitness accounts we know just one
ship was burned, none were sunk and no one was killed. The damage
was nevertheless extensive and his description of the pirates being
'giddy' with their own power chimes with other accounts of this attack.
Of no one was this more true than Roberts himself. 'He made the
masters all prisoners and beat some of them heartily for their cowardice
in not making any resistance,' one account recorded. He berated them
for their 'incivility in not waiting upon him to make him welcome at
his entrance', and threatened to hang one of them as punishment. He
was particularly contemptuous of Captain Babidge of the *Bideford
Merchant*, the admiral of the port, who had abandoned his ship 'with
Jack, ensign and pendant flying, the guns all loaden'. The pirates
showed their contempt by boarding his vessel, striking his colours,
raising their own and then firing his guns. They cut down his main-
mast and did the same to several other ships and slashed the cables and
rigging of the remaining vessels. Over the next few days, as his men
plundered the port, Roberts fired a gun each morning 'at which . . . all
the masters [were] obliged to go on board to receive their orders for the
day. One [order] was that no house, chest or locker . . . should be
locked while he remained there, under pain of severe punishment.'

As so often, the pirates benefited from the fact the common men
showed little enthusiasm for defending their masters' property. Many
were sympathetic. Roberts never left the *Good Fortune* but his men
came on shore, forty or fifty at a time, and got 'all hands drunk along

with such fishermen as remain in the harbour', according to one report. Around half a dozen men joined the pirate crew, while four or five others were forced.

This was a very different Roberts from the clumsy, blundering commander of Devil's Islands and the disgraced, demoted captain last seen scuttling away from Barbados. This was once again the Roberts of Pernambuco, in firm command of his vessel and his crew, defeating overwhelming odds through sheer daring, and clearly revelling in the power he had regained. He'd used the previous three months in the Caribbean well and his crew was once more a formidable fighting force. Even Governor Spotswood of Virginia was forced to comment on 'the boldness of this fellow'.

The summer migration northwards to the fishing grounds of Newfoundland was common among pirates. It was part of what was known as the 'pirate round' and was always followed by a return to the warmer waters of the Caribbean, West Africa or the Indian Ocean in the autumn. As in West Africa, pirates went to Newfoundland primarily in search of large, ocean-going vessels and men. They were rarely disappointed.

The banks south and east of Newfoundland were the richest source of cod in the world. The Vikings and then the Basques had fished there long before Columbus discovered America and the English moved into the region in the Elizabethan era. Along with the expansion of the coal trade between Newcastle and London, the Newfoundland fishery was the main stimulus for the dramatic growth of the English merchant fleet in the late sixteenth and early seventeenth centuries. In 1719 the fishery employed 119 ships along with 680 smaller boats. But conditions for the 3,000–4,000 men who worked there each summer were harsh.

The trade was dominated by the small West Country towns of Barnstaple, Bideford, Poole, Dartmouth and Topsham. The men were hired from the countryside around at spring fairs, contracts often signed at the Dartmouth Inn or Newfoundland Tavern in Newton Abbot, the deal lubricated with liberal helpings of cider, beer and Jamaica rum. Most bound themselves over to their masters for periods of between one and five years. The ships departed each spring, heading first to the Cape Verde Islands or the Caribbean to pick up salt to preserve their catch. They left Newfoundland in the autumn bound for Spain, Portugal and the Mediterranean, their principal markets, returning to England with cargoes of wine, oil and gold.

The fishing was done with lines rather than nets and was tough, exhausting work. No sooner was the ship full than they'd return to harbours such as Trepassey and 'pew' the fish onto the landings using pitchforks – an operation similar to forking hay on to a rick. There, separate teams of 'headers', 'splitters' and 'salters' would take over while the fishing vessel headed straight back out to the banks. This continued all summer long. There had been a time when fishermen received a share of the catch – a last echo of the mediaeval tradition whereby sailors on all merchant vessels had a share in the cargo. But by 1720 this practice was dying out. More and more fishing was also being done in deeper waters far off-shore. This was unpopular with English fisher-men and increasingly the West Country ships were stopping off in Ireland to recruit men there from the impoverished peasantry.

By 1720 settlements were springing up along the coastline of south-east Newfoundland and local planters and master fishermen were starting to compete with the West Country merchants for control of the industry. It was a development the West Country men resisted, petitioning parliament for the settlers to be removed. Eventually a com-promise was reached whereby settlements were permitted but were not granted full colonial status. The result was a series of forlorn, inhospitable outposts dotted along Newfoundland's rocky coastline, of which Trepassey was just one. There were no connecting roads and behind them lay nothing but a barren hinterland, deforested to build huts and landing stages and inhabited only by dwindling bands of hostile, Beothuk Indians. There were no schools, the church had almost no presence and the only government was provided by the masters of the larger vessels and the captains of the two Royal Navy ships which were sent out each summer to convoy the fishing fleet.

During the bleak North Atlantic winters there was no government at all and the population shrank to a little under 2,000 people, almost all of them men. During these months the island was notorious for its lawlessness. 'Theft, murder, rape or disorders of any kind may be committed without control,' wrote one visitor in 1715. In 1720 the residents of Petty Harbour complained to the government that they laboured 'under severe difficulties for the want of administration and justice amongst us and in the winter season . . . [we] are in danger of our lives from our servants whose debauched principles lead them to commit wilful and open murder upon their masters'.

But the masters did little to help themselves, often selling their men vast quantities of rum as a means of driving them into debt. This was intended to bind the poor fishermen to their employers and so stem the steady drain of men from Newfoundland to New England where wages were higher and there was an abundant supply of cheap, fertile land. Many fishermen were reduced to virtual slavery as a result of the masters' control of the supply, not just of alcohol, but all other commodities. Not surprisingly, many fled at the first opportunity. Provision ships and fishing vessels from New England were frequent visitors to the island and their captains were more than happy to 'spirit' men away, hiding them in casks when necessary. The pirates who came without fail each summer were on much the same mission and many of the impoverished fishermen of Newfoundland were equally happy to sign up for service beneath the black flag.

In 1720 Roberts was helped by the fact that the two Royal Navy vessels that normally spent the summer in Newfoundland were late arriving. He also quickly built up his strength. He and his men had arrived off the east coast of the island about a week or two before the raid on Trepassey. They seized a number of vessels there, forcing several men to join their crew. Among them was an elderly fisherman from Dartmouth called Moses Reynolds who would spend three months with them and later give the authorities a detailed description of their activities during this time. He is the first source to refer to Roberts as 'John', and also provided an early example of the vengefulness that would become one of Roberts' most marked characteristics.

While off eastern Newfoundland, in the weeks before the raid on Trepassey, the pirates seized a ship from Bristol, whose captain had formerly traded out of Barbados. Captain Rogers, who had chased them off Barbados, had also come from Bristol, and, according to Reynolds, they decided to give the captain a beating, apparently seeing this as a way of exacting vicarious revenge on both ports. He was only saved when he told them the gossip on Barbados was that Rogers' expedition against them had been successful and that the *Good Fortune* had been sunk. Why he said this is unclear – both Captain Rogers and Captain Graves had been open about their failure when they'd returned to Bridgetown. But the story so delighted the pirates that, 'in their merriment', they handed the captain back his ship and sent him on his way.

About a week before the attack on Trepassey they mounted a smaller raid on the harbour of Ferryland. There they burnt the local admiral's ship and one other. Roberts' confidence was already high and he cheerfully informed his victims at Ferryland that he intended to sail to Trepassey. But, although the authorities had notice of his coming a day or two before his arrival, they 'were so confounded that they could not put themselves in a posture of defence', according to a press report.

At Trepassey, Roberts achieved his ambition of acquiring a larger vessel, taking over a galley (a large ship with oar ports) from Bristol. He spent ten days converting it into a fighting ship, forcing carpenters from the other boats to work into service, and loaded it with 18 guns. He kept the *Good Fortune* as his support vessel and now had 30 guns under his command. A few days later he raided the small harbour of St Mary's; after his experience at Barbados he may have been pursuing a policy of destroying ports in his rear. Then, at the start of July, he headed south-east towards the Grand Banks, the main fishing area, knowing that he had the shipping there at his mercy.

The pirates quickly snapped up a number of large French fishing boats. Captain Johnson claimed Roberts seized nine or ten vessels and sank all of them apart from one. This would have meant the indis-criminate slaughter of their crews, and, again, Johnson was relying on the sensationalist reporting of the *Boston Newsletter*. Moses Reynolds, who was still with them, said they took 'five or six' ships, none of which they sunk, taking 'only . . . wine or brandy or ammunition'. Reynolds also noted that 'they would not force or permit any French or any other nation to be with them, only English'.

Roberts decided to keep one of the French vessels, a sizeable ship of 220 tons, for his own use, loading it with 26 guns and naming it the *Royal Fortune*. He did not yet feel strong enough to man three vessels, or even two large ones, and so abandoned the Bristol galley he had taken such trouble to convert at Trepassey just a few days before, keeping the smaller *Good Fortune* as his consort. He now had 34 to 36 guns in total, more than he'd had on the *Royal Rover* prior to the desertion at Devil's Islands.

The pirates then headed out into the Atlantic, beyond the Banks, and parked themselves in the latitude of New England, a couple of hundred miles south-east of Newfoundland. Here they sat for around a week hoovering up not just fishing vessels but also large merchant ships passing between Britain and the New England ports. They took around a dozen prizes in all. From them they seized goods –

particularly tobacco – and provisions. More importantly, they scooped up large numbers of men, some forced, others willing volunteers. Many were from the West Country and they would form an important block in Roberts' crew from this time onwards.

One of the ships taken at this time was the *Samuel*, a London-based ship headed for Boston under Captain Samuel Cary, seized on 13 July 1720. The *Boston Newsletter* later gave a lurid description of Cary's ordeal which has become one of the best-known accounts of capture by pirates:

> The first thing the pirates did was to strip both passengers and seamen of all their money and clothes which they had on board, with a loaded pistol to every one's breast ready to shoot him down who did not immediately give an account of both, and resign them up. The next thing they did was, with madness and rage, to tear up the hatches, enter the hold like a parcel of furies, where with axes, cutlasses etc., they cut, tore and broke open the trunks, boxes, cases and bales, and when any of the goods came upon deck which they did not like to carry with them aboard their ship, instead of tossing them into the hold again they threw them over-board into the sea. The usual method they had to open chests was by shooting a brace of bullets with a pistol into the key-hole to force them open. The pirates carried away from Captain Cary's ship aboard their own 40 barrels of powder, two great guns, his cables etc. and to the value of about £9–10,000 sterling worth of the choicest goods he had on board. There was nothing heard among the pirates all the while, but cursing, swearing, damning and blaspheming to the greatest degree imaginable, and often saying they would not go to Hope Point [the pirates' name for Execution Dock in Wapping] in the River of Thames to be hung up in gibbets a sun-drying as Kidd and Bradish's company did, for if it should chance that they should be

attacked by any superior power or force, which they could not master, they would immediately put fire with one of their pistols to their powder, and go all merrily to hell together!

They 'ridiculed and made mock' at the King's various offers of pardon for pirates, saying 'they had not got money enough' and would accept a pardon only when they had. Predictably the liquor store was one of the first targets and they 'made themselves very merry . . . with some hampers of fine wines'. Like Captain Snelgrave before him, Captain Cary noted their aversion to the use of corkscrews. 'It seems they would not wait to untie them and pull out the corks with screws, but each man took his bottle and with his cutlass cut off the neck and put it to their mouths and drank it out.'

Cary's account is quoted in almost every modern book on pirates. Given that other elements in the *Boston Newsletter*'s report are exaggerated, it may be embellished, not just by the newspaper, but also by Cary himself, anxious, like most pirate victims, to dispel any suspicion of complicity. But Roberts' men were clearly in aggressive mood. On a ship seized shortly afterwards the captain was 'used barbarously' because, like Captain Rogers in Barbados, he came from Bristol. On another they 'abused several women', according to the *Boston Gazette*. It's not clear what this means. Pirates sometimes raped slaves and other non-Europeans they captured, but very rarely white women, and it's likely the paper would have been more specific if this had been the crime.

The pirates took four men from the *Samuel*, leaving behind a fifth because he was Irish. One of them in particular attracted Roberts' attention – the first mate, a Scot called Henry Glasby. Glasby was a highly experienced seaman and, most importantly, a skilled navigator. As a former mate, Roberts could navigate, but given his scanty education his abilities were probably limited. Navigation required a high level of both numeracy and literacy and, like Royal Navy captains, Roberts carried a 'sailing master' who took responsibility for plotting the ship's course. Roberts had been using a man called Nicholas Thomas in this capacity when he first arrived at Newfoundland. He now had two ships and so needed two sailing masters. Glasby was a man of exceptional ability and Roberts was determined to add him to the crew. But, like most senior officers, Glasby had no interest at all in turning pirate. He tried to hide but the pirates found him, beat him and threw him aboard their vessel. He refused to sign the articles but was 'cut and abused very much'. In the end he complied and this most reluctant of pirates would play a central role in Roberts' story from this time on.

Roberts' thoughts were now turning to their next destination. The pirates told Captain Cary they were headed 'to the Southward, to the Island of New Providence, possessed by Negroes, in South Latitude 17, which they say is a place of the Pirates' General Rendezvous, where they have a Fortification and a great Magazine of Powder etc. where they intend to spend their money with the Portuguese Negro Women'. They were winding him up – there was no such island. But such whimsical notions were common among pirates. In their mind's eye they had converted Madagascar into a pirate paradise and they often fantasised about establishing pirate kingdoms. A couple of years earlier one of Captain Bellamy's men had urged him to set up a colony in North America to be peopled with Indians and 'the discontented and desperate people of the neighbouring English and French colonies'. 'Had they all united,' wrote Captain Johnson, 'and settled in some of those Islands, they might, by this time, have been honoured with the name of Commonwealth, and no power in those parts of the world could have been able to dispute it with them.'

These were no more than fantasies. The anarchic, centrifugal impulses within pirate crews were such that it was all captains like Roberts could do to hold their own men together, never mind form a confederation of pirate crews. But this didn't prevent the authorities indulging in lurid fantasies of their own. In their darkest moments they conjured up ghastly visions of a pirate-slave alliance that would rise up to overwhelm the civilisation of the New World. 'The negro men', warned Governor Bennet of Bermuda in 1718, 'are grown so very impudent and insulting of late that we have reason to suspect their rising [and] . . . should fear their joining with the pirates.' As they began to receive reports of his activities off Newfoundland, Bartholomew Roberts was terrifying to the authorities because he seemed the type of intelligent, able leader who might be able to harness pirate energies and make such dark fantasies reality.

In fact, Roberts and his men were headed not for a pirate utopia, but for Africa. By now Roberts's crew numbered around 130 men. But he was keen to build up his strength further and, like Howel Davis before him, he knew the warm waters of the Gulf of Guinea, clogged with crowded, disease-ridden slavers, were a perfect recruiting ground. The winds and the currents of the North Atlantic move in a great, clockwise swirl and, from their position south-east of Newfoundland, the African coast was just a few weeks sailing away. They set sail around 19 July, bound initially for the island of Brava at the southern end of the Cape Verde islands, where they intended to careen before beginning their assault on the mainland.

On long voyages like this life aboard quickly settled into a rhythm. Like the merchant ships they came from, pirates operated a watch system. Normally the presence of large numbers of slaves eased the workload, perhaps sparing some of the more senior pirates from the need to stand shifts. But they had lost most of their slaves at Devil's Islands and, as they headed east, their daily routine was closer to that of a conventional ship than at any other time in Roberts' pirate career.

The crews on the two ships were divided into a 'starboard' and a 'larboard' watch, which took alternating four-hour shifts. While one watch worked, the other rested, although generally both were on deck during the afternoon. The first shift began at noon and a senior officer kept time using an hour glass, ringing a bell every half hour. 'Eight bells' signalled the changing of the watch. The 'dog watch', between 4 and 8 p.m., was divided into two, two-hour shifts so that the shifts served by each watch alternated every day.

Even without slaves the pirates' lives were easier than those of merchant sailors. They were not racing to keep to a tight schedule. And, as on Royal Navy vessels, the extra men needed for a fighting ship eased the general workload. On merchant ships sailors were obliged to spend hours on general maintenance – mending ropes, sewing sails and, in tropical waters, endlessly scraping, sanding, oiling and painting the timbers to keep the ship's wooden body from decaying. But Roberts' men could largely neglect repairs, knowing they could always steal equipment from their next prize and, when necessary, take a new ship.

The pirates were better fed since their store room was constantly replenished, even if the requirements of conservation meant they suffered the same drab diet as other sailors when at sea – salt beef and pork, ship's biscuits, flour, oatmeal, dried peas, butter, suet, cheese and salted cod. The one-legged, one-eyed veterans who served as cooks were probably no more accomplished on pirate vessels than their counterparts in the Royal Navy. But pirates could, at least, be sure that there were no extra helpings for the officers. 'At meals the quartermaster overlooks the cook to see the provisions equally distributed to each mess,' wrote one pirate captive in 1724. Like all sailors they supplemented their rations with as much fresh food as possible. They may well have fished for sharks, although it's unlikely they adopted the slavers' practice of using 'dead negroes' as bait – if only for want of dead negroes.

One pirate captive, taken off the Cape Verde islands in 1722, recalled a tranquil moment one day when the ship was at anchor:

'Nobody had anything to do, but the lookers'out at the top mast head; the mate of the watch, the quartermaster of the watch, helmsman & co. being gone down to drink a dram, I suppose, or to smoke a pipe of tobacco, or the like.' Life aboard the *Royal Fortune* and the *Good Fortune* followed a similarly relaxed rhythm and Roberts' men filled their leisure in a variety of ways.

As item XI of Roberts' articles showed, his ships carried musicians. They were mainly recruited from the slavers where it was their job to provide accompaniment for the curious practice of 'dancing the slaves', described by the captain of a slave ship in the 1690s: 'We often at sea, in the evenings, would let the slaves come up into the sun to air themselves, and make them jump and dance for an hour or two to our bag'pipes, harp and fiddle, by which exercise to preserve them in health.' This grim dance of death provides a stark contrast to the scene aboard a pirate ship described by a pirate captive in the Indian Ocean in 1720. The pirates would practise with their weapons on deck, he wrote, 'while their musicians play divers airs so that the days pass very agreeably'.

Roberts' crew included at least a drummer, a trumpeter, an oboe player and a fiddler. They played on the raised poop deck at the rear of the ship in times of battle, as when the *Good Fortune* sailed into the harbour at Trepassey. They also played at celebrations and were expected to be on hand whenever the crew felt the need of them, other than Sundays. Like cooks, many musicians were invalids. Their fiddler, James White, was described as 'decrepit and ill'shapen, unfit for any purpose with them but music'.

It would be fascinating to hear the music produced by these racially hybrid pirate crews. The songs sung by conventional sailors to accom' pany such strenuous physical activities as raising the anchor, setting the sails and working the pumps bore a strong resemblance to African work songs with their use of call and response patterns. The famous rhyme in *Treasure Island*, which the evidence suggests may be authentic, was one:

Fifteen men on the Dead Man's Chest
Yo ho ho and a bottle of rum
Drink and the Devil had done for the rest,
Yo ho ho and a bottle of rum.

A single voice sang the first and third lines, the men singing the second and fourth together as they pulled on the ropes or windlass. 'Sailors' laments' have also been described as an early form of the blues. If sailors' music generally bore a strong African influence, this was heightened further among pirate musicians who lived side by side with large numbers of slaves for such lengthy periods of time and were largely cut off from the musical influences of their homelands. Pirate ships were one of the earliest crucibles for the great fusing of African and European music which would be such a feature of the musical life of the Americas for the next three hundred years.

Pirates also loved to gamble, and although the practice was banned on Roberts' ships it would be surprising if he was entirely successful in enforcing this rule. But, above all, pirates loved to drink. As the new sailing master, Henry Glasby, adapted to life among the pirates in the weeks after his capture he was staggered by the ferocious, incessant consumption of alcohol. They 'loved drinking and mirth', he later said, and there were many occasions when there were 'all hands drunk, and nobody fit for duty'. A number of the men were so constantly inebriated – or 'fuddled' – that they were unable to take part in attacks. And Joseph Mansfield – the former highwayman they had recruited at Dominica – probably spoke for many when he said later 'the love of drink and a lazy life' were 'stronger motives with him than gold'.

119

Glasby – a sober, disciplined personality, not unlike his new commander – was accustomed to heavy drinking on merchant ships. But this was something else. Unlike ordinary seamen pirates had access to fine wines and brandies. But their preference was always punch. Made from a combination of sugar, water, lime juice and rum, and sometimes nutmeg, it accompanied every aspect of pirate life. New recruits were plied with it and huge bowls were prepared every time a meeting was called. One pirate captive in 1724 noted that every man drank hot punch first thing in the morning, the look-out in the tops having it hauled up to him on a rope. However, their addiction to the drink did have one fortuitous side effect. The lime juice it contained meant that there are scarcely any references to pirates suffering from scurvy, which plagued most deep-sea sailors at this time.

Truly helpless alcoholics stood out and were disapproved of. Christopher Lang 'was a drunken fellow and of no esteem among the gang, they abusing him and often calling him Drunken Dog', one captive said. John Jessup was 'so drunk they cut him often out of his share'. And, when at sea, Roberts' men reined in their drinking slightly – otherwise they would have been unable to work their ships. But life aboard was not for the faint-hearted and, as he sat alone each evening, Glasby's feelings were similar to those expressed by a captive taken by pirates off New England in 1722:

I soon found that any death was preferable to being linked with such a vile crew of miscreants, to whom it was sport to do mischief, where prodigious drinking, monstrous cursing and swearing, hideous blasphemies, and open defiance of heaven, and contempt of hell itself, was the constant employment, unless when sleep something abated the noise and revellings.

Glasby was soon determined to escape.

Roberts too was still repelled by the constant drunkenness of his men and knew that drink posed the greatest threat to their survival. His career can be seen as the struggle of an intelligent, disciplined man against the anarchy inherent in the pirate way of life and, by this time, his captaincy was evolving in unusual ways. He had abandoned Davis's practice of dividing the crew into Lords and Commons. But, wisely, he had retained what Johnson called a 'privy-council of half a dozen of the greatest bullies, such as were his competitors' – men like Thomas Anstis, Valentine Ashplant and Little David, whom he was careful to keep close. His personal authority was growing. 'Roberts, by better management than usual, became the chief director in everything of moment,' wrote Johnson. He gained sole authority over the treatment of prisoners, which set him apart from other pirate captains, and used this to rein in the worst excesses of the crew, 'a much more rash and mad set of fellows than himself'. You sense he sometimes pined for the company of educated men and he liked to invite captured captains to his cabin for a quiet drink and a chat, making sure they understood they owed their good treatment to him and to him alone. But he was under no illusion that this would save him if ever he were caught. 'There is none of you but will hang me, I know, whenever you can clinch me within your power,' he would tell his guests, with a wry smile, as they left.

His style of captaincy represented a radical departure from pirate tradition. At times he was autocratic to the point of being dictatorial. But alcohol was the one area where he found it impossible to stamp his authority. Indeed, his reluctance to 'drink and roar at their rate' irritated the men. In the highly communal world of the pirate ship, his refusal to get drunk, combined with his solitary and detached personality, aroused suspicion and hostility. But success eased tensions, and as the two pirate ships headed east they were laden with booty.

We can picture them as they sped across the ocean. The *Royal Fortune* was perhaps 100 feet in length and 25 feet across, with a hold around 10 feet deep. It had three masts, each bearing two square-rigged sails. The *Good Fortune* was around two-thirds of its size, with one or at most two masts. They kept close company, the long boats occasionally passing between them, the sound of music and wild revelry drifting across the waves from time to time, alternating with periods of exhausted calm. By early August they had entered the tropics and, during the long, sultry afternoons, the pirates leant on the ship's rail, watching the shoals of flying fish. Long-tailed white 'tropic birds' began to follow the ships as they neared land, and the appearance of two islands, shaped like women's breasts and known to sailors as the 'Two Paps', signalled they were nearing their destination at the southern end of the Cape Verde Islands. But then disaster struck.

Somehow they missed Brava, where they had planned to careen – an act of sabotage perhaps by the new sailing master? South of the Cape Verde Islands the winds and currents switched once more towards the west and, before they knew it, the great clockwise swirl of the North Atlantic had carried them back out into mid-ocean with no chance of beating their way back. This was a catastrophe. They'd taken a couple of ships on their way south. One, a Portuguese vessel, yielded 700 moidores – equivalent to around £950. From another they took a French doctor, slitting one of his ears to force him to work for them. But they had taken no provisions to get them beyond the Cape Verde Islands. They worked on the assumption that their next meal was always just over the horizon. But there was not a sail in sight and they now had no choice but to continue westwards, hoping to reach South America before their food and water ran out.

They had just one hogshead of water – 63 gallons – for the 130 or so men aboard the two ships; this in a tropical climate where the only food they had was salted. Captain Johnson gave a pitiful description of their condition:

They continued their course and came to an allowance of one single mouthful of water for twenty-four hours; many of them drank their urine, or sea water, which, instead of allaying, gave them an inextinguishable thirst that killed them. Others pined and wasted a little more time in fluxes and apyrexies [fevers], so that they dropped away daily. Those that sustained the misery best, were such as almost starved themselves, forbearing all sorts of food, unless a mouthful or two of bread the whole day, so that those who survived were as weak as it was possible for men to be and alive.

He was exaggerating slightly to ram home a moral point – 'With what face could wretches who had ravaged and made so many necessitous look up for relief?' A captive who was with them at this point recorded only that they were 'short of water' and mentioned no deaths. But when finally they spotted land at some point towards the end of August they were in a desperate state, having travelled over 2,000 miles since missing the Cape Verde Islands. Dispatching a boat to fetch water, they found they were in the mouth of the Meriwinga River – now known as the Maroni River, which forms the border between French Guiana and Surinam. It was almost exactly the same spot where, eight months previously, they'd found themselves after adverse winds dragged them west from Devil's Islands.

The pirates slaked their immediate thirst and then headed north-west to Tobago where they fully watered the two vessels. They then sailed to the Grenadines in the southern Windward Islands and on 4 September anchored once more at the lovely island of Carriacou where they had careened prior to their journey to Newfoundland. They were still in desperate need of provisions. But they found the lagoon at Carriacou swarming with giant turtles. There was a British sloop called the *Relief* there on a hunting expedition and the pirates forced its captain, Richard Dunne, to hand over his catch. They built fires on the beach and once more lounged in the shade of the palms, gorging themselves on the succulent meat, the sweet green juices running down their beards.

They stayed at Carriacou for two weeks, slowly regaining their strength. They careened their vessels and as Roberts sat on the sand, looking out over the turquoise sea, listening to the sound of his men carousing, he was able to reflect on an astonishing fifteen months. Within a few months of being captured he'd both become captain and pulled off the extraordinary coup at Pernambuco. He'd then suffered the disaster of Devil's Islands, been demoted and come within a hair's breadth of death or capture at Barbados. He'd then regained the captaincy and led the hugely successful campaign off Newfoundland, only to come close to destruction again crossing the Atlantic. Even by the standards of eighteenth-century pirates, whose lives contained more ups and downs than most, it had been a roller-coaster.

But as he looked about him he knew he was still the head of a considerable force. Captain Dunne of the *Relief* later said the *Royal Fortune* 'had 28 guns on its upper and quarter deck and six swivel guns on its gunwale'. It also had six pairs of 'organs' – primitive, multiple-barrel guns that fired a number of musket balls simul-taneously – which were mounted in the fighting tops. The smaller *Good Fortune* had six guns. The combined crews still numbered around 130 and this put Roberts a cut above most pirates operating in the Caribbean and made him more than a match for all but the largest ships the Royal Navy had on station in the region. And it would be a bold merchant captain who would set off in pursuit of him in the way Captain Graves and Captain Rogers had done from Barbados the previous February. The time for the authorities to crush Roberts was when he had been weak, between December 1719 and May 1720. They had missed their chance.

7

'TO CREOLES WE ARE A FOE'

WEST INDIES
SEPTEMBER 1720–JANUARY 1721

'YOU MAY ASSURE YOURSELVES HERE AND HEREAFTER NOT TO EXPECT ANYTHING FROM OUR HANDS BUT WHAT BELONGS TO A PIRATE'

*R*OBERTS NOW ENTERED A period of sus-tained success, a period in which he scooped up prize after prize and grew steadily in strength. It was a period of revenge on those who had hunted him in the past, and for a lifetime of petty slights and humiliations – and, for the traders of the eastern Caribbean, one of havoc and devastation. By the end of it his reputation as the greatest pirate of the age would be firmly established.

Roberts spent most of the next seven months in the Windward and Leeward Islands. He may have had a pre-existing grudge against the authorities there. 'He used to say,' Walter Kennedy claimed, 'nothing from the King of England should content him, but the government of the Leeward Islands, and if he could not peaceably obtain them, he would e're long hold them by force.' Perhaps Roberts had bitter memories of the merchant captains and island governors in this part of the world from his time spent serving as mate aboard a sloop out of

Barbados. But there were sound practical reasons for an ambitious pirate to base himself here. This was where most of the British and French colonies in the Caribbean were located, the most prosperous and fastest growing in the region.

The island of St Christophers (modern St Kitts) in the Leeward Islands, first settled in 1624, was the mother colony for both powers. For the early settlers it had the advantage that it was remote from the main centres of Spanish power on Hispaniola and Cuba – a function partly of geography, but also winds. The eighteenth-century mariner's life was dominated by the concepts of 'windward' and 'leeward'. Windward was the direction *from* which the wind was blowing, leeward the direction *towards* which it was blowing. In the eastern Caribbean the prevailing winds blew from the east. Hence the first islands they hit were known as the Windward Islands, and the more sheltered islands to the north-west were the Leeward Islands. Both were to windward of the main Spanish settlements and any ship approaching them from Cuba or Hispaniola had to beat against the wind. St Christophers was more easily reached from London than from Havana.

From St Christophers the English moved into Barbados in 1627, Nevis in 1628 and Montserrat and Antigua in 1632, while the French moved into Guadaloupe and Martinique in 1635. The first settlers lived by planting tobacco but the economy of the region was transformed with the arrival of sugar from the 1640s onwards. By the end of the century the English colonies had overtaken Brazil as the largest producers in the world and the plantation owners of the West Indies were the *nouveaux riches* of the age. 'Splendour, dress, show, equipage, everything that can create an opinion of their importance is exerted to the utmost,' wrote one observer; 'an opulent West Indian vies in glare with a nobleman of the first degree.'

But their wealth brought them little contentment. The heat and humidity, the hurricanes and earthquakes, the ever-present threat of malaria and yellow fever and the terrifying levels of mortality – all combined to make the Caribbean an alarming, alien place to them even after almost a century of settlement. Virginians and New Englanders by this time were becoming Americans, creating a stable society of small farmers and traders. But the West Indian planters, perched precariously atop their rigidly hierarchical social structure, remained steadfastly English.

They sought the comfort of familiar objects and strove ludicrously to replicate the lifestyle of English country squires in the sweltering heat of the Caribbean. They wore wigs and waistcoats and enveloped themselves at night in curtains to protect themselves from the noxious breezes. They built brick houses in the 'English style', tall and narrow with glass windows rather than shutters – claustrophobic and stuffy. They ate vast meals of roast beef – imported, salted, from Britain – in the middle of the afternoon, followed by prodigious drinking bouts lasting late into the night. And they bored visitors rigid with their endless small talk about the price of sugar and the wickedness of the slaves. To visitors from New England they cut ridiculous figures, with their 'carbuncled faces, slender legs and thighs and large prominent bellies'. Most kept black mistresses, rearing what one governor of the Leeward Islands called a 'slavish sooty race' of mulattoes through their 'unnatural and monstrous lusts'.

Above all, the plantation owners lived in perpetual terror that the chained captives on whom their fortunes rested would one day rise up and rebel. On Barbados by 1713 there were 45,000 slaves, and on the British Leeward Islands by 1720 there were 37,000. They out-numbered the white population by more than three to one and the slightest whiff of revolt provoked punishments of such savagery that they leave the modern reader bewildered at their sadistic ingenuity. A French priest visiting Barbados in 1700 described seeing men 'put into iron cages that prevent any movement and in which they are hung up to branches of trees and left to die of hunger and despair'. Other slaves were killed by being passed alive through the cane mills. For lesser offences they were whipped and beaten, their limbs cut off and their tongues torn out. Melted wax was poured into their wounds. One plantation overseer in Jamaica in 1678 observed an execution that was far from atypical in its barbarity:

> His legs and arms were first broken in pieces with stakes, after which
> he was fastened upon his back to the ground. A fire was made first
> to his feet and burned up by degrees. I heard him speak several
> words when the fire consumed all his lower parts as far as his navel.
> The fire was upon his breast (he was burning near 3 hours) before
> he died.

Only through such terror did the planters believe they could find security.

But for the governments in London and Paris these were dream colonies. They complemented but did not compete with the home economies – satisfying the demand for sugar, yet relying entirely on imports for all their needs. For Roberts the significance of this was simple – almost everything produced or consumed in the islands had to be transported by ship. Where Drake and the Buccaneers who followed him were the maritime equivalent of bank robbers, aiming for the occasional, spectacular bullion heist, Roberts and his contemporaries were muggers, preying on the everyday activity – the steady, vibrant hum – of an ultimately far wealthier mercantile empire.

But before he could begin his assault Roberts had to deal with unrest in the crew. While at Carriacou seven men escaped in a captured sloop, taking £800 in gold with them. Then, a few days later, Henry Glasby, the new sailing master, disappeared, along with two other men, one white and one black. A search party was immediately dispatched. Trying to hide on Carriacou would be futile – the island was only a few miles across. More likely they were frantically paddling to one of the nearby islands in a makeshift canoe when the pirate long boat drew effortlessly level and the search party silently levelled their muskets. They were dragged back and the machinery of pirate justice quickly swung into motion.

By the time their trial began the pirates had left Carriacou, sailing northwards towards the island of Dominica. There they watered and, on 19 September, seized a French sloop 'laded with claret, white wine and brandy', according to Captain Dunne of the *Relief,* who was still with them. The trial took place immediately afterwards and was well lubricated with alcohol.

The pirates crowded round, grim faced, in the dark, humid steerage. Judges were appointed and a jury of twelve men was formed. Bowls of punch were filled, pipes prepared, and then the three terrified men were dragged out. Articles of indictment against them were read. The men begged and pleaded for mercy. But the case was clear cut and the judges were about to pronounce sentence of death when there was a dramatic intervention from Valentine Ashplant, one of the senior men. Johnson described the scene:

> Taking his pipe out of his mouth [he] said he had something to offer
> to the court in behalf of one of the prisoners, and spoke to this effect.
> 'By God, Glasby shall not die; damn me if he shall.' After this
> learned speech he sat down in his place, and resumed his pipe. This
> motion was loudly opposed by all the rest of the judges in equivalent
> terms, but Ashplant, who was resolute in his opinion, made another
> pathetical speech in the following manner. 'God damn ye
> Gentlemen, I am as good a man as the best of you; damn my soul if
> ever I turned my back to any man in my life, or ever will by God.
> Glasby is an honest fellow, notwithstanding this misfortune, and I

love him, Devil damn me if I don't. I hope he'll live and repent of what he has done. But, damn me, if he must die, I will die along with him.' And thereupon he pulled out a pair of pistols and presented them to some of the learned judges upon the bench who, perceiving the argument so well supported, thought it reasonable Glasby should be acquitted, and so they all came over to his opinion and allowed it to be law.

Glasby was probably as astonished as everyone else at his miraculous escape. Just why Ashplant should have formed such a violent attachment to him is unclear. It's conceivable they were old acquaintances. But the episode is another example of the strangely intense emotions that swirled around within pirate ships. Roberts may also have been happy to see his sailing master spared.

While Glasby was cleared the two men who had escaped with him were not so fortunate. Allowed only the liberty of choosing their own four-man firing squad, they were taken aboard the French sloop that had been seized that day, perhaps to avoid bringing bad luck on the pirates' own vessel. There they were tied to the mast and shot dead.

The day after the trial and execution the pirates captured Captain Cane, whose sloop they had seized at Cayenne in November 1719, for the second time. They believed he was complicit in Kennedy's desertion and beat him savagely before stealing rum and sugar – the key ingredients of punch – from his ship. By contrast, when two days later they released Captain Dunne, the turtler they'd seized at Carriacou, he was generously rewarded for his services with sails, ropes, fishing lines, brandy, sugar, 'a handkerchief with some spice in it' and some calico 'to make his wife a gown and petticoat'. With him they sent Moses Reynolds, the old Newfoundland fisherman who had been a prisoner with them since June. Reynolds was also given parting gifts, apparently in admiration for his steadfast refusal to sign their articles.

Their thoughts now turned to their next move. At Tobago Roberts had gathered important intelligence. There was not a single British warship in the entire eastern Caribbean. HMS *Rose* and HMS *Shark*, normally based in Antigua, were undergoing a lengthy re-fit in the shipyards of Boston. And the Navy had suffered a major disaster during the summer – the loss of HMS *Milford*, the 30-gun ship normally based in Barbados, which had run aground on rocks during a storm as it convoyed a fleet of merchantmen from Jamaica around the western tip of Cuba on 18 June. Thirteen merchant vessels had gone down with her, with heavy loss of life. It would not be replaced until the following May. The pirates had a free run.

They headed boldly for the British Leeward Islands. Antigua, Nevis, St Christophers and Montserrat were replacing Barbados as the centre of British power in the region at this time and their governor, Walter Hamilton, based in Antigua, was a determined enemy of pirates. But he was a beleaguered, forlorn figure. He had been in his post, on and off, for ten years and had pleaded repeatedly for the Admiralty to send him a ship of 36 or 40 guns 'to protect the trade from these vermin'. But he'd been forced to make do with ships of 14 and 20 guns in which he had little faith. He described one as a 'mere bauble', unable to carry more than four or six guns 'when it blows but anything hard'. With HMS *Rose* and HMS *Shark* both in New England he was now thrown back entirely on his own resources.

Those who ought to have had the strongest interest in suppressing the pirates – the local planters – offered little help. The concentration of land in ever larger plantations over the previous quarter-century had squeezed out the poorer whites and left the island's citizen militia undermanned. The plantation owners were reluctant to release their own servants for militia drill if it interfered with sugar production. And the island assemblies had economised on the construction of forts.

With the two warships absent all four islands were extremely vulnerable – as Roberts well knew.

The pirates made initially for Basseterre, the main port in St Christophers. It had been completely destroyed during the War of the Spanish Succession but was now being quickly rebuilt and had one of the most beautiful locations in the Caribbean. The fertile sugar plantations that surrounded the town were cradled by three gently sloping hills, beyond which the peak of Mt Misery, the island's highest point, could just be discerned, constantly shrouded in cloud.

As at Trepassey in Newfoundland, the authorities had advance warning of Roberts' arrival. Lt General William Mathew, the senior military officer on St. Christophers, received word that there were pirates in the area on the evening of Saturday, 24 September. He immediately ordered the various batteries around the coast to keep their guns 'ready and in order, and to be very watchful'. This proved unfortunate for Captain Dunne of the *Relief*, who tried to slip ashore in the north of the island the following morning to unload the goods the pirates had gifted him. He was spotted and promptly arrested. General Mathew was busy taking an inventory of Dunne's sloop when, around 1 p.m. the following Tuesday, 27 September he received word that Roberts and his men had sailed brazenly into Basseterre. He immediately issued orders for the island militia to be mobilised and then rode as fast as he could to confront them.

Mathew arrived to find 'everything in confusion', he reported to Governor Hamilton in Antigua a couple of days later. The pirates, flying 'black flags etc' had seized one ship and set two others on fire. The battery that was supposed to defend the town was 'without powder or ball rammer' and, in any case, had just two guns 'fit for any service'.

General Mathew managed to beg, borrow and steal eight barrels of gunpowder, four small cannons and a few cannon balls from the inhabitants of the town. Combining these with the two functioning cannons from the battery he subjected the pirates to 'a small cannonading for about an hour'. But it was a farcical effort. 'What with bad gunners, unsizable shot etc. we did them little hurt,' he wrote.

The two ships the pirates had set on fire were the *Mary and Martha* from Bristol and an un-named ship belonging to a Captain Andrew Hingston. Both captains were ashore when the pirates arrived. Packed with sugar, the *Mary and Martha* was blazing fiercely. But Hingston's vessel was burning more slowly. There were 500 barrels of beef aboard and General Mathew was keen to try and save it, but found Hingston to be unenthusiastic. His 'behaviour savoured much of knave or coward', Mathew complained, perhaps suspecting the captain was more interested in collecting the insurance. Eventually Mathew sent his own men aboard and extinguished the fire.

The third ship, the one the pirates had seized but not set alight, was the *Mary* of Boston, commanded by a Captain Henry Fowle. Fowle, also ashore when the pirates arrived, had gone out himself in a boat and begged Roberts to spare his vessel. Roberts agreed, but on condition Fowle stay with them overnight and write a note requesting provisions be prepared for them to collect the following morning. Fowle agreed and his letter was sent ashore that evening. In it Fowle wrote that he was being 'treated very civilly' and asked that 'one dozen of sheep, one dozen of goats, two bullocks and what small stock you can get', be got ready.

With it was a second letter, written by Roberts himself and addressed to General Mathew. The original is lost, but a copy was made and sent to London. It is one of the few letters written by a pirate that survives from this era and in it we hear Roberts' authentic voice:

Royall Fortune
Sept. 27th, 1720

Gentlemen

This comes expressly from me to lett you know that had you come off as
you ought to a done and drank a glass of wine with me and my company I should not a harmed the least vessell in your harbour. Farther, it is
not your gunns you fired that affrighted me or hindred our coming on
shore but the wind not proving to our expectation that hindred it. The
Royall Rover you have already burnt and barbarously used some of our
men but we have now a ship as good as her and for revenge you may
assure yourselves here and here-after not to expect anything from our
hands but what belongs to a pirate. Farther Gentleman, that poor fellow
you how have in prison at Sandy Point [presumably Captain Dunne] is
entirely ignorant and what he hath was gave him and so pray make conscience for once, let me begg you, and use that man as an honest man
and not as a C[riminal?]. If we hear any otherwise you may expect not
to have quarters to any of your Island.

Yours

Bartholomew Roberts

Here we see Roberts' perception of himself – a gentleman highwayman, dispensing alternately vengeance and largesse to his victims,
according to his own sense of honour and justice. The men
'barbarously used' were the six from the *Royal Rover* hanged on the
neighbouring island of Nevis as Kennedy's crew broke up in the early
months of 1720. His desire for revenge on the governor confirms that he
considered those who had stayed on the *Royal Rover* as less culpable

for the desertion at Devil's Islands than those who had gone to Britain with Kennedy. This is the only document from this middle period of Roberts' career that features the name Bartholomew rather than John, and it was clearly the name he himself preferred to be known by.

The two pirate vessels pulled away slightly from Basseterre overnight. At nine the next morning the sloop *Good Fortune* returned and dropped off Captain Fowle to fetch the provisions the pirates had requested. It then pulled away again. To his dismay Fowle found General Mathew was not prepared to meet the pirates' demands and would not let him return to their ship. Overnight Mathew had managed to get the defences of Basseterre in order, bringing in thirteen large guns from nearby towns. When the *Good Fortune* returned about 11 a.m. it was met with cannon fire. 'We had time to give her two rounds of all our guns of which seven hit her,' wrote Mathew. It suffered damage to its sails and rigging and 'one 24 pound ball took her in the bow. She made no return but got out as well as she could.'

Shaken, the pirates fled to a small bay at the very southern tip of St Christophers, taking Fowle's ship, the *Mary*, with them. None of them had been killed, but they were angry. Fowle knew they had piled timber in the cabin of his ship ready to set it on fire and expected to see it ablaze at any moment. But the pirates were feeling magnanimous. They guessed that Fowle had been prevented from returning and felt he was 'an honest fellow that never abused any sailors'. They spared the *Mary* but plundered it of provisions and water, slashed the rigging, destroyed Fowle's books and instruments, staved in the men's sea chests and 'left him and his men only with what they had on their backs', according to a press report. But the substantial cargo of sugar was left largely intact.

The pirates also took time to write a verse in chalk on the timbers:

For our word's sake we let thee go
But to Creoles we are a foe.

The term 'Creole' referred to Europeans and Africans born in the West Indies and Spanish America and the verse implies the pirates saw a distinction between Fowle, who was a New Englander, and the authorities in the Caribbean, who were the main focus of their antagonism. It was accompanied by 'a death's head and arm with a cutlass'. They had been in whimsical mood. When General Mathew recovered Captain Hingston's ship at Basseterre he found that, before setting it alight, the pirates had chalked the enigmatic couplet:

In thee I find
Content of mind.

From St Christophers the pirates headed for the island of Nevis, which lay immediately to the south-east, intending to pay the governor a visit in Charlestown 'and burn the town about his ears for hanging the pirates there'. But the winds were against them and they were forced to turn northward again, sailing around the western coast of St Christophers, pursued all the while by General Mathew 'with 70 horse and dragoons' galloping along the shoreline. They were last seen heading towards the French island of St Bartholomew.

Although they had sown terror and confusion at Basseterre the raid had been a failure for Roberts and his men. They'd got no provisions and had suffered damage to the *Good Fortune*. They had more luck at St Bartholomew, which the French shared with Carib Indians. The French settlement was tiny and easily intimidated and, like Cayenne in French Guiana, it had a Buccaneer tradition. 'They met with much handsomer treatment,' wrote Captain Johnson, 'the governor not only supplying them with refreshments, but he and the chiefs caressing them in the most friendly manner. And the women, from so good an example, endeavoured to outvie each other in dress, and behaviour, to attract the good graces of such generous lovers, that paid well for their fortunes.'

Their reception provided welcome relief to many in Roberts' crew. Although they had sped away from Carriacou prior to Newfoundland in search of 'wine and women', this was the first time they had been able to indulge their libidos since leaving Cayenne ten months previously, and no doubt they squandered much of what they had gained over the previous few months. Once again, there is no record of Roberts partaking of these pleasures.

At St Christophers we are given a name for the first time of the man captaining the *Good Fortune*, the pirates' smaller vessel. He was Montigny La Palisse, a Frenchman from St Malo. It's surprising they'd chosen a foreigner. As Moses Reynolds had observed at Newfoundland, Roberts' men strove to keep the crew 'English' (a term that incorporated Welsh and Scots) and at Carriacou Captain Dunne of the *Relief* also noted that the pirates were 'mostly Englishmen'. La Palisse was democratically elected. But he may well have had the backing of Roberts, keen to see someone without a strong personal following in this post. Having a second vessel strengthened Roberts, but it also created a rival centre of power and managing the relationship with his subordinate captain was to be one of the main challenges facing him from now on.

From St Bartholomew the pirates headed north and spent the next five or six weeks plundering the shipping lanes between the West Indies and Europe and North America. By 30 October they were close to Bermuda, where they took a brigantine called the *Thomas*. They forced the captain and most of his men to join their crew, leaving only the ship's owner, Thomas Bennett, and a sailor whose arm they had broken aboard. At midnight they set the *Thomas* adrift to fend for itself. But then they took pity and sent the *Good Fortune*'s long boat across, telling Bennett they would not leave him to 'perish in the sea'. Bennett and the injured sailor were taken aboard the *Royal Fortune*, where Bennett remained a prisoner for the next three months.

Bennett later provided the authorities with descriptions of a number of men among Roberts' crew whom he believed had been forced. His intention was that these could be used in their defence if they should ever be captured and brought to trial. In fact a number of these men went on to become hardened pirates and the descriptions provide a snapshot of Roberts' crew at this time.

> Thomas Wills of Bideford [Devon] . . . aged about twenty six years, very much pock broken, about five foot three inches
> John Carter of Bideford aforesaid aged about twenty three years of a very fresh complexion about five foot two inches
> James Harris of Bideford aforesaid, aged about twenty seven years, fresh complexion, middle sized
> William Williams a Cornish man aged about 26 years, a short thick man, very swarthy
> Lesby, a North Briton [Scot] aged about 28 years, a tall thin man, much pock fritten
> Seerden of Piscataqua in New England, cooper, aged about 35 years, red haired and very much pock broken. Middle sized

As throughout this period in and around the Caribbean, none of their prizes yielded a spectacular haul of treasure. Many were sizeable trading ships but their bulky cargoes were of little use to the pirates. And although they often carried stashes of cash or gold for trading purposes, these rarely amounted to more than a few hundred or at the very most a few thousand pounds. They were useful primarily for the food, drink and equipment they provided, items which enabled the pirates to continue with their everyday lives, and, above all, for new recruits.

The crew was growing steadily and at some point in the autumn of 1720 Roberts traded up once more, swapping the *Royal Fortune* they'd taken on the banks of Newfoundland for a large French prize from Martinique. It was bigger, but in other respects it wasn't a great exchange. The new ship – which they also named the *Royal Fortune* – was soon reported to be leaky. Despite this Roberts and his men continued to cover extraordinary distances. Even in this period, which saw no ocean crossings, they covered well over 1,000 miles in travelling from St Christophers to Bermuda. And in early November they turned south again, sailing a further 2,500 miles or so to Surinam on the northern coast of South America. From there they travelled 500 miles to Tobago to water.

It was at Tobago that the pirates were told for the first time of the Governor of Martinique's attempt to capture them at Carriacou just before their trip to Newfoundland, which they had so narrowly escaped. The governor had merely been doing his job. But the pirates quickly worked themselves up into a lather of indignation and Roberts, filled with entirely unreasonable rage, swore revenge. Until now their efforts in the Caribbean had been focussed on the British colonies. But, as the New Year dawned, they turned their sights on the French.

France had just two substantial colonies in the eastern Caribbean – Martinique and Guadeloupe, lying at the heart of the Windward and Leeward Islands chain. Martinique was the larger of the two and the governor there, Marquis Isaac de Pas de Feuquières, had authority over both, as well as smaller islands such as St Bartholomew. Martinique had something approaching what contemporaries regarded as 'society'. 'Many families there now make a very splendid appearance,' wrote a visitor at this time. It was 'the rendezvous for the officers of men-of-war, and of the garrison, and the residence of the General, the Governor, the Intendants, the magistrates and of the sovereign court of judicature . . . Here are also the agents of the French African Company, and those of many substantial merchants and factors in France'. The women, he added, were 'as handsome as any in Europe, well fashioned and genteel'. As in the British islands, slaves heavily outnumbered the white population.

Guadeloupe, very much the satellite colony, was felt to attract a slightly lower class of settler. Between the two lay the island of Dominica, formally ceded to the Carib Indians but containing a smattering of French settlers and clearly in the French sphere of influence. To the south lay St Lucia, fiercely contested between the British and French, but still empty at this time apart from the occasional Indian village.

Revenge was not the only motivation for targeting the French colonies. Roberts and his men had been threatening revenge against Barbados ever since their skirmish with Captain Rogers and Captain Graves ten months before. But they never returned there nor, after the raid at St Christophers, to any of the larger British islands. For all their bravado pirates rarely went out of their way to pick a fight and the British colonies had shown that, however ineptly, they were prepared to offer resistance. In targeting the French, Roberts and his men were homing in instinctively on the weaker of the two powers in the eastern Caribbean. The French Navy, like the Spanish Navy, had been left severely weakened by the War of the Spanish Succession and had almost no presence in the region. Their experiences at Cayenne and St Bartholomew had taught the pirates that French governors tended to be more pliant as a result.

The *Royal Fortune* and the *Good Fortune* made their way first to St Lucia, just south of Martinique. There, on 13 January 1721, they anchored on the north-western shore at a place called Pigeon Island. It was a popular spot for collecting wood and the pirates quickly snapped up six prizes, including four French sloops from Martinique, three of which they burned, dumping the crews on the island. They also destroyed a sloop from Barbados, handing its crew the remaining French sloop. But they kept one prize for themselves – a brigantine from Rhode Island under Captain Benjamin Norton.

Roberts was keen to replace his old sloop, the *Good Fortune*, which he'd now had for more than a year since first seizing it from Captain Cane at Cayenne in November 1719. It had served them well. It had taken them through the disaster of Devil's Islands and for six months after that it had been their only vessel. But it had suffered damage at both Barbados and St Christophers and it was becoming overcrowded. They loaded its ten guns on to Norton's brigantine, along with eight guns they had down in the hold of the *Royal Fortune*. Then, perhaps with a small ceremony marking the occasion, they sank it. They gave their new consort the same name as its predecessor.

The sinking of the *Good Fortune* brought definitively to a close the period when Roberts and his men had been a struggling, small-scale pirate crew. When he'd arrived at Trepassey in Newfoundland just over six months before Roberts had had 12 guns and sixty men under his command. He now had 52 guns and somewhere between 140 and 180 men in two large vessels. This was a crew with a reputation and an identity all of its own. Roberts marked the occasion by having his tailors stitch a new flag.

All pirate ships in this era flew black flags, something that had been common practice since the turn of the century. Previously witnesses had described Roberts' flags as containing 'death's head and co.' or 'death's head and cutlass', which sounds close to the skull and crossed swords, or bones, which, by his time, was becoming the convention. But many were far more elaborate. 'Roger' was a contemporary name for the devil and the term 'Jolly Roger', which had evolved from 'Old Roger', referred to the full-length skeleton that featured in most. Many also included an hour-glass and a heart dripping blood, conveying a crude and simple message – surrender now or face the consequences. But Roberts wanted something more distinctive, something that would convey his thirst for vengeance.

According to Johnson, the new flag depicted Roberts himself standing upon two skulls, under which were written the letters ABH and AMH, signifying, 'A Barbadian's Head' and 'A Martinican's Head' – the two islands which had attempted to hunt him down. It was made from silk. A French witness gave a slightly different description. The flag, he said, had 'a picture on each side and infamous inscriptions writ in French on them. The said pictures and their inscriptions are representations of the General of Martinique and of Barbados.' Whatever its exact design, the new flag represented a brazen challenge to the colonial authorities of the Caribbean. It would be hoisted from the bowsprit at the front of Roberts' ship for the rest of his career.

On 16 January 1721 the pirates set sail from St Lucia and headed northwards for Martinique.

8

THE GREAT PIRATE ROBERTS

WEST INDIES
JANUARY–APRIL 1721

'HE PUT ON A ROUGHER DEPORTMENT AND

A MORE MAGISTERIAL CARRIAGE . . . AND IF

ANY SEEMED TO RESENT HIS USAGE, HE TOLD

THEM THEY "MIGHT GO ASHORE AND TAKE

SATISFACTION OF HIM . . . AT SWORD AND

PISTOL, FOR HE NEITHER VALUED NOR

FEARED ANY OF THEM"'

Y THE STANDARDS OF the early eighteenth-century Caribbean, Martinique was a formidable island. Eyeing it warily from Antigua, Governor Hamilton estimated it contained 5,000–6,000 men able to bear arms as well as 300–400 regular troops. The coast was guarded by a number of forts and Roberts was smart enough not to attempt the sort of frontal assault he had employed at Trepassey and St Christophers. Instead he used trickery in order to gain his revenge for the governor's pursuit of him at Carriacou.

Martinique was a popular destination for Dutch slave ships. Officially they were banned, the authorities anxious to preserve a monopoly for French traders. But such was the demand they always found a market. It was the custom of the Dutch to appear off Martinique flying a Dutch flag, and then to withdraw to Dominica to the north. The planters of Martinique would surreptitiously fit out sloops to follow them and engage in illicit trade.

Roberts knew this and imitated them, raising a Dutch flag, sailing along the coast of Martinique, and then pulling away to Dominica. Once there he cast anchor and scanned the horizon. Sure enough, the French took the bait, and soon a steady stream of sloops was making its way from Martinique. It was only when they drew close enough to see the grinning pirates crowding the decks that the French realised their mistake, and by then it was too late. Gleefully the pirates gobbled up prize after prize, ordering them, as soon as they had been secured, to lie still at anchor as if trading so as not to alarm new arrivals. In all they took fifteen vessels, Roberts telling his captives 'they were a parcel of rogues' and that he 'hoped they would always meet with such a Dutch trade as this was'. They also took a number of English vessels which happened to be in the area.

On 18 January the pirates spotted a rather more formidable prize – the *Puerto del Principe* from Flushing in Zeeland, which turned out to be a real Dutch slave ship. Weighing in at somewhere between 250 and 300 tons it carried seventy-five men and was well armed with 22 guns. It had on board seventy to eighty slaves as well as substantial quantities of sugar, cocoa, ivory and cotton. The pirates anticipated a rich haul and quickly moved in, raising their new flag and firing their gun to signal the Dutch to surrender. But the Dutch were not prepared to give in without a fight. They returned fire, and when the pirates pulled alongside preparing to board they managed to run out fenders to push them away. Roberts' men were not used to such effrontery. This was the first ship to offer resistance since the *Sagrada Familia* off Brazil fifteen months before and the pirates responded with a ferocious bombardment. A number of the Dutch crew were killed before they finally surrendered.

According to the Governor of Bermuda, Benjamin Bennet, writing to London a month later, the pirates then embarked on a grotesque orgy of torture and murder quite unlike anything that had gone before under

Roberts' captaincy. 'What men the pirates found alive on board they put to death after several cruel methods,' Bennet claimed. They then subjected their captives from the French sloops to even more horrific treatment. They were 'barbarously abused . . . Some they almost whipped to death, others had their ears cut off, others they fixed to the yard arms and fired at them as a mark.' They sank fourteen of the fifteen sloops, sparing just one so it could return to Martinique with its 'poor tormented' crew to tell the story. These passages have been regularly quoted by historians ever since and have done much to shape an image of Roberts as a brutal sadist. But they are almost certainly untrue.

There is not a single reference to this slaughter in any of the other numerous sources we have for this period – including statements from French captives themselves, who began arriving back in Martinique as early as 19 January. In a letter describing Roberts' activities, written on 28 January, Governor de Feuquières makes no mention of the massacre. And the Dutch authorities, in a lengthy letter to the British describing the attack, also seemed unaware of it. It was never mentioned at any of the subsequent trials of members of Roberts' crew, despite the fact that it would have been one of the worst crimes they ever committed. And, Captain Johnson, who, as a general rule, was quite happy to revel in tales of pirate atrocity, makes no reference to it whatsoever. Governor Bennet was located over 1,000 miles to the north and was relying on secondhand sources. His letter is inaccurate in a number of other respects – for example, he places the capture of the *Puerto del Principe* at St Lucia – and Johnson doubtless rejected his account as highly unreliable hearsay.

It's possible wild rumours were sparked because some of the prisoners disappeared. If so, there may well be a more obvious explana﹑tion for this – rather than being slaughtered, they had joined the pirates. Roberts' crew was expanding fast at this time and we know of at least one man from the *Puerto del Principe* who was with them later.

From Dominica Roberts headed north to Guadeloupe to complete his humiliation of the French authorities, taking the *Puerto del
Principe* and two of the captured sloops with him. They drew fire as
they passed the island's forts, but it had little effect and they were able
to seize a sloop and a large ship, whose crew fled ashore at the sight of
the black flag. The sloop they burnt, but the ship they took with them
to plunder at leisure, finding it contained a substantial cargo of
sugar. A few days later they were reported chasing shipping off St
Thomas at the eastern end of the Leeward Islands. They then
disappeared from view.

The impact of this raid was devastating. Trade in the Windward
and Leeward Islands had been brought virtually to a halt and for the
French it was an abject humiliation. Roberts had brazenly plundered
shipping in the very heart of the French Caribbean for more than a
week, and then waltzed away scot free. He was a plague that could no
longer be tolerated. On 21 January 1721 Governor de Feuquières wrote
to the British authorities in Barbados proposing that the two nations
combine 'to purge our seas from such a cursed race'. It was a highly
unusual move that reflected the threat Roberts now posed. And, for de
Feuquières, it must have been a difficult letter to write. 'Unfortunately
for us we are without any ships of war to enable us to send in chase of
those villains,' he admitted. He even had to ask the authorities in
Barbados to pass on his message to Governor Hamilton in the British
Leeward Islands because Roberts had left him with no 'ships in a
condition to undertake the voyage'. All he could offer was 'good
soldiers' and a vague promise of 'all that is in my favour to contribute
to the extirpation of those villainous robbers'.

Nevertheless, on Barbados his proposal was received favourably.
Governor Lowther had been removed and replaced in control by
Samuel Cox, former president of the island council, who was rather
more resolute. 'Common humanity', but also self-interest, demanded

that they take action, Cox wrote to London a few days later. 'We may soon expect him to windward of this island, which might be attended with fatal consequences.' The British were in a stronger position to help than they had been a few weeks previously. De Feuquières had seen HMS *Rose* and HMS *Shark,* finally returning after six months in New England, sail past Martinique a few days before and was hoping his letter would catch them at Barbados. In fact they had already left for their home base in the Leeward Islands when it arrived. But a few days later Captain Thomas Durrel of HMS *Seahorse* sailed into Bridgetown.

Durrel had been sent by the authorities in Boston to escort New England shipping northwards in response to repeated reports that the region was 'very much infested by pirates' and that 'the trade of the place did not care to venture without a convoy to protect them'. He was an enthusiastic and diligent officer and immediately offered to sail after Roberts. But, on examining de Feuquières' letter, he hesitated. HMS *Seahorse,* like HMS *Rose,* carried just 20 guns and was no match for the pirate force described by the French Governor. The island council would need to supply him with ninety well-armed men, at their own expense, he told them. Even then, he would have to sail to Martinique to see what assistance the French had to offer before he could even think of confronting the pirates.

The request for reinforcements proved problematic. The expedition against Roberts the previous February had involved considerable expense for no reward and the merchants of Barbados were not keen to stump up funds again. The island council was forced to borrow money. Then, when Captain Durrel attempted to recruit, Bridgetown miraculously emptied of sailors. They 'had armed themselves and had gathered into a great body and gone up the country, whereby the intent of the press warrants . . . was in great measure frustrated', Durrel irritably reported on 31 January. Given Roberts' strength, the

The greatest of pirates, Bartholomew Roberts, whose career saw the capture of 400 prizes and the dominance of the Caribbean. This illustration is taken from the first Dutch edition of Captain Johnson's *General History of the Pirates* (1725). Although largely forgotten today, for Johnson Roberts was a far more important pirate than his better known contemporary, Blackbeard.

Roberts at Whydah, West Africa, in January 1722,
a black and white print from the first edition of
Captain Johnson's *General History of the Pirates* (1724).
It was at Whydah that Roberts' crew committed
their one truly grotesque crime – the burning of a
slave ship with 80 slaves still chained below decks.
Roberts himself preferred the diplomatic route to
conflict resolution.

A modern representation of the last of Roberts'
three *Royal Fortunes*, the most powerful pirate ship of
the age. Roberts' flags bore complex designs and
descriptions varied. According to Johnson, the
figure confronting the skeleton on the main mast
should be brandishing a 'flaming sword ...
intimating a defiance of death itself'.

A contemporary illustration of a 17th-century Buccaneer on Hispaniola. Buccaneers were the forebears of pirates of Roberts' era and passed on to them their strange democratic culture and a misogyny which concealed a degree of hearty homosexuality. Isolated from women, Buccaneers lived in male couples.

above A modern painting of Roberts' final battle with HMS *Swallow* off Cape Lopez in Central Africa in February 1722. The crew were drunk, having taken a prize the day before, and mistook the *Swallow* for a merchant ship. They were in no fit state for combat, much to Roberts' fury.

left Pirates storming a merchant ship, as represented in this 19th-century painting by the artist Frederick Waugh. Boarding a ship was costly in terms of casualties, but essential if a vessel and its cargo were to be captured intact. Pirates were masters of the art.

Roberts' nemesis – Captain
Chaloner Ogle of HMS
Swallow. As Roberts became
more and more brazen
through 1720 and 1721,
pressure on the Royal Navy
from slave trading and
plantation-owning interests
intensified. It was Captain
Ogle who finally hunted
Roberts down.

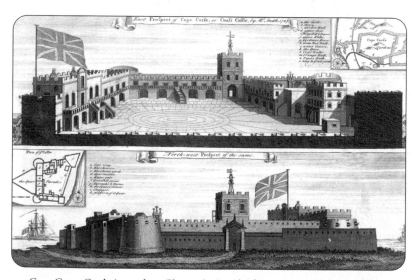

Cape Coast Castle in modern Ghana, the Royal African Company's main fort on
the African coast, where Roberts' crew were brought to trial in April 1722.

The execution of a pirate in 1718. The drop – which broke the victim's neck – was not perfected until the 19th century and it could take 45 minutes to die. This was the fate that befell 52 of Roberts' men at Cape Coast Castle.

A death warrant from the trial of Roberts' men at Cape Coast Castle. These six men – William Magnes, Thomas Sutton, David Simpson, Valentine Ashplant, Christopher Moody and Richard Hardy – were regarded as the hard core of the crew and were executed first to forestall any attempts at escape.

reluctance of local men to take part in the expedition was not surprising – particularly if there were wild rumours circulating of a massacre on Dominica. In the end the militia had to be mobilised to force men aboard.

On 2 February Durrel finally set sail for Martinique, only to find the wind had switched direction and that he was confronted with a 'great . . . rolling . . . sea' driving him back towards Barbados. He wrestled with this for a couple of days but was forced to limp back into Bridgetown on 5 February with the rigging around his bowsprit flapping loose and his main top-mast badly damaged. Cox conveyed the sorry news to Governor de Feuquières. The New England fleet could wait no longer and two weeks later Durrel set sail for Boston.

But by now de Feuquières had managed to communicate with Governor Hamilton in the Leeward Islands. Hamilton had been fuming in impotent rage ever since Roberts' brazen attack on St Christophers four months previously. With HMS *Rose* and HMS *Shark* now finally back on station, he saw the French offer as a perfect opportunity to rid himself of the man he by now referred to as 'the great pirate Roberts'. De Feuquières had sent an aide, Monsieur Malherbe, to coordinate measures and by 19 February he and Hamilton had drawn up a detailed memorandum of understanding between the two nations. 'It is agreed that the two governments will send a sufficient quantity of forces to run by sea after the pirates to take them, to fight and destroy them, or at least put them to flight,' it began. It was agreed any booty captured would be divided proportionate to the number of men each side provided and that any ship failing to lend assistance to its ally would be 'chastised and punished'. The French were now in a slightly stronger position and contributed a ship and two sloops. Combined with HMS *Rose* and HMS *Shark* this made a ramshackle flotilla of five small vessels. But between them they just about outgunned Roberts' two ships.

On 20 February Hamilton summoned Captain Whitney of HMS *Rose*, the larger of the two British men-of-war, to a meeting at St John's in Antigua. HMS *Rose* was at anchor off the island. But, to Hamilton's fury, Whitney failed to show up. When, by midday, there was still no sign of him Hamilton fired off an angry note asking him to explain his absence. Whitney wrote back saying he was busy with his accounts, but that he would be happy to sail with the French if Hamilton would be so kind as to inform him 'where the pirates are' – a response that must have had Hamilton tearing his hair out. At the same time Whitney casually informed him that he was about to sail to St Christophers to take in water.

Whitney had already had one unsuccessful encounter with pirates when he'd been driven from the harbour at New Providence in the Bahamas in July 1718. He'd also quarrelled repeatedly with Captain Woodes Rogers, the Governor there. He was not one of the more diligent Navy officers in the Caribbean and was perhaps less than enthusiastic about confronting the Caribbean's most formidable pirate for little apparent gain.

Hamilton responded by issuing a direct order to Whitney to proceed, in company with HMS *Shark*, to Martinique. 'I don't question but you will observe the order and do everything for His Majesty's Service,' he wrote. Whitney was forced to obey. But when he arrived in Martinique on 1 March, to his enormous satisfaction he found the French had changed their mind. 'Affairs have changed face,' Governor de Feuquières told him. Roberts, he believed, was now off Saint Domingue (modern Haiti) 750 miles to the north-west, and 'no longer disposed to do you any harm or us any harm'. There was no reason at all to think Roberts had abandoned his hostility to the French and the British. But a number of French Navy vessels had now arrived in the region. Two frigates were on their way to cruise off Saint Domingue and de Feuquières also mentioned a large ship called the

Dromadaire which he said was cruising to windward of Martinique with 400 men on board. Their presence freed him from his humiliating dependence on the British and he was happy to suspend what he called 'the little armed expedition' they had planned.

'I was very much surprised after so much noise of pirates,' wrote Captain Whitney, with infuriating smugness, to Hamilton when he returned to Antigua a week later. He suggested the whole furore had been cooked up by smugglers, keen to distract attention from their activities, and described de Feuquières' envoy, Malherbe, as 'a petty fogging merchant of little account'. He concluded by demanding £28, 16s to pay for food for the soldiers he had had aboard. De Feuquières had also found Captain Whitney 'impertinent' and had been informed by Malherbe of the 'repugnance' the two Royal Navy captains felt at being ordered to Martinique. He apologised to Hamilton for the change of plans and sent him two barrels of red wine, but it can have been little consolation.

'They write from St Christophers that Captain Roberts, who is now the most desperate pirate of all that range those seas, calls himself admiral of the Leeward Islands,' reported a London paper a few months later. For Hamilton it was galling. 'Your Lordships may perceive that I am confined by Captain Whitney's capricious temper,' he wrote to London a few weeks later, once more begging for a larger warship, with a more resolute commander, to be sent out.

De Feuquières was right that Roberts was now at Saint Domingue, or, to be more precise, Hispaniola, the Spanish-owned, eastern half of the same island. After leaving the Leeward Islands the pirates had gone initially to Isla Mona, which lay between Puerto Rico and Hispaniola. There they intended to careen. But, finding the seas too rough, they continued westwards and eventually anchored in the Bay of Samaná on the north-eastern coast of Hispaniola. It was a smart move to get away from the region where they had caused so much havoc. And, a century on from when the first Buccaneers had settled there, Hispaniola was still an ideal hideaway.

It remained an economic backwater. As in most of the Spanish Americas, sugar had never really taken a hold and many of the locals continued to live by hunting wild pigs and cattle which they sold to their French neighbours in the more prosperous, western part of the island. There were also thriving communities of escaped slaves dotted around the interior. An English visitor in 1721 portrayed Hispaniola as a natural wilderness; 'the sea and rivers [were] full of fish and the country spread with forests of cabbage and palm trees'. In 1717 there were no more than 20,000 people in the entire colony and there were many hidden coves where pirates could take refuge without fear of discovery. The Gulf of Samaná was a particularly well-known pirate haven, and Roberts and his men were once more able to relax among golden sands and nodding palms.

They careened their vessels and spent several weeks on the island, engaging 'in their usual debaucheries', according to Johnson. 'They had taken a considerable quantity of rum and sugar, so that liquor was as plenty as water, and few there were who denied themselves the immoderate use of it.' Roberts' reputation was now spreading and while there he received a curious visit from two sloops, whose commanders, Captain Porter and Captain Tuckerman, came to the great pirate as disciples. They addressed him, wrote Johnson, 'as the Queen of Sheba did Solomon, to wit, that having heard of his fame and achievements, they had put in there to learn his art and wisdom in the business of pirating, being vessels on the same honourable design with himself'. They were also looking for handouts, 'being in want of necessaries for such adventures'. Won over by the 'peculiarity and bluntness' of these two men Roberts gave them 'powder, arms, and whatever else they had occasion for'. He also handed them sixteen to eighteen negroes in return for three or four men from their own crew –

a revealing exchange in terms of the relative values Roberts' men attached to white sailors and slaves. Roberts 'spent two or three merry nights with them and, at parting, said he hoped the Lord would prosper their handy work'.

Roberts and his men referred to Porter and Tuckerman as 'private pirates' – men who profited by trading with pirates without indulging in direct acts of piracy themselves. They 'said they got much more money in that private way than public pirates', one of Roberts' men later recalled. Tuckerman was arrested a few months later at Port Royal in Jamaica after getting drunk in the company of a number of senior military officers and firing off his guns in the harbour. The term 'private pirates' could well have been applied to a number of the merchant captains Roberts and his men had dealt with, including Edward Cane, who they'd taken at Cayenne, and now Benjamin Norton, whose brigantine they had seized at St Lucia and who was still with them at Hispaniola.

Roberts generally had cosier relations with North American captains than those from England or the Caribbean. Less dependent on trade with the mother country, and still a relative backwater economically, the inhabitants, and even some of the authorities, in North America, retained a sympathy for pirates – a source of cheap, stolen property – long after their counterparts in the West Indies. New York had effectively been a pirate haven in the 1690s and, as late as 1718, the Governor of North Carolina was openly sheltering Blackbeard.

It's highly likely Captain Norton was commander of the brigantine that Roberts had chased, on Cane's recommendation, from Devil's Islands back in December 1719, with such disastrous consequences. Like Cane he was from Rhode Island and was on the same stretch of coast at the time. Cane probably urged Roberts to chase Norton knowing that, once captured, he would be glad to do business. Norton was viewed with deep suspicion by the Rhode Island authorities. When he had fitted out his vessel the previous autumn for the voyage to the West Indies it was felt, by 'common observation' to be 'more fit for [piracy] than trade', a colonial official later wrote – a conclusion Roberts himself obviously reached in deciding to take over the vessel.

At Hispaniola Norton cut a potentially lucrative deal with Roberts. In return for his brigantine Roberts agreed to give him the Dutch slaver the *Puerto del Principe*, laden with much of its original cargo. It was agreed Norton would take the Dutch ship to New England and seek to sell the contents. The two men probably planned to meet up again so the pirates could get a cut and Roberts could add the *Puerto del Principe* to his fleet, possibly with Norton as commander. On 7 March Norton nosed his way out of the Bay of Samaná and headed north.

Roberts was now approaching the very zenith of his power. Even without the *Puerto del Principe* his two ships carried more than 50 guns and perhaps as many as 350 men between them. He was the most formidable pirate the Caribbean had seen since Buccaneer times and more than a match for any of the British warships he was likely to encounter. His name was feared along the entire Atlantic seaboard, from Newfoundland to Brazil, and the addition of the *Puerto del Principe* would make him all but invincible. As he relaxed on the beaches of Hispaniola, the tall, dark Welshman, now almost forty years old, knew he could ravage the shipping lanes virtually at will.

But the rapid expansion of the crew over the previous twelve months had also brought with it problems. Most of the new men were volunteers. But a number were forced. Bitter and resentful, they were constantly looking for a chance to slip away, and discontent among this group was coalescing around Henry Glasby. At Hispaniola, he tried to escape for a second time, this time taking ten other men with him.

Under cover of darkness, or perhaps during an unusually heavy drinking session, they slipped away into the jungle. Glasby had with him a pocket compass and they were doubtless aiming for the Spanish settlements further south. But the sailing master who could navigate his way so skilfully across the wide, empty oceans was soon lost in the dense, dark forests of Hispaniola. Two days passed, and they found themselves going in circles, plagued by mosquitoes, spiders and snakes. Just when it seemed they were doomed to stumble in the gloom forever they suddenly popped back out on to the beach – at almost exactly the same spot from which they had started. They were quickly spotted by a group of Roberts' men and hauled back to camp. 'They made such excuses for their absence as they thought might most please,' Glasby said later, and somehow managed to talk their way out of the situation – an indication of the pirates' desperation for a good navigator, rather than their gullibility. From this time on Glasby was a prisoner aboard the *Royal Fortune*, forbidden to board prizes or to go ashore, and Roberts took the precaution of keeping the long boats permanently chained up.

There was discontent too among the more willing recruits. Although Roberts had dispensed with the division between Lords and Commons, there was still a clear pecking order in the crew. The more experienced men were referred to as 'Old Standers', and retained the arrogance of an aristocracy. One of them, James Philips, 'was morose and drunk, carrying his pistols sometimes about him to terrify newcomers if they offered to speak, saying they ought to serve their time first', according to a captive. A new recruit later recalled that 'he was allowed only a quarter share at his first coming, till he roused off his dullness and stupidity, and then received a whole share'. New men often found themselves relegated to the *Good Fortune*, and Glasby observed that the second ship had 'not so liberal a share in fresh provisions, or wine'. Their subordinate status chafed, and it was an ominous sign when Thomas Anstis, the belligerent West Countryman who had temporarily supplanted Roberts at the start of 1720, was elected to replace Motigny La Palisse as captain of the *Good Fortune*.

Roberts was also having difficulty with the Old Standers. Success seemed to breed insubordination. "Twas with great difficulty they could be kept together under any kind of regulation, for, being almost always mad or drunk, their behaviour produced infinite disorders, every man being in his own imagination a captain, a prince, or a king,' wrote Johnson. Roberts was forced to become increasingly dictatorial. According to Johnson, when he

> saw there was no managing of such a company of wild,
> ungovernable brutes by gentle means, nor to keep them from
> drinking to excess – the cause of all their disturbances – he put on a
> rougher deportment and a more magisterial carriage towards them,
> correcting them when he thought fit. And if any seemed to resent his
> usage, he told them they 'might go ashore and take satisfaction of
> him, if they thought fit, at sword and pistol, for he neither valued
> nor feared any of them.'

It was a style of leadership that was departing more and more from the traditions of pirate democracy and put him at odds with many in the crew. Around the time of the visit to Hispaniola Roberts found himself having to back these words with actions. According to Captain Johnson, a drunken member of the crew insulted Roberts. In response, Roberts, 'in the heat of his passion, killed the fellow on the spot' – the first record we have of Roberts personally killing anyone. The dead pirate had a mess-mate called Thomas Lawrence Jones, 'a brisk, active young man', who had been almost two years in the crew. When he heard of the incident, 'he cursed Roberts, and said he ought to be served so himself'. Hearing this, Roberts attacked Jones, running him through with his sword. The wound was not fatal and Jones, in retaliation, seized Roberts, 'threw him over a gun, and beat him handsomely'.

The incident adds another dimension to Roberts' personality. For all his sobriety and restraint he was a man of violent passions when roused and the murder and its aftermath threw the crew into uproar. Some sided with Roberts, others against him and it was only the intervention of the quartermaster that prevented an armed confrontation. A vote was taken and, according to Johnson, 'the majority of the company were of opinion that the dignity of the captain ought to be supported on board; that it was a post of honour, and . . . should not be violated by any single member'. Jones was sentenced to receive two lashes from every member of the crew. Both Jones and the dead man belonged to the *Good Fortune*. The incident exacerbated tensions between the two ships and would have important repercussions.

Roberts was sitting atop a powder keg of simmering grievances. Old Standers resentful at his increasingly autocratic style, and perhaps ambitious for power themselves; Old Standers who'd simply had enough, and were keen to slip away; new recruits resentful at not being fully accepted into the pirate brotherhood; and forced men — it was a dangerous cocktail, one which confronted all pirate captains as their crews expanded. It took all Roberts' energies to hold them together.

Strangely, the only group that Roberts didn't need to watch like a hawk were the slaves. He'd captured a large number since returning to the Caribbean and, by this time, close to a third of the crew were black. Most were 'French Creole negroes', according to one captive — a description that makes clear they were not taken fresh from the holds of slavers, but were men living and working in the French Caribbean. Some may have been seized from plantations. But the majority were probably sailors, captured, already trained, from prizes. Ships in West Africa and the Caribbean at this time carried small numbers of slaves trained as mariners and these would have been ideal recruits for

Roberts. With the exception of the black man shot for attempting to escape with Glasby at Carriacou, there is not a single reference to them giving him any problems.

Unlike Howel Davis, Roberts armed his slaves — reflecting not a desperation for recruits but his desire to become as powerful as possible as quickly as possible. For the slaves this must have involved some *quid pro quo* in terms of living conditions if the pirates were to be sure of their loyalty. It was not a life for the squeamish. But, for a slave in the early eighteenth century, it was probably as good as it got. Compared to the grind of life on the plantations it brought variety and relative freedom. And if pirates got a buzz from power, we can only guess at the emotions of the slaves, accustomed to a life of terror and grovelling servitude, and now licensed to point guns at white men and watch them quiver in fear. Living, sleeping, fighting side by side for months on end, the two races, both outcasts in their own way, surely developed some limited camaraderie. But the slaves' great virtue was still that they were cheap, since they received no share of the booty.

By mid-March the pirates were hungry for further plunder and left Hispaniola heading east. De Feuquières' assessment that Roberts was 'no longer disposed' to do harm to either the French or the British was wrong. They headed straight back to the Leeward Islands and parked themselves to the windward of Guadeloupe. There, on 26 March, they seized the *Lloyd*, a richly laden merchant ship from London bound for Jamaica.

Going aboard the pirates found the captain was Andrew Hingston, whose ship they had partially burned at St Christophers six months before. Despite General Mathew's suspicions of complicity between Hingston and the pirates at that time, it wasn't a joyful reunion. 'They took away most of my rigging and sails, all my anchors, blocks, provisions, powder, small arms &c,' lamented Hingston. 'What of the cargo was not fit for their service they threw overboard.'

They also took twelve of his eighteen-man crew. Finding that the chief mate, who was Hingston's brother, had tried to conceal two gold rings in his pocket, the pirates strapped him to the rigging and 'whipped him within an inch of his life'.

By now Roberts was displaying extraordinary confidence. He took the *Lloyd* north to the British island of Barbuda and spent five days plundering it at leisure, despite the fact that Antigua, where Governor Hamilton was based, was only 30 miles to the south. According to Governor Bennet in Bermuda he was also displaying murderous brutality. In a letter to London, Bennet claimed that, shortly before taking the *Lloyd,* the pirates had captured the Governor of Martinique on a French ship and 'hanged [him] at the yard arm'. He cited Hingston as his source, though Hingston never mentioned this in his own correspondence. Bennet's account was included in the same package of letters where he described the supposed massacre at Dominica in mid-January, and was just as untrue. The Governor of Martinique – de Feuquières – was most definitely still alive, as was his number two, the Intendant of Martinique, Monsieur Bernard. But, again, Bennet's story has been much quoted by historians ever since as evidence of Roberts' barbarity.

On 1 April the pirates took Hingston and the *Lloyd* further north and released him at sea 'in a very sad condition'. The following day the hapless captain was captured again, this time by a French pirate in a small sloop who stole what few possessions he had left and then dumped him in the Virgin Islands. He was eventually picked up by Captain Whitney in HMS *Rose,* who may or may not have been embarrassed to discover that the pirate he had so casually dismissed six weeks earlier was still active and, according to Hingston, now in command of 54 guns and more than 350 men. Whitney immediately set off in pursuit – of the far smaller French pirate, who he also failed to catch.

Governor Hamilton was furious. 'If you had followed my orders at your return from Martinique to cruise for some days to windward of these islands, you might in all probability have come up with the pirate Roberts,' he pointed out in a letter to Whitney. Given the imbalance in their forces Whitney was doubtless relieved he hadn't. But it seemed a further period of humiliation now awaited the authorities in the Windward and Leeward Islands. The merchants of the Leeward Islands felt so beleaguered that they sent a petition to London at this time, begging for greater naval protection: 'The pirates are now so strong and numerous in these parts that, not only the trade to and from these islands suffers very much, but likewise all intercourse is broke off betwixt these islands to their very great damage.'

But the capture of the *Lloyd* was a parting shot rather than the start of a new rampage. News travelled fast in the highly mobile world of the eighteenth-century Caribbean and Roberts was doubtless aware of the three new French warships in the region. He may also have been aware that there were two fresh British warships on the way – the 40-gun *Faversham*, which was to replace HMS *Milford* on station at Barbados, and the 40-gun *Launceston,* which was coming out on surveying duty. He was bold but he wasn't stupid and he knew when the time had come to move on. After releasing Hingston he continued north and he had soon left the squabbling officials of the West Indies far behind, hitching a ride on the great clockwise swirl of the Atlantic and bound once more for Africa.

9

AFRICA AGAIN

The Atlantic and West Africa
April–July 1721

'HE PINED WITH A VACUUM OF THE GUTS,

AND DIED; LEAVING THIS ADVICE TO HIS

COUNTRYMEN, RATHER TO RUN A REMOTE

HAZARD OF BEING HANGED AT HOME, THAN

CHOOSE A TRANSFER HITHER'

*T*HE PIRATES QUICKLY CAUGHT the trade winds and soon the stifling heat of the Caribbean gave way to the fresher breezes of the North Atlantic as they curved their way towards Africa. With the sails set and the wind behind them there was little to do aloft and life aboard quickly settled in to its normal rhythm. But this was no time to relax. They were travelling the main shipping routes and encountered a steady stream of prizes.

On 9 April, just off Bermuda, they captured the *Jeremiah and Anne*, a Virginia-bound sloop that had come from London via the Cape Verde Islands. They took at least seven new men. Glasby observed with disgust that one of the new recruits 'got so drunk with the pirates he was forced to be hoisted out with a tackle and into the [*Royal*] *Fortune* again in the same way'. Roberts told the captain 'that he expected speedily to be joined by a ship of 46 guns, and that he would make Virginia a visit and revenge the death of the pirates which have been executed here'. This was a reference to the six men hanged by Governor Spotswood in early 1720 following Kennedy's desertion, and the 46-gun ship was presumably the *Puerto del Principe* under Captain Norton, which was still making its way to New England at this point. The threat was bluster. It seems they planned to rendezvous with Norton off Africa, not America. But it succeeded in spreading panic along the North American coastline. Governor Spotswood wrote to London begging for a 40 or 50-gun warship to be sent out – 'for there is not one of the guardships on this coast fit to encounter such a one as this Roberts has now under his command' – and quickly erected batteries at the mouths of the James, York and Rappahanock Rivers.

Eight days later, on 17 April, they seized a Dutch ship, the *Prince Eugene*, in mid-Atlantic. A Danish crewman later provided the most detailed description we have of the firepower aboard Roberts' ships. The *Royal Fortune* now had 42 guns aboard. The largest were capable of firing 12-pound cannon balls, the smallest were four-pounders. The *Good Fortune* carried 18 guns, a mixture of four-pounders and six-pounders. This was broadly in line with Royal Navy warships of similar size. But both vessels also carried large numbers of smaller two- and three-pounders. The *Royal Fortune* had seven of these located in the tops of the main and foremast, while the *Good Fortune* had twelve on its quarterdeck. The *Royal Fortune* also had two swivel guns in the tops of its mizzen-mast. Any merchant ship offering resistance would be faced with a blizzard of fire, from the waterline to the mast-tops.

Scudding across the Atlantic in the bright, spring sunshine Roberts had every reason to be confident. But then, at dawn on 20 April, three days after the capture of the *Prince Eugene*, he emerged from his cabin to find the sea around his ship empty. The *Good Fortune* had deserted overnight.

For its captain, Thomas Anstis, this was revenge for his demotion following the battle off Barbados the year before. But he'd also been unhappy with Roberts' treatment of the second ship. 'What made Anstis a malcontent,' Captain Johnson wrote, 'was the inferiority he stood in, with respect to Roberts, who carried himself with a haughty and magisterial air, to him and his crew, he regarding the brigantine only as a tender [support ship], and, as such, left them no more than the refuse of their plunder.' Johnson almost certainly got his version of events from members of Anstis' crew – above all Thomas Lawrence Jones, the man whose mess-mate Roberts had murdered earlier in the year, who was in the Marshalsea Prison when Johnson was writing *A General History*.

Jones was one of the ringleaders and the murder, and his subsequent beating was the catalyst for the desertion. Jones had won over Anstis and the other leading men and the decision was put to the rest of the *Good Fortune*'s crew just a few hours beforehand. Finding a majority in favour of deserting Roberts they 'came to a resolution to bid a soft farewell', and slipped away into the darkness shortly after midnight. They had planned to throw overboard anyone who resisted, but this proved unnecessary.

Anstis and the men in the *Good Fortune* headed straight back towards the Caribbean. Over the next few months they took a number of prizes and were soon a formidable crew in their own right, with well over 100 men. Like Roberts they bolstered their strength by adding a second ship. But Anstis proved rather less adept at containing the tensions within a large, successful pirate crew than Roberts and he was soon deposed by a one-handed pirate called John Fenn (sadly, it's not recorded whether Fenn wore a hook). Shortly afterwards the crew voted to plead for a royal pardon and by the end of 1721 they were hunkered down on a deserted island off Cuba awaiting a response from London.

This was a major blow. Roberts had lost perhaps a third of his strength, including a number of highly experienced men. And, although he didn't know it at the time, at almost exactly the same moment that the *Good Fortune* was deserting, the *Puerto del Principe* had been captured by the authorities in New England. Captain Norton had taken it to Tarpaulin Cove in Massachusetts, 'a by-place fit for roguery', according to a colonial official, to dispose of the cargo. But the sheer quantity of goods being unloaded, including large numbers of slaves, aroused suspicion and the ship was seized, although Norton himself managed to escape. There would be no rendezvous off Africa and now, instead of ravaging the coast at the head of three large ships, as planned, Roberts was back down to one.

But the Welshman was never one to be easily discouraged. He always showed extraordinary resolve and determination in these situations. He had been through far worse before and come through, and he knew he still had between 150 and 200 men under his command, perhaps a third of them loyal black slaves. He made a half-hearted pursuit of the *Good Fortune* but soon gave up and the *Royal Fortune* resumed its course towards Africa. Roberts was confident the slavers would be as full of willing recruits as ever and he was resolved to build up his strength once more.

A few weeks later, close to the Cape Verde Islands, they seized an English galley called the *Norman,* bound from Liverpool to Antigua. For those in Roberts' crew who may have been wavering in their commitment to life under the black flag the *Norman*'s captain, Samuel Norman, provided a timely reminder of the arbitrary power they had escaped in the merchant navy. Norman achieved notoriety the following year when he became one of the few eighteenth-century merchant captains accused of buggery. His fourteen-year-old cabin boy claimed he had ordered him to wash 'his legs, thighs and privy parts' and had then inserted his 'yard' into his 'fundament'. The vast imbalance of power between captain and cabin boy meant such crimes were almost never reported and the cabin boy only spoke up on this occasion because he was encouraged by the rest of the crew. Even then the case never came to court. Norman was already an unpopular captain when Roberts encountered him and at least three men joined the pirates from his crew, including one glorying in the name of Thomas Withstandyenot.

From the Cape Verde Islands the pirates turned eastward and at some point towards the end of May the vast bulk of the African continent loomed before them once more. For the men aboard – particularly the Newfoundlanders, many of whom had never sailed in African waters – it was a sobering moment. All sailors knew of the dreadful mortality these seas exacted on European ships. And, as they gazed at the endless, flat coastline they knew they were entering an environment very different from the bright specks of the Caribbean islands that they had flitted between for much of the last eighteen months, one that was far more alien and forbidding. Here European settlements were few and far between, and were confined to tiny, dilapidated forts, clinging to the periphery of the continent. Between lay vast tracts of land inhabited only by Africans, regarded by most Europeans as savages and cannibals. But for Roberts, the sight of the familiar old coastline through the soupy, humid atmosphere was welcome. There were no colonial governors, ready to fit out expeditions to hunt him down. And he knew fear of the locals would make most of his men think twice before deserting.

But the West African coastline was not quite the defenceless wilderness it had been when Howel Davies had ravaged it with Cocklyn and La Bouche two years earlier. In the autumn of 1719 the government in London had finally agreed to the frantic pleas of the slave traders for protection. Two fourth-rate men-of-war – HMS *Swallow* and HMS *Weymouth* – had arrived off Africa just a few weeks before. Each had 50 guns and between them they carried 500 men – the sort of force Governor Hamilton in Antigua and Governor

Spotswood in Virginia had been begging for for years. The French also now had two warships off West Africa, one of 50 guns and one of 24. Their job was not an enviable one. These four vessels had to patrol a disease-ridden coastline stretching 3,000 miles from Cape Verde in modern Senegal to Cape Lopez in modern Gabon. But for the first time Roberts would be confronted with ships that he had good reason to fear.

With the arrival of HMS *Swallow* and HMS *Weymouth* off the African coast a colourful new set of characters enter Roberts' story. *Swallow* – the lead British vessel – was commanded by Captain Chaloner Ogle. At forty years old he was almost exactly the same age as Roberts, but his life could not have followed a more different trajectory. He came from a naval family and, while Roberts had laboured for years as a common seaman, Ogle had entered the Royal Navy in July 1697 as a 'king's letter-boy'. This was a fast-track traineeship for officers, introduced by King Charles II in 1661 as a means of encouraging 'the families of better sort among our subjects' to send their sons to sea. By the age of twenty-one Ogle was a lieutenant and he received his first command the following year, serving with distinction in the Mediterranean throughout the War of the Spanish Succession. He was a rising star.

The captain of HMS *Weymouth* was an able young commander called Mungo Herdman. Serving under Herdman as first mate was a morose, solitary, forty-five-year-old Scot called Alexander Selkirk. Seventeen years earlier Selkirk had been marooned on the deserted island of Juan Fernández off Chile after falling out with his shipmates during a privateering mission to the South Seas. He lived there alone for more than four years. When his ammunition ran out he hunted goats with knives fashioned from the iron hoops of barrels washed up on the sea shore, leaping from rock to rock in his bare feet. By the time he was rescued by Captain Woodes Rogers – later governor of the

Bahamas – in 1709 he had almost lost the power of speech. He was the inspiration for Daniel Defoe's *Robinson Crusoe*, published in 1719.

Aboard HMS *Swallow* was a thirty-six-year-old surgeon called John Atkins. An intelligent, thoughtful man, Atkins later wrote a lengthy memoir of the voyage. He was prone to philosophical digressions, likening the departure from Land's End – 'shooting into an Abyss of Waters' – to death – a 'launch into a greater Abyss; eternity'. But he was also a perceptive and in many ways enlightened observer of what he saw in Africa. He dismissed the conventional wisdom that Africans were cannibals, which he saw as a myth created to 'justify dispossession'. And he was a rare critic of slavery, at least in the form it took in the West Indies. The plantation owners used slaves as 'beasts of burden', he wrote, feeding them the same diet as horses. As a result he felt it was 'inhumanity' to take Africans from their home-land. He was also an acerbic critic of the Royal African Company, which served as the representative of the British Crown in West Africa and was about to find itself locked in an epic, eight-month struggle with Roberts and his men.

The Royal African Company had been established in 1672 and granted a monopoly of all Britain's trade with Africa. The monopoly had been ended in 1698 and since then the company had been in freefall. Nevertheless it was still obliged to maintain forts along the African coast to protect the trade. The burden was crippling it, and the company's treatment of its staff and sailors made it a particular object of hatred to the pirates. Atkins left a vivid description of the appalling conditions at Cape Coast Castle, the company's main base in Africa, where HMS *Swallow* and HMS *Weymouth* arrived on 18 June 1721. Located on the Gold Coast, at the heart of the slave-trading region, it contained 'merchants, factors, writers, miners, artificers and soldiers', Atkins wrote. 'Excepting the first rank, who are the council for managing affairs, [they] are all of them together a company of white negroes, who are entirely resigned to the Governor's commands, according to the strictest rules and discipline and subjection.' Salaries were scarcely enough to keep them from starving, and they were forced to borrow from the company, turning them, like the fishermen of Newfoundland, into debt slaves. For those who somehow managed to avoid this, the governor had a series of fines at his disposal. 'They are all liable to be mulcted for drunkenness, swearing, neglects and lying out of the castle, even for not going to church.' For more serious misdemeanours punishments ranged from confinement in the dungeons, to 'drubbing' and 'the wooden horse' – a torture whereby a man was forced to sit astride the angle of a three-sided length of wood for hours on end, with weights attached to his legs.

Mortality rates were horrific, worse even than those on the slaving ships. During the course of 1719 a total of sixty-nine new employees were sent out to the Gold Coast. Of these almost half were dead within four months and almost two thirds within a year. Just three weeks before Atkins arrived at Cape Coast Castle a ship pulled in to the company's station at Whydah carrying a rare phenomenon on the African coast – an entire family. The new surgeon, Dr Levens, had brought out with him his wife, his two children and a maid. All five were dead within six weeks, along with the majority of their fellow passengers.

Cape Coast Castle generally contained between fifty and a hundred white men, crowded together in cramped, insanitary quarters. The numbers at the lesser forts strung out along the coast were much smaller, often less than five, and conditions there were even worse. 'I have . . . visited your forts at Anamaboe, Winneba, Tantumquerry and Accra,' the company's chief surgeon wrote to the board in London in 1725, 'and indeed they more resemble haunted houses than garrisoned forts, having one ghost above stairs and perhaps 2 or 3 at most below, spinning out a life that is a real burden to them, in miserable conditions.'

'I observed,' recalled Atkins, 'most of our factors to have dwindled much from the genteel air they brought; wear no cane nor snuff-box, [are] idle in matters of business, have lank bodies, a pale visage, their pockets sewn up, or of no use, and their tongues tied.' Many took refuge in drink, and senior officials didn't hesitate to ascribe the high mortality among their employees to their own debaucheries. The governor at James Fort in Gambia in the 1730s described one man who 'died a martyr to rum; for when he was not able to lift a mug to his mouth, he made shift to suck it through a pipe, and died with a pipe and a mug full of Bumbo close to his pillow'.

The writers – or clerks – were often in their teens. Atkins recalled visiting the office of 'Poor T-d . . . a youth well recommended', at Cape Coast Castle one day. 'A negro woman came bawling about his ears for a plantain he had stole from her. He would feign have concealed the meaning of her music, but at length I understood it was the only morsel he had eat for three days past, one night's debauch, and several mulcts having run him out of pocket.' 'Poor T-d' was dead before Atkins left the fort. 'He pined with a vacuum of the guts, and died; leaving this advice to his countrymen, rather to run a remote hazard of being hanged at home, than choose a transfer hither.'

There were compensations. In 1727 one trader wrote a lengthy eulogy to the greater sexual freedom of African society. He recalled being given a concubine for the night by a minor local king. 'At midnight we went to bed, and in that situation I soon forgot the complexion of my bedfellow, and obeyed the dictates of all-powerful nature. Greater pleasure I never found, and during my stay, if paradise is to be found in the enjoyment of a woman, I was then in the possession of it.' This more relaxed attitude to sex, he claimed, was responsible for the total absence 'of those detestable and unnatural crimes of sodomy and bestiality, so much practised among Christians'.

But this was small consolation for the almost certain death that awaited. Like the sailors aboard the slavers, many of the soldiers and artisans at the forts were effectively conscripts, dragged half-conscious from the bars and brothels of London, Liverpool and Bristol, unaware of the dreadful rates of mortality that awaited them precisely because so few returned to tell the tale. Further up the ladder, those who went out as traders were playing a game of Russian roulette, hoping they could fight off the malaria and the dysentery long enough to return home rich men. It was almost always a miscalculation and they weren't among the best and the brightest that Britain had to offer. As one historian put it: 'One might guess that a good many men entering the African service had already failed at some other job.'

There were rare exceptions, men who, through sheer dint of their ability to stay alive while all those around them dropped like flies, attained an almost mythical stature. Such a man was General Phipps, the Governor of Cape Coast Castle, the company's senior official in Africa, whose duel with Roberts over the coming months would be a very personal one. He'd somehow managed to survive almost twenty years in the job and reigned supreme, the 'first person' in all things at the fort, according to Atkins. The absolute power he wielded in his 'petty sovereignty' and the 'fawning submission of the Negroes' had made him 'haughty towards all under him'. He resided 'forever within his battlements' like a giant in his 'enchanted castle'. On the rare occasions when he invited guests to dinner he had developed the strange habit of taking the food, uninvited, from their plates. You had to 'keep a good look-out, or lose your dinner', wrote Atkins, 'though he knows there is no victuals anywhere else'.

In the midst of the poverty and squalor of the coast Phipps lived like a king. His salary was £2,000 a year. This compared with £300 a year for the best-paid factors, or traders, and on top of this he was able to trade on his own account. Atkins noted that, although meat was a rarity at the castle, Phipps never went short, supplying himself both from trading vessels and the surrounding African villages. He also had a large 'orchard' or 'garden', almost ten miles in circumference, close by, which provided oranges, lemons, limes, citrons, guavas, paw paws, plantains, bananas, coconuts, cinnamon, tamarinds, pineapples, Indian cabbage and some European crops. Little of this found its way to the plates of his employees.

Cape Coast Castle itself was considerably grander than any of the other British forts along the coast. Built of stone, bleached white in the sun, it contained 28 guns, jutting aggressively out from the ramparts towards the sea, it having been built, like all the forts in Africa, for defence not against the Africans but against other Europeans. Below ground, cut from solid rock, were dark, gloomy dungeons, into which the slaves were lowered, up to a thousand at a time, to await shipment. 'The keeping of the slaves thus underground is a good security to the garrison against any insurrection,' wrote a French trader in 1682. Rather more compassionately, Atkins noted there was just a single iron grill 'to let in light and air on those poor wretches'. Each was branded on the right breast with the letters 'DY', for 'Duke of York', the Royal African Company's original founder, later King James II.

Above ground Phipps had spacious lodgings. They were linked directly to the chapel and the main hall, so he could overlook his employees both at prayer and at work. He also had a private bastion, or walkway, with 'a very pleasant prospect to the sea'. From here he could watch ships coming down the coast and, with a telescope, identify the vessels anchored at El Mina, the main Dutch fort on the coast, which lay just nine miles to the east.

He spent his time firing off lengthy, cantankerous letters to London. Besides pirates, competition with independent traders – or interlopers – and with the Dutch were his main preoccupations. But

he also moaned incessantly about the quality of the men sent out to
serve him.

John Brooks, shipwright died on the 6th, and I can but observe to
your honours that had he lived he would have been of little service
being old and past his labour . . .

. . . Edward Gold and Peter Roberts who came over in the
Carlton under the denomination of brickmakers know nothing of the
business having been only labourers . . .

. . . What with the impertinence, ignorance and rascality of the
factors and writers I am become a perfect slave.

The men beneath him were all 'scoundrels' and 'idiots', who shared
the annoying habit of dying before they could pay off the debts he had
taken such care to drive them into.

But he had one soft spot – his mulatta concubine, and the four
little children he had had by her. It was common for Europeans on the
coast to take local 'wives', and they tended to prefer women of mixed
race. Phipps' partner was the daughter of a Dutch soldier at El Mina.
A merchant captain in the 1690s recalled watching the concubines of
European traders dance 'frenziedly' to the sound of music played on
elephant-tusk horns. 'This is a pleasant way of marrying,' he
commented, 'for they can turn them off and take others at pleasure,
which makes them very careful to humour their husbands, in washing
their linen, cleaning their chambers, and the charge of keeping them is
little or nothing.' But Phipps was an exception. He doted on his
concubine and was forever trying to persuade her to return to England
with him, without success. She went barefoot, Atkins wrote, and
was always 'fetished with chains and gobbets of gold at her ankles,
her wrists, and her hair' and felt she would 'fit awkward' in
England. Although she went with him to chapel occasionally, she

complied 'without devotion . . . being a strict adherent to the negrish customs'.

Phipps had, however, persuaded her to send their children – 'of fair, flaxen hair and complexion' – to school there. The oldest two had already gone. The youngest two, a boy and a girl, were still with him, and he was forever ordering clothes and other trinkets for them from London. When Atkins was there he was awaiting the arrival of a servant girl to wait on his daughter, along with some shoes, and some clothes to put his 'boy in breeches'. Atkins was made very aware that Phipps set no store at all in the skills of surgeons like himself. Examining him one day when he fell ill, Atkins was disturbed to discover the old general wore African charms around his wrists and his neck.

Phipps' ships would suffer grievously at Roberts' hands over the next eight months. But as the general became acquainted with Captain Ogle and Captain Herdman in mid-June 1721, there was still no word of the pirates' arrival on the coast. And so, on 26 June, HMS *Swallow* and HMS *Weymouth* left Cape Coast Castle and set off east towards the Bight of Biafra.

By this time Roberts and his men were already at Sierra Leone, 1,000 miles to the west. They had hit the coast originally at the Senegal River, further north, where the trade – mainly tree gum rather than slaves – was dominated by the French. There they had been challenged by two small cruisers which the French kept at the mouth of the river to deter foreign ships. The pirates immediately raised their black flag, at which 'their French hearts failed', and they quickly surrendered, according to Captain Johnson. The two cruisers were found to contain 26 guns and 140 men between them and the pirates decided to take them with them, first dumping the crews on the African coast.

They arrived at Sierra Leone on 12 June. At this time it was a backwater in the slave trade. But Cape Sierra Leone, combined with the broad estuary of the Rokel River, provided one of the few natural harbours in West Africa and the Royal African Company had a small fort there. The governor, an old Irishman called Robert Plunkett, was a grizzled veteran in the mould of General Phipps. He had been in Sierra Leone at least five years and his letters back to London rivaled those of his superior in their spleen and vindictiveness. He complained that his surgeon was a 'morose, ignorant fellow' and his writer 'both fool and madman', and felt Phipps was always short-changing him in the supplies he sent from Cape Coast Castle – the food 'perishing . . . the rum well-watered'. The ruins of his fort can still be seen today, the stone walls being slowly wrestled to the ground by the roots of giant trees, the guns lying scattered in the grass, their carriages long since rotted. It had been pillaged by Davis, Cocklyn and La Bouche during their stay in April 1719 and Plunkett had been taken prisoner. The legend on the coast was that they had spared his life in admiration for his ability to outswear them.

Roberts and his men decided not to storm the fort. Located on an island high up the river it contained little worth stealing, and Plunkett was clearly resolved to resist. Roberts knew that, if they left him alone, he would have little option but to leave them alone and, as ever, he was not interested in picking a fight for the sake of it. Instead, the pirates got to work converting the larger of the two French cruisers to be their new consort. They named it the *Ranger* and loaded it with around 30 guns. They elected as captain a Welshman called James Skyrm, who had been first mate on a sloop from St Christophers, captured the previous October. At the same time they careened the *Royal Fortune*. They were at Sierra Leone for more than six weeks and, as ever during these stopovers, they enjoyed themselves.

It was a hauntingly beautiful spot. The main watering hole was at a cove called Frenchman's Bay and was one of the best-known in West Africa. 'The water comes cascading down from the mountain, among an infinity of rocks, making no small amount of noise against the profound silence of these vast forests,' wrote one visitor. The 'sweet and clear' waters gathered in a pool just yards from the sea, around which 'large and handsome trees' provided a 'delectable shade'. All around stood high hills, almost 3,000 feet tall, which trapped the sound of thunder during the rainy season and sent it echoing around the bay. Down at the water's edge it was possible to gather great clumps of oysters from the branches of mangrove trees at low tide. There were dangers too. HMS *Swallow* had stopped here in April en route to Cape Coast Castle and John Atkins saw a sailor, 'mellow in drink', almost eaten by a crocodile as he walked in the shallows. He saved himself only by ramming his fist down the animal's throat.

As Howel Davis and his men had discovered two years before, it was one of the few places in the world where there was still a community of Englishmen prepared to welcome pirates. Plunkett and his men at the fort lived cheek by jowl with around thirty independent traders – 'men who, in some part of their lives, have been either privateering, Buccaneering or pirating, and still retain and love the riots, and humours, common to that sort of life', according to Johnson. The best known was John Leadstone, or 'Old Crackers', a former Buccaneer. 'He keeps the best house in the place,' wrote Johnson, 'has two or three guns before his door, with which he salutes his friends (the pirates, when they put in), and lives a jovial life with them, all the while they are there.' The traders kept African servants, both male and female – 'the women so obedient that they are ready to prostitute themselves to whomsoever their masters shall command them'.

Again, there is no record of Roberts indulging. But his crew were not so reticent and some nights Roberts and Henry Glasby – still a prisoner on the *Royal Fortune* – were almost the only people left aboard. We can picture these two sober, solitary figures leaning on the ship's rail, slightly apart, gazing into the tropical night and listening to the distant sound of the men's revelry, an unspoken empathy between them.

A crew member called William Williams, who had been captured off Newfoundland, took the opportunity to escape but was later caught and subjected to two lashes from every member of the crew. Other than that, as Roberts had calculated, most of his men were 'too much afraid of the negroes' to attempt anything. He even gained a couple of recruits. One of them, William Davis, had deserted from a slaving galley shortly before and had lived among the Africans at Sierra Leone for a time. He'd been given an African wife, but had sold her for some punch, after which he fled to the Royal African Company's fort for protection from her family. Governor Plunkett handed him back to them, telling them 'he did not care if they took his head off', but they opted to sell him instead and he was living as a virtual slave when Roberts arrived. He was a poor recruit, soon proving himself to be an 'idle, good-for-nothing fellow'.

Roberts took no prizes at Sierra Leone. Two years before Davis, Cocklyn and La Bouche had captured thirteen vessels here. But it was now the rainy season and the estuary was known as a particularly unhealthy spot at this time — something that didn't seem to worry Roberts and his seasoned men. But by the end of July he was impatient to move on. He had a new ship to fill with recruits. He'd also gained important intelligence from the traders at Sierra Leone.

Old Crackers and the others had told him of the arrival of HMS *Swallow* and HMS *Weymouth*. But they'd also told him that the two Royal Navy vessels had no plans to return to this stretch of the coast until Christmas. The prevailing winds and currents along the African coast ran west to east. Ships rarely attempted to travel in the opposite direction. Instead, having reached their destination towards the Bight of Biafra, they tended to drop south of the equator to either Cape Lopez or the island of Annobón and then pick up the south-east trade winds.

The slavers used these to take them out into the Atlantic. HMS *Weymouth* and HMS *Swallow* would use them to take them back across the Gulf of Guinea to Gambia, before cruising east again. So long as he remained behind the two men-of-war as they made this circuit Roberts calculated that he was safe. The two French warships were also far to the east at this time. At the start of August the *Royal Fortune* and the *Ranger* sailed out of Sierra Leone knowing that they had the coast at their mercy.

10

KNIGHTS ERRANT

'HE ABUSED HIM, CALLING HIM A . . . SON OF A BITCH, THAT HE STARVED THE MEN, AND THAT IT WAS SUCH DOGS AS HE AS PUT MEN ON PYRATING'

*T*HE AFRICAN SLAVE TRADE began in the sixteenth century in West Central Africa – the region around the modern nations of Congo and Angola – and then spread north-west in a wave. At its peak in the second half of the eighteenth century slaves were being exported at a rate of 5,000 a year from areas as far north as Senegal and Gambia. By 1721 this wave had reached the Gold Coast, which was exporting 7,000 slaves a year. The area immediately to the east of it – known simply as the Slave Coast – was the most important supplier. The town of Whydah, in modern Benin, was the greatest slave port of the age, exporting 20,000 in peak years. The area immediately to the west of the Gold Coast was the frontier, the slave trade's Wild West, only just being opened up by aggressive interlopers from Bristol and Liverpool. Comprising the modern nations of Liberia and Côte d'Ivoire, it was generally known as the Windward Coast. This was the region Roberts and his men were now entering.

As they edged their way cautiously eastwards the pirates were confronted with a flat, featureless landscape of endless jungle. The African villages, when they could be glimpsed between the trees, consisted of small gatherings of mud and wattle huts. The people painted themselves with a dark, reddish paint and sharpened their teeth. Few spoke English or Portuguese and they were generally regarded by Europeans as being less civilised than those of the Gold Coast. The Africans were equally wary of Europeans. John Atkins had met the local chief at Cape Mesurado – the site of modern Monrovia – when he'd passed this way three months before on HMS *Swallow*. He was distinguished by 'an old hat and sailor's jacket, [and] a greater number of thick brass rings on his fingers and toes than his attendants'. He came out to greet them in a canoe, but 'seemed shy of entering the ship . . . his town's people having often suffered by the treachery of the ships'. Kidnapping – or 'panyarring' – was a plague here, Europeans often saving themselves the trouble of buying slaves by simply abducting the traders. The Royal African Company blamed Liverpool and Bristol interlopers, complaining they saw little need to build up a long-term relationship with the Africans.

The Africans responded in kind. It was here that some of Howel Davis's men had been murdered while ashore in May 1719, prompting him to seize a number of local men, string them from the yard-arm and use them for target practice by way of retaliation. Europeans rarely left their ships. Instead the locals sent smoke signals when they had goods to sell and the ships anchored off shore. The Africans rowed warily out to them, carrying slaves or ivory. They 'will play for hours together in their canoes about the ship, before they dare venture', wrote Atkins. Once they were on board the ships' captains kept their crews heavily armed, gathered in the stern, in case of attack. As elsewhere along the African coast, the slave trade was creating a brutal, dog-eat-dog world among the Africans. 'It is their villainies and robberies upon one another that enable them to carry on a slave trade with Europeans,' Atkins commented cynically, 'and as strength fluctuates, it is not infrequent for him who sells you slaves today, to be a few days hence sold himself at some neighbouring town.'

But Roberts was an old hand here. When the Africans tilted their heads back and put a drop of salt water in their eye on first meeting, he knew he was expected to reciprocate as 'an engagement of peace and security'. For him this was an ideal hunting ground. There were no European forts. And although the Windward Coast was a minor source of slaves in itself, all ships bound for the Gold Coast and the Slave Coast had to pass this way. Fresh from Europe, they were still packed with trade goods, rather than slaves, which were a burden. More importantly, the bulk of their crews – Roberts' real quarry – were still alive, having not yet been exposed to the mosquitoes of the African coast.

Roberts' career had now come full circle. Having been liberated himself from the slavers two years before, he was now the liberator. The pirates hadn't passed Cape Mesurado before they'd snapped up at least three prizes – the *Martha,* the *Robinson* and the *Stanwich,* all interlopers from Liverpool. On each Roberts lined the men up and invited them to join his crew, expecting the usual surge of willing recruits. But he was disappointed.

The pirates took at least fifteen men from the three ships. But they had to force most of them. By now David Simpson – 'Little David' – the quick-tempered, powerfully built Scot who had unsuccessfully challenged Roberts for the captaincy at Princes Island back in July 1719, was quartermaster. He beat many of the men on to the pirate ships. And when Roger Pye, a young sailor on the *Stanwich,* begged to be released on the grounds that he was newly married and had left his wife with child Simpson was deaf to his pleas. Henry Glasby intervened repeatedly and the captains of the *Martha* and the *Stanwich* both recorded that he was responsible 'for what good usage they met with'. But he was powerless to prevent the men being taken.

Like Howel Davis before him, Roberts disliked forcing men. But he was always sceptical of those who claimed to be reluctant to join the pirates. He assumed they were putting on a show for witnesses, or, if genuine, that they would quickly be seduced by pirate life – as he himself had been. He was usually right. But the Liverpool men proved stubbornly resistant. Roger Gossuch from the *Martha*, in particular, irritated the pirates by remaining 'melancholy' and 'meditating on Godly books'. They were an awkward presence within the crew from then on, providing a hard knot of malcontents always looking for an opportunity to escape. It was the first indication Roberts had that the boundaries of his world were narrowing and that, with four warships patrolling the African coast, life beneath the black flag no longer carried the same automatic appeal for men aboard the slavers.

The capture of the *Stanwich* yielded an intriguing encounter. The ship was captained by John Tarlton, part of a fast-rising dynasty of Liverpool slave merchants, who had on board a young doctor called George Wilson. When the ship was first captured Tarlton was unwell and sent Wilson aboard the *Royal Fortune* to speak to Roberts. Roberts took a shine to the young man. He instantly invited him to become his mess-mate – in other words to share his quarters and eat and sleep with him. Wilson replied that he had a wife and child, at which Roberts laughed. Whether Wilson moved into Roberts' quarters we don't know, but he certainly joined the crew, if only briefly. Two days later he was swept ashore at Cape Mesurado while rowing across to the *Stanwich* to fetch his chest. The pirates sailed on without him. Whether this was an accident or an escape was unclear. But it was not the last time Roberts and Wilson would meet.

Sailing east, the pirates had more luck with their next prize, a Royal African Company ship called the *Onslow,* which they came across riding at anchor in the mouth of the River Sestos on 8 August. At 410 tons it was one of the largest ships they ever encountered. It carried 26 guns and a crew of fifty and had room on board for up to 600 slaves. But − unusually − the bulk of the men were ashore when the pirates arrived and it surrendered meekly.

The *Onslow* should not have been there. Royal African Company ships were meant to make straight for Cape Coast Castle and the *Onslow* had only stopped so the captain, William Gee, could indulge in private trade. General Phipps, when he heard, was furious, and blamed the loss of the ship entirely on Gee's 'imprudence'. It had £9,000 worth of goods on board, the vast bulk of it trading items intended for delivery to Cape Coast Castle and the Royal African Company's station at Whydah. They included guns, gunpowder, pewter crockery, cowry shells (used as currency at Whydah), hats, bells, beads and 240 mirrors, as well as large quantities of textiles and copper and iron bars. It was also carrying tobacco, pipes and malt spirits which, surprisingly, the Royal African Company provided for the slaves on their journey across to the Caribbean.

There were a number of passengers aboard, including a Captain Trengrove, who was coming out to run the gold mine the company was attempting to open up next to Cape Coast Castle. He had brought a number of miners with him, as well as his wife, Elizabeth. There were also a large number of soldiers and artisans intended for Cape Coast Castle and a clergyman called Roger Price. The pirates jokingly invited Price to join their crew, 'promising he should do nothing for his money but make punch, and say prayers', but he declined. Good naturedly, they returned almost all the goods they had stolen from him, although they kept a corkscrew, for which their need was obvious, and 'three prayer books', for which it was less so.

Roberts and Little David cast an eye over the cargo and quickly realised the real prize here was the ship itself. The *Royal Fortune*, by now, was 'leaky and crazy' — a term used to describe an old and decrepit ship. They exchanged it with Captain Gee for the *Onslow* and quickly set about making alterations, knocking down the bulkheads below deck and removing the quarterdeck to make it sleek, streamlined and easy to move around in times of battle, a classic pirate ship in every way. They mounted it with 40 guns and decided to keep the name *Royal Fortune*.

In contrast to the Liverpool men captured earlier, the employees of the Royal African Company were as eager as ever to turn pirate. While the alterations were being made Roberts called the captured crew together and asked, according to a witness, 'whether they were willing to go with him, for that he would force nobody'. Initially there was much whispering and shuffling of feet, at which Roberts laughed and cried out, 'These fellows want a show of force!' He and Little David obligingly dragged a number of them off to sign the articles, after which they quickly became enthusiastic pirates. No sooner was this performance over than a number of the soldiers from the *Onslow* came forward and asked if they might also be allowed to join the pirates. A few months before the garrison being sent to the Royal African Company fort at Gambia had mutinied *en masse* and turned pirate. And the soldiers on the *Onslow* had had their 'ears . . . tickled' by the sailors, who portrayed the pirates as 'knights errant' out 'to relieve the distressed'. However, the pirates were unsure. A large group of landlubbers were of little use. They put them off with excuses for some time, but eventually agreed to accept them, 'out of charity'. But the soldiers were only to be allowed a quarter-share of loot.

At least fifteen men joined from the *Onslow*. A number of them quickly revealed a bitter resentment towards their former officers. One, John Stephenson, was all 'for cutting the chief mate's ears off'. Another, Peter Lesley, got drunk and started ordering his former ship-mates to throw the cargo overboard. Both had to be restrained by the pirates, anxious not to be distracted from the more serious business of plunder. Little David was forced to give Lesley a lesson in pirate etiquette, asking him 'how he dare do this', and pointing out that he, as quartermaster, was responsible for the goods on a prize. But Little David himself was also in aggressive mood. One captive recalled him being 'particularly cruel beyond the rest of the pirates, driving them about with his cutlass and bragging he was as good a man as Roberts'. Another pirate, William Mead, approached Captain Trengrove's wife Elizabeth, 'swearing and cursing' and 'forced her hooped petticoat off'. On the advice of another pirate, she took refuge from him in the gun room.

The pirates threw the miners' tools overboard – which probably didn't bother the miners, though it angered Captain Trengrove. And they read the private correspondence intended for General Phipps at Cape Coast Castle, leaving letters scattered about the deck. At least some of the cargo was also thrown into the sea. The pirates were keen to take over their new ship as quickly as possible and couldn't be bothered to carry everything across to the old *Royal Fortune*. At the same time they couldn't be bothered to take everything out of their old ship and so, between what they left in the hold, and what was carried across from the *Onslow*, Captain Gee found he still had a decent cargo when he took over the pirate's vessel. To the fury of General Phipps he promptly set off west as soon as he was released despite the ship's leaky condition, dumping his passengers at Sierra Leone and heading for the West Indies. 'It may be supposed that his designs are to make up his own bulk [trade on his own account] without any further regard to your interest,' Phipps wrote to the Royal African Company board in London when he heard the news. Phipps was particularly upset at the loss of some silk shoes which were being sent out for his 'little one'.

Roberts was now in the most powerful ship that he, or any other pirate of the age, ever acquired. He'd recruited perhaps fifty men since the desertion of the *Good Fortune* and, in terms of numbers, he was beginning to approach his former strength. But, as ever, there were rumblings of discontent within the crew, and Henry Glasby picked this moment to make yet another escape attempt. He was in touch with conspirators aboard the *Ranger,* the new consort. The plan was that he would request a transfer to their ship. They would then get the Old Standers aboard drunk and make their escape. But Roberts and Little David were suspicious. They put Glasby's request for a transfer to a vote, and it was rejected, and so the plan was thwarted. But from this time on the *Ranger,* like the *Good Fortune* before it, was the focus of all conspiracies – whether by forced men or hardened pirates resentful at Roberts' increasingly autocratic rule – and Roberts took care to spread the malcontents, particularly the Liverpool men, between the two vessels.

As they headed east the flat, featureless jungle was replaced by a scrubby, hilly landscape, signalling their arrival at the Gold Coast. At the end of August they seized a Dutch vessel called the *Semm* close to the port of Axim. The pirates had a policy of taking all Englishmen they found in foreign ships. But, although there were three Englishmen aboard, after the glut of men he'd taken from the *Onslow,* Roberts was relaxed and prepared to let them go. But one of them, a sprightly twenty-five-year-old from Exeter called Charles Bunce, turned and gave Roberts a low bow and wished him a 'good voyage'. Again, it tickled Roberts' sense of humour. 'This fellow wants only a little encouragement!' he laughed, and ordered all three Englishmen stopped. Bunce proved a lively presence aboard, and quickly acquired the nickname 'Captain Bunce' for his habit of prescribing the number of salutes that should be fired on various occasions. Even more useful to Roberts was a man called Robert Armstrong who, it turned out, had deserted from Captain Ogle's ship, HMS *Swallow,* shortly before. Roberts now had someone on board who could advise him in detail on the strengths and weaknesses of his main adversary.

The pirates seized at least two other ships close to Axim, including a second Dutch vessel. By now they were just 50 miles from Cape Coast Castle and on 8 September General Phipps got word of their presence for the first time. In alarm, he quickly dispatched warnings to the forts and trading stations to the east. All along the coast the shipping took fright, either anchoring beneath the forts for protection, or scattering out to sea, like a herd of antelope before an approaching leopard. The pirates sailed brazenly past Cape Coast Castle on 9 September and pounced on a Portuguese sloop which had been slow to heed Phipps's warning at Tantumquerry a day or so later. By 19 September they were at Whydah. But the coast was empty. And at the end of September the two pirate ships slunk into the great, labyrinthine river estuary of Old Calabar to digest their prey at leisure.

Despite the presence of four warships in the region Roberts' rampage had been every bit as destructive as that of Davis two years previously, and General Phipps was seething. The two French men-of-war were further east. And HMS *Swallow* and HMS *Weymouth* had not been on the coast at all. Instead they were careening on Princes Island, the small Portuguese colony where Howel Davis had been killed two years before. Events there were about to leave the authorities in a still more vulnerable position.

Swallow and *Weymouth* had arrived at Princes Island on 28 July, just as Roberts was beginning his rampage along the coast. They anchored on the south-western side of the bay at St. Antonio and, like Howel Davis two years before, immediately set about careening and taking in wood and water. As with Davis's crew, the men soon began to enjoy themselves.

While the warships were on their sides the crew slept in tents ashore. This left them 'more at their own wills and disposals than it is proper they should ever be trusted with', wrote the surgeon, Atkins.

They were 'ungovernable in their actions and appetites, pilfering from the Negroes, and debauching their wives'. They drank vast quantities of palm wine, many pawning their own clothes and possessions to buy it, and often 'lay down in these inebriations' semi-naked and slept in the open air, exposed to the elements. Atkins blamed these debauches, in part, for what happened next.

It was the habit of Europeans in the tropics to build their settlements in sheltered, leeward spots. This gave them protection from hurricanes and typhoons. But it also meant they were airless, muggy and oppressive, particularly in the rainy season. Ringed with densely forested mountains, St Antonio was typical. Captain Ogle had taken care to arrive before the rains. But in 1721 the rains came early – with fatal consequences.

'Little winds, calm and rain,' noted Ogle in his log for 10 August. It was the same the following day. 'Much rain,' he wrote on 25 August. Slowly the tops of the mountains disappeared beneath a thick bank of cloud and the air became heavy and humid. The sun remained 'extraordinary' hot during the day, wrote Atkins. But this was followed by chilly evenings and 'prodigious dews' in the night, 'sufficient in a few hours to wet all the beds through a double tent'. Soon the men began to fall ill. 'Both ships people began to be very sickly by the rains and damp ashore,' Ogle noted on 26 August. He hired houses in the town as a temporary hospital and sent John Atkins to treat them.

Atkins noted the men were seized by 'frenzies, convulsions and . . . sweats'. Their temperatures soared and they raged with thirst, but insisted on wearing 'two or three coats, to resist the coldness of the air that, to me, seemed more like the steam of a hot oven'. By now they'd finished careening HMS *Swallow* and it was upright again and back on the water. Atkins ordered those men still healthy to return on board and persuaded Ogle to stop working the men in the middle of the day.

By these measures he slowed the spread of the sickness among HMS *Swallow*'s crew. But by early September the bulk of the men from HMS *Weymouth* had already succumbed.

Atkins tried everything he knew. He bled them. He gave them laxatives. He gave them emetics to induce nausea and vomiting. He applied crushed beetles to their arms and legs to draw out blisters. He smeared the resin of spruce trees on to the soles of their feet and the palms of their hands. And he forced them to drink solutions made from ground sea shells and 'hartshorn' – the ground antlers of a hart – which he believed would help absorb excess liquids. But he merely added to their suffering. What the men had was malaria and what they needed was quinine, and Atkins could not know this. Most were dead within six days of falling ill.

By early September the men were dying in large numbers. Ogle proposed that they take quarters in the town and send for reinforce/ments from England. But Atkins was astute enough to realise that the only solution was to get away from the pestilential air of St Antonio as fast as possible. Ogle eventually agreed. But the more men fell sick, the slower the work of careening progressed. Then, on 5 September, they discovered a fracture in HMS *Weymouth*'s keel. It had run aground on a sandbar at Gambia earlier in the year and the damage was worse than they had realised. They were forced to carry out a makeshift repair, and it slowed them further. It wasn't until 20 September, five dreadful weeks after the sickness had first broken out, that they were finally ready to leave. By then 100 men were dead and 200 sick. HMS *Weymouth*'s crew was so depleted that they had to borrow twenty slaves from another ship in the harbour in order to haul the anchor.

Once at sea the death rate abated slightly. But on HMS *Weymouth* the sickness seemed to have entered the very timbers of the ship and a trickle of men continued to die. They limped northward to seek help from General Phipps at Cape Coast Castle. But when *Weymouth* arrived there on 22 October, slightly ahead of *Swallow*, it was greeted with cannon fire, the jittery gunners mistaking them for Roberts and his men returning. It was the first indication they'd had of the havoc the pirates had wrought along the coast in their absence.

When finally *Weymouth* was allowed to anchor, fortunately unharmed, General Phipps was appalled by the state of the crew. 'The ship's company are so sickly and very weak that they have few hands enough to hoist the sails,' he wrote. The death toll aboard the two ships had now risen to 160. Herdman mustered his men on 25 October and found he had fewer than sixty fit for service, having set out from England with a complement of 240. When HMS *Swallow* arrived a few days later it had just eighty healthy men out of an original crew of 274. The two French men-of-war appear to have left region by this time – certainly they played no further part in either Ogle's or Roberts' calculations. And, as Ogle, Herdman and Phipps conferred in the general's spacious apartments overlooking the ocean, it was clear they were in a drastically more vulnerable position than they had been three months previously.

They compounded their problems with an error of judgement. The pirates had not been heard of since sailing past Whydah in mid-September. From this the three men concluded they had probably left the coast, most likely for Brazil or the East Indies. It was agreed *Weymouth* would stay at Cape Coast Castle while its men recovered. But on 10 November *Swallow* left the fort, heading not east after the pirates but west, beating against the wind, in order to replenish its crew by pressing men from the merchant ships along the Windward and Gold Coasts.

In fact, Roberts and his men were still holed up at Old Calabar, 750 miles to leeward. Since ships rarely travelled east to west along the coast, the failure to send HMS *Swallow* in pursuit of them meant it would be months before the men at Cape Coast Castle learned of their presence there. The pirates would be free to relax, careen their ships, and draw up plans for a further assault upon the coast.

Old Calabar was an ideal hiding place. Located in the south-east of what is now Nigeria, it was a labyrinth of narrow creeks and inlets. Green and grey parrots shrieked among the thick foliage of the river banks and the canoes of the local Africans, adorned with the skulls of ancestors, nosed their way through the thick, steaming mangrove swamps which clogged the upper river. Even by the standards of West Africa this place had a reputation for fearsome levels of mortality, particularly during the rainy season, which was only just ending. As at Sierra Leone, this didn't bother the pirates. But it deterred other Europeans. Slaves from here also had a reputation for fits of despondency and for committing suicide ('*Ibos pend' cor' a yo'* – 'The Ibo hang themselves' – is still a phrase in Haiti), which further reduced trade. Finally, there was a sandbar across the mouth of the river. This restricted access to a narrow and intricate channel and no ship could go up the river without a skilled pilot.

When they arrived at the end of September the pirates encountered a Captain Loan in a brigantine called the *Joceline* and pressed him into service as their guide. He took them over the bar and guided them to the upper river. 'Here . . . they sat easy and divided the fruits of their dishonest industry, and drank and drove care away,' wrote Captain Johnson. Captain Loan later claimed he'd had a good part of his cargo stolen. But it's more likely that, as Johnson states, he was rewarded for his services and invited to join in the revelry. Certainly none of the men from his ship were forced, although two joined the pirates voluntarily.

Although a minor slaving centre, Old Calabar yielded a handful of prizes in the six weeks the pirates were there. As they caroused they sent a long boat downriver from time to time to look for ships coming over the bar, and any vessel straying into their lair was instantly devoured. One of the first, a 90-ton brigantine called the *Hannibal*,

taken on 1 October, was a Royal African Company ship. Its commander, Captain Christopher Ousley, had on board a company factor
called John Wingfield, and the pirates immediately recognised in both
men the type of officers who had made their lives a misery as sailors on
the slavers. They suffered accordingly.

One of the pirates struck Captain Ousley so hard with the flat of
his cutlass that it broke. Another man, John Philps, called Wingfield
a 'son of a bitch' and told him 'that he starved the men, and that it was
such dogs as he put men on pirating'. When Wingfield, somewhat
ungallantly, pointed out that 'the captain was always victualler', Philps
'swore that if he spoke another word he would throw him overboard'.
Another pirate stole all of Wingfield's clothes and made a point of
wearing them for the next week, parading backwards and forwards in
front of him. The pirates were all for burning the ship, but Henry
Glasby managed to persuade them not to. Taking Wingfield aside later
he 'expressed a great deal of sorrow for being among such a company
of rogues', and Wingfield observed that 'he acted among them with
reluctance and . . . could not avoid it'.

The pirates ransacked the *Hannibal*, throwing its cargo overboard
and turning it into a storage vessel, or 'hulk', while they cleaned their
own ships. The malignant air of the river estuary soon took its toll on
the *Hannibal*'s crew. Captain Ousley was dead within a couple
of weeks, and by the time the *Hannibal* finally limped back to the
Gold Coast a few months later only Wingfield and six others were
still alive.

Shortly afterwards the pirates seized two more prizes, the *Mercy* and
the *Cornwall*, both from Bristol. They had taken no one from the
Hannibal — the crew was probably already too sickly to be worth
bothering with — but these two ships yielded at least fifteen men. Most
were forced. One tried, unsuccessfully, to gain his freedom by putting
on a cod Irish accent, it now being common knowledge along the coast

that Roberts and his men always refused Irishmen. But many of the new recruits were soon enthusiastic pirates.

The pirates took the surgeons from both the Bristol ships. William Child from the *Mercy* was reluctant, later pointing out to an Admiralty court that 'his being in a pirate ship was not only much against his inclination but his interest, having a good employ whereon to build, and friends to advance him in the world in an honest and reputable way of livelihood'. But the *Cornwall*'s surgeon, Peter Scudamore, was an altogether more intriguing character.

Previously the pirates had a policy of changing their surgeons regularly and never forcing them to sign their articles. But Scudamore, who was thirty-five and from Bristol, actually asked to sign, and according to witnesses 'gloried in being the first surgeon that had done so'. Afterwards he boasted he was now 'as great a rogue as any of them'. For a man of his social standing this was extremely unusual. Scudamore also had navigational knowledge and had picked up a smattering of various languages. He was no run-of-the-mill ship's surgeon and the life of a pirate had clearly captured his imagination. His captain later signed an affidavit stating that nine of the men taken from his ship were forced, but explicitly excluded Scudamore, who he said 'was a great villain'. He was soon elected the pirates' chief surgeon, and set about his work with zeal, stealing medicines from captured vessels and anything else that took his fancy.

The pirates had now switched quartermasters, voting out Little David, whose brutality had alienated his shipmates, and replacing him with William Magness, a thirty-five-year-old from Minehead in Somerset. Magness, who had been taken from a sloop as the pirates left the West Indies earlier in the year and had risen fast through the ranks, was a less aggressive figure. But there were still a number of unreconciled, forced men in the crew, incessantly plotting their escape. At Old Calabar five of the Liverpool men seized in August formed a conspiracy to take one of the ships' boats and slip away in the night. The vigilance of Roberts' look-outs thwarted them. But a man from the *Jeremiah and Ann,* taken at Bermuda in April, did manage to get ashore and run away. The rumour among the crew was that he had given all his money to Roberts 'to wink at it'.

The incessant plotting was wearying for Roberts. It drained his energy and sapped the morale of the crew. It wouldn't be surprising if he had accepted a bribe to be rid of a single malcontent. What he couldn't tolerate were mass desertions. These stopovers, when the ships were careening, were always a difficult time. It had been the same at Cayenne, Carriacou and Hispaniola. The men were drunk. They had time on their hands. And it was easier for them to slip away on land than at sea.

Once again, it wasn't just the forced men who were conspiring. Cabals were also being formed among the more hardened pirates, chafing under Roberts' increasingly authoritarian rule. This was a problem that was intensifying with time and Roberts knew that it was now a real threat to his power. But he was in a quandary. If he were to turn his men into an efficient fighting force that could sustain itself over time and withstand the assaults of the authorities, then he had to rein in their anarchic impulses, above all their incessant drinking. But to do that he had no choice but to become more dictatorial and autocratic. This clashed with the democratic traditions of pirate culture, the liberty and freedom which had drawn most of his men to the pirate way of life in the first place, and so provoked discontent. It was a dilemma he never fully resolved.

He was also having problems with the local Africans. Known as the 'Efik', they were an aggressive, entrepreneurial people. An English trader in 1714 described them as 'the greatest thieves in the world . . . They would . . . steal slaves out of the port-holes that they had sold us the day before and sell them again to the other ships.' At that time they

were still relatively unfamiliar with Europeans and the trader was surrounded by a crowd shouting 'Bacarada Oh! – White Man!' – every
time he went ashore. But in 1719 the region had been visited by the
pirate Edward England, whose men, according to Johnson, 'lived
there very wantonly for several weeks, making free with the negro
women, and committing such outrageous acts, that they came to an
open rupture with the natives, several of whom they killed, and one of
their towns they set on fire'. This may well have occurred at Old
Calabar itself. It was certainly nearby and word of the outrage spread
along the coast.

It was another indication of the pirates' shrinking world. Even
Africans were now hostile. When Roberts and his men tried to buy
supplies they were refused. The Efik had worked out their new visitors
were the same breed as Edward England and wanted nothing to do
with them. In retaliation the pirates launched an attack on the main
African town, forty men landing under cover of fire from the ships'
guns. The Efik drew up in a body of men, 2,000 strong, to confront
them. They managed to kill two or three of the pirates. But when the
others continued to advance they fled, with heavy losses. The pirates set
fire to the town and returned to their ships. This obviously made any
further stay in the river difficult. With the mutinous mutterings within
the crew growing louder, Roberts was soon keen to be back out to sea.

At some point in November he forced Captain Loan to pilot them
back down the river. Before parting Henry Glasby took the
opportunity to slip 'two or three moidores' into Loan's hand 'to carry
to his wife'. Then the *Royal Fortune* and the *Ranger* sailed out into the
Bight of Biafra.

The plan was to drop south of the equator and pick up the south-
east trade winds to carry them back towards the main trading areas
further west along the African coast. But, having failed to trade at Old
Calabar, they first needed to make a couple of stops to obtain supplies.

The pirates headed initially to Cape Lopez. The king there liked to dress in European style with 'hat, wig and breeches' and was a figure of amusement to visiting sailors, but rather more welcoming than the men of Old Calabar. Cape Lopez was a popular watering hole with European ships before they headed west and they were also able to buy wood, ready chopped by the local people.

On 14 December, immediately before or after this stop, the pirates seized a Dutch ship called the *Gertruycht* a few miles off the mouth of the River Gabon. They found two British men aboard. One, a drummer, they forced to join them. The other they left because he was Irish. The pirates irritated the Dutch mate by taking 'some very good sausages [and] ludicrously stringing them about their necks for a time, and then throwing them away'. They left the Dutch with just enough food to get back to El Mina on the Gold Coast.

They then headed for the island of Annobón to take in additional supplies. By this time Roberts was so nervous of the mutinous impulses within his crew that he took the unusual step of allowing only one man in each mess ashore at a time – effectively keeping the other men behind as hostages. He finally set off across the Gulf of Guinea around Christmas 1721, preparing for another rampage.

The sickness suffered by HMS *Swallow* and HMS *Weymouth* at Princes Island had had one unforeseen consequence. It had drastically weakened the two Royal Navy ships. But by forcing them to divert to Cape Coast Castle it had also thrown out Roberts' calculations. He was working on the assumption that they were now back at Sierra Leone, as Old Crackers and the other traders had told him in July. But they weren't. They were on the Gold Coast. Captain Ogle and Captain Herdman may not have known where Roberts was. But he now didn't know where they were.

11

DEFIANCE
OF DEATH
ITSELF

'I SHALL HAVE THE SATISFACTION OF

SITTING UPON HIS COURT MARTIAL IN MY

LACED SUIT'

HE *ROYAL FORTUNE* AND the *Ranger* hit land at Cape Lahou on the modern Cote d'Ivoire, at the eastern end of the Windward Coast, intending to rampage eastward along the Gold Coast and the Slave Coast. Roberts believed this placed him several hundred miles ahead of HMS *Swallow* and HMS *Weymouth* at Sierra Leone. In fact, the two warships were on the other side of him, to Leeward, just a couple of hundred miles away and directly in the path the pirates intended to take.

HMS *Weymouth* remained in a desperately weak condition. Alexander Selkirk, the original Robinson Crusoe, had died a sad, obscure death off El Mina on 13 December and the ship still had no more than seventy men fit for service. It had not strayed far from Cape Coast Castle over the previous two months. But HMS *Swallow* was approaching its former strength having recruited numerous men from the slavers to replace those who had died. Few needed to be pressed;

according to Atkins – they were 'escaping to us themselves from ill treatment (they said), bad or short diet', although he noted that 'more again, on the same pretence, took on with the pirates'. Had Roberts arrived just two weeks earlier he'd have landed right on top of HMS *Swallow* as it patrolled the Windward Coast. But Captain Ogle's ship was now headed back towards Cape Coast Castle.

By now the pirates had a new flag, which they raised from their mizzen peak, to accompany the representation of Roberts which flew from the bowsprit. It was an elaborate design. On the left was a full-length skeleton clutching crossed-bones in one hand and an hour-glass in the other, a 'dart' by its side, and 'underneath a heart dropping three drops of blood', according to Johnson. On the right, confronting the skeleton, was a figure clutching a flaming sword, 'intimating a defiance of death itself'. Like the first flag, it was made of black silk.

On the first day of 1722 the pirates seized a ship called the *Tarlton* close to Cape Lahou. It was from Liverpool and captained by Thomas Tarlton, brother of the John Tarlton whose ship the *Stanwich* they had captured back in August. They forced six men, who, like the other Liverpool men, were reluctant recruits. One even fell to his knees and begged to be released, but Roberts merely mocked him for his 'crocodile tears'.

A day later, a few miles to the east, they seized the *Elizabeth*, a London ship under the command of Captain John Sharp. Like the *Tarlton*, it fell without a shot fired, but the boarding party was an aggressive one. A number of reluctant recruits were beaten aboard the pirates' ships. And when the ship's surgeon tried to intervene to prevent them stealing some of his property they threatened to 'cut his ears off'. The surgeon reported that they barged into the captain's cabin, hung up their cutlasses, 'and fell to drinking and swearing, the vices he saw they were all enamoured of'. Despite the theft of a corkscrew from the *Onslow* the previous year, he noted they were still 'knocking off the heads of bottles' with their cutlasses. Henry Glasby again took advantage of the chaos to have a quiet chat with Captain Sharp, telling him 'how miserable his condition was with such a crew, lamenting very much'.

There was a pleasant surprise awaiting Roberts aboard the *Elizabeth*. Travelling as a passenger was George Wilson, the young surgeon from the *Stanwich* that Roberts had taken such a shine to the previous August. Despite the strong suspicion Wilson had deserted the pirates on that occasion Roberts was delighted to see him, and the relationship he formed with the young surgeon over the next few weeks is revealing of the inner impulses and passions which drove him.

'God Damn you! What, are you here again?' Roberts shouted across with a grin when he first spotted Wilson aboard the *Elizabeth*. He ordered that he be brought across in the first boat and Wilson, apparently equally pleased to see Roberts, hastily borrowed a shirt and drawers from the ship's surgeon to be more presentable. Once aboard the *Royal Fortune* Roberts greeted Wilson warmly and gave him a laced hat and shirt, the small matter of his apparent desertion in August quietly forgotten.

Wilson had had various adventures since his last meeting with Roberts. After being washed ashore at Cape Mesurado he'd lived in a wretched state among the Africans for five months. During that time Thomas Tarlton, the captain of the ship the pirates had captured the day before, had anchored nearby. Wilson had sent word of his desperate condition and begged him to at least send some food. Tarlton, firmly convinced Wilson had deserted his brother on the *Stanwich* and joined the pirates willingly, refused. Wilson was eventually rescued by a French ship which took him to Sestos, from where he was picked up by Captain Sharp in the *Elizabeth*.

On coming aboard the *Royal Fortune* Wilson immediately caught sight of Thomas Tarlton, who was still a prisoner on the pirate ship, and flew into a rage. On hearing the story Roberts instantly took upon himself 'the correction of Mr. Tarlton', who, until then, had been treated well, and began 'beating and misusing him grievously'. Tarlton was later hidden by the other Liverpool men aboard to spare him further abuse.

A number of witnesses later testified that Roberts and Wilson soon became 'intimate', even swearing a suicide pact together. 'They two [used] often to say that if they should meet with any of the Turnip Man's ships [an insulting term for King George I] . . . they would blow up and go to hell together,' one claimed. Roberts' attachment is all the more striking because Wilson was lazy in his work and unpopular with the rest of the crew – so much so that, on one occasion, Roberts himself threatened to cut Wilson's ears off, chiding him 'that he was a double rogue, to be there a second time'.

In this era it was common for men to show emotions and express affection for each other in a way that would later be regarded as inappropriate. But Roberts and Wilson hardly knew each other. In total, their relationship would last for no longer than six weeks. They had no time to develop a deep and profound friendship and it's hard to see what their 'intimacy' was based on if it wasn't physical.

By 5 January the pirates had reached Assinie on the boundary between the Windward Coast and the Gold Coast, where they took a small Royal African Company ship called the *Diligence*. Once again, they showed a particular hostility to the company's ships. Having thoroughly plundered it they sank it, leaving the crew with little option but to join them. Many were far from reluctant. One, a man called John Jessup, had originally been on the *Onslow* and had declined to join the pirates when it was taken in August. But five months in the service of the Royal African Company had changed his mind. His captain later testified that 'he . . . got drunk with the pirates and continued on a jovial life, swearing 'twas better being among them than at Cape Coast Castle'. The new recruits also included two slaves whom the Royal African Company had trained as seamen.

The next day, close to Cape Apollonia, they came across another Royal African Company ship, the *King Solomon*, a sizeable vessel of 200 tons laden with goods and provisions for Cape Coast Castle. Its captain, Joseph Traherne, was keen to resist. The *King Solomon* had 12 guns and a crew of more than thirty and the pirates sent across a long boat with just twenty men to seize it. Traherne grabbed a musket and fired on them, shouting to his men it was a 'shame they should be taken by half their number, without any repulse'. But the men stared sullenly at him and threw their guns to the ground, leaving him with no option but to surrender. Climbing aboard, the pirates were furious that Traherne had even contemplated resistance. 'Don't you see them two ships?' shouted one, gesturing to the *Royal Fortune* and the *Ranger*, anchored three miles away. They were 'commanded by the famous Captain Roberts', he told him, as if this were explanation enough why resistance was futile.

As on the *Onslow* back in August, the pirates quickly found themselves inundated with volunteers, including soldiers bound for Cape Coast Castle. At least nine were accepted. As on the *Onslow*, many were clamouring for revenge. One, John Divine, who turned out to be a ex-pirate himself, showed the pirates his 'allowance', or rations, 'to incense them against' Captain Traherne. 'It was their time before, but now it was his,' Divine was heard to mutter, menacingly, to some of his former officers. As on the *Onslow*, the pirates restrained them. But they planned to burn the ship. One of the boarding party decked himself out in Traherne's wig and clothes, ordered a bottle of wine, and merrily took the wheel to pilot the *King Solomon* over to the two waiting pirate vessels so it could first be plundered at leisure. But there Roberts' colder, more calculating personality asserted itself.

Roberts reached an accommodation with Traherne, who, it seems, paid a ransom to save not just his ship but also his cargo, which included a full-length mirror, intended as a gift for an African king. The pirates stripped it of everything else, from cables and sails to a backgammon set, taken by Peter Scudamore, the volunteer surgeon from Old Calabar.

As the *King Solomon* was being plundered its mate was astute enough to take note of the simmering tensions between the two pirate ships. Watching the pirate Isaac Hynde force two men on to the *Ranger*, he heard him say, 'the [*Royal*] *Fortune* had men enough, and [we] must have as many'. It was clear that the two ships saw themselves as much as competitors as collaborators.

Immediately afterwards they took a Dutch ship called the *Flushingham* close to Axim. They forced one man, a Philip Haak. He was a 'decrepit little fellow, unfit for their purpose,' his captain said, but he was a trumpeter, which they needed, and they were deaf to his pleas to be released. 'They killed all the fowls' aboard the ship, 'and fell to drinking very hard . . . prophanely singing at supper time Spanish and French songs out of a Dutch prayer book.'

The two pirate ships were now within 50 miles of HMS *Weymouth*, which was at Cape Three Points. From his captives Roberts now knew of the presence of the two warships on this stretch of the coast. But he had also been informed of their sickly condition. He decided to gamble. He had been planning to sail along the coast as far as Whydah. This was peak season at Africa's richest slave port and he knew he was assured a rich crop of prizes, particularly Portuguese vessels carrying Brazilian gold. He was not prepared to abandon his plan, but he decided to veer away from the coast and make direct for Whydah across open sea, leapfrogging the two warships lying in his path. The raid there would be his parting shot, a final spectacular. Afterwards he would head south, careen, and leave Africa for safer waters.

He made extraordinarily fast time. After abandoning the *King Solomon* at Axim on 8 January the *Royal Fortune* and the *Ranger* covered the 400 miles to Whydah in just three days. On 11 January the great port loomed into view. As throughout West Africa there were no jetties or harbour walls — just one long strip of sand against which the surf ceaselessly thundered. The town itself was set back a little way from the coast, and there was no fort, the local king refusing to allow one. The only indication of the torrent of human misery that flowed through this spot was a cluster of tents on the beach, used by ships' captains as a base from which to conduct trade. A double sand bar made this the most dangerous port on the entire coast and, once ashore, the captains preferred to stay there, sending slaves out to the ships whenever the surf abated slightly. Accidents were common and huge sharks roamed the waters. 'Whenever the dead are committed to the sea, which happens almost every day while ships are in this road,' a visitor in 1727 recalled, 'the sharks give such due attendance that the corpse can no sooner touch the water than it is immediately torn to pieces and devoured before our faces.'

The sea was slightly calmer in January than in other periods, which encouraged trade, and the pirates encountered twelve slaving ships. Five were Portuguese, four English and three French. The French in particular were formidable vessels, each containing 20 to 30 guns and more than 100 men. Some of the pirates were itching for a fight. 'Damn you — give the French ship a broadside and board him at once!' a new recruit seized just days before from the *King Solomon* shouted at Roberts. But it was unnecessary. Not only the captains but the bulk of the crews were ashore and all of the ships quickly surrendered — except one, a small Royal African Company sloop called the *Whydah*, that managed to slip away.

This was a rich haul — more than they had taken in the entire previous week in the waters west of Cape Coast Castle. The pirates set about plundering them of supplies and anything else useful aboard while Roberts opened negotiations with the captains to ransom the ships and their cargoes. It was a lengthy process, letters having to be sent back and forth by canoe through the crashing surf. But they eventually agreed on a ransom of eight pounds of gold dust per ship which, when multiplied by eleven, was worth around £5,600. Some of the foreign captains requested receipts and the pirates were happy to oblige. The documents they were given were reproduced by Captain Johnson:

> THIS is to certify whom it may or doth concern, that we GENTLEMEN OF FORTUNE, have received eight Pounds of Gold-Dust, for the Ransom of the Hardey, Captain Dittwitt Commander, so that we Discharge the said Ship. Witness our Hands, this 13th of Jan. 1722 – Batt. Roberts, Harry Glasby.

Others were written out by Little David and Thomas Sutton, the pirates' gunner, who jokingly signed themselves 'Aaron Whifflingpin' and 'Sim. Tugmutton'. It was all most civilised and good-humoured. But the master of one ship refused to pay – Captain Fletcher, of the English interloper *Porcupine*. Roberts' response was blunt. His ship would be burned.

Roberts was now in a hurry. While the process of ransoming had dragged on his men had intercepted a letter from General Phipps at Cape Coast Castle to the local Royal African Company agent. It informed him of the pirates' presence on the coast and told him that, at that very moment, HMS *Swallow* was making all speed for Whydah.

Word had reached Cape Coast Castle that Roberts was once more in the area on 9 January, at about the same time the two pirate ships were passing the fort, some miles out to sea, on their way to Whydah. By chance HMS *Swallow* had arrived at Cape Coast Castle the previous day. As more detailed information arrived over the following thirty-six hours Captain Ogle rightly guessed that Roberts would be unable to resist raiding Whydah before he left the coast. HMS *Weymouth* was still to the west and, in any case, in no fit state to confront the pirates. And so, the following evening, 10 January, HMS *Swallow* set off alone in pursuit. General Phipps could scarce contain his excitement. Captain Ogle 'can not well miss of them', he gloated to a friend in London. 'I shall have the satisfaction of sitting upon his court martial in my laced suit.'

On learning of Ogle's approach, Roberts called his men together. As ever after the seizure of a prize, many were drunk. Some, at least, were eager for a fight even with a fully armed British man-of-war and Roberts knew he would have to be careful how he handled them. Reading out Phipps' letter, he said he knew that they were 'brave fellows', but that on this occasion discretion was the better part of valour. There was some drunken posturing from a small number. But the majority agreed that they should leave as quickly as possible.

Roberts now dispatched a small group to burn the *Porcupine*. The party was led by a pirate called John Walden. Known as 'Miss Nanny' for the 'hardness of his temper', he had been taken off Newfoundland in the summer of 1720 and was a pirate in the mould of Little David – cruel and quick tempered. Walden was under firm orders to take off the last of the *Porcupine*'s crew and the eighty slaves who were chained in pairs below decks. But the pirates' haste now led them to commit what was, by some distance, the most barbaric crime they ever committed.

With Walden was the *Porcupine*'s mate, clutching the keys to the slaves' shackles in his hand. While the pirates took off the remaining crew and began to smear the decks with tar, he was sent below to unchain them. But he was nervous, fumbling. The pirates became impatient and beat him, but this only slowed him further. Eventually Walden had had enough. He ordered everyone out and set the ship ablaze – with the slaves still chained below deck.

As the pirates' boat pulled away the slaves' screams echoed across the water. Still chained together in twos, some managed to stagger up on deck and hurl themselves into the sea – only to be instantly devoured by sharks and torn limb from limb alive in front of the pirates' eyes.

Just what Roberts made of this as he watched from the *Royal Fortune* we don't know. He, after all, had been a slaver, and, whatever camaraderie might have developed with the slaves in his own crew, it was in his bones to view Africans first and foremost as commodities rather than human beings. The atrocity was against his orders. But there is no record of Walden or anyone else being disciplined for their actions. And before the pirates left Whydah Roberts had to tolerate a second act of insubordination, this time from an element of the *Ranger's* crew.

A group of the *Ranger's* men were ransacking a 20-gun French vessel as the pirates prepared to leave. It was a former privateer from St Malo and, as they plundered it, the pirates admired its sleek design. It was larger than their own ship and, by the time the order came to depart, a decision had been made: they would seize it, despite the fact Roberts had already received a ransom from the French captain. Roberts was aware the *Ranger's* men were seeking to build up their own strength, independent of the *Royal Fortune*. But there was little he could do about it.

As night fell on Saturday, 13 January 1722, the two pirate ships pulled away from Whydah, taking the French prize with them, leaving the *Porcupine* blazing in their wake. Captain Ogle arrived in HMS *Swallow* twenty-four hours later.

Roberts had got away with it again. He had sailed into the very jaws of two of the most powerful British warships ever sent in pursuit of pirates, and yet had managed to pillage shipping along a 500-mile stretch of coast, leaving them twisting and turning in his wake, bewildered by the speed of his movement, and sailed away unharmed having taken a total of nineteen prizes. For all the simmering tensions within his own crew, he must have felt invincible. There was even a bonus. As they pulled out into open sea the pirates came across the *Whydah*, the small Royal African Company sloop which had escaped them two days before, enabling them to indulge once more their detestation of the company and its ships. They plundered it and Miss Nanny was again given license to set it alight. Watching the flames take hold, one of the Liverpool men asked James Philips, an Old Stander, the 'reason of such wicked practice that served no purpose among them'. 'It was for fun,' Philips replied.

The *Whydah*'s crew was loaded on to a slaver called the *Neptune*, which happened to be passing, but which the pirates decided not to plunder. The pirates then made their way to Cape Lopez where they set about converting the French prize into their new second ship, naming it, like its predecessor, the *Ranger*.

The plan now was to make for Brazil in the hope of repeating the capture of the *Sagrada Familia* over two years before. Since Kennedy's desertion with their gold Roberts' rampages had been confined to waters which, though rich in prizes, rarely yielded the sort of spectacular haul that would enable a pirate to retire. And retirement was what Roberts now had in mind. They planned to raid off Brazil for eight months, 'share 600 or 700 pounds a man, and then break up', Roberts' confidant George Wilson told a new recruit. It was increasingly rare in this period for pirates to survive to enjoy their ill-gotten gains. Shrewd operator that he was, Roberts sensed that he had pushed his luck for long enough, and was dreaming of a life of ease, free of the constant stress of having to keep control over an unruly crew of 250 men. He would probably have made the move earlier if the *Good Fortune* hadn't deserted or the *Puerto del Principe* hadn't been captured, which forced him to stay longer off Africa to build up his strength.

But Captain Ogle hadn't finished with him yet. At Whydah he was told that Roberts was carrying substantial quantities of gold. If any extra incentive were needed he now had it, and he was determined not to let the pirates slip through his grasp. 'I judged they must go to some place in the Bight [of Biafra] to clean and fit the French ship before they could think of cruising again,' he wrote. There were only a limited number of places where this could be done. Ogle strengthened his crew with thirty recruits from the *Porcupine* and the French ship the pirates had seized. Then, on 19 January, he sailed out of Whydah planning to explore them one by one.

He went first to Princes Island, where he had buried so many of his men four months earlier. Finding no word of the pirates he hurried quickly away. He went next to the River Gabon, but, again, drew a blank. Then, as dawn broke on 5 February, he saw the outline of the three pirate ships, riding at anchor, framed against the headland of Cape Lopez.

He'd arrived just in time. The pirates had careened the *Royal Fortune* and had almost completed fitting out the new French ship. Two days later they'd have sailed for Brazil. But Ogle might be forgiven if at this moment he paused and drew breath. They'd loaded the new *Ranger* with 32 guns, giving Roberts 72 guns in total. The pirate crew now numbered 253 men, and Ogle believed it to be larger. Ships taken at the start of January had told him there were close to 300 men aboard the two pirate vessels, including '100 blacks, trained up'. Ogle had just 50 guns and a crew of no more than 250. He was confronting the most powerful, experienced pirate crew in the Atlantic and the outcome was by no means certain.

But, for once, Roberts' luck deserted him. There was a sandbank between HMS *Swallow* and the three pirate ships. As Ogle approached from the north he was obliged to veer west, out into open sea, to avoid it. Seeing this, the pirates thought he had taken fright at the sight of them, and was trying to escape. They concluded that *Swallow* was a merchant ship, probably Portuguese and full of sugar.

Roberts now made a fateful decision. Sugar, of course, was one of the key ingredients of punch and they were running short. The men on the new *Ranger,* in particular, had had none for the past few days and this was adding to tension between the two crews. 'There is sugar in the offing,' he bellowed across to them. 'Bring it in that we may have no more mumbling!' He was handing the prize to the second ship. It was a sound piece of team management. But it meant that, from that moment, Roberts' forces would be fatally divided.

The *Ranger* was 'on the heel' when HMS *Swallow* appeared, meaning its contents had been shifted to one side, tilting it so its hull could be scrubbed. Its crew quickly righted it and, while they were doing this, Roberts took the precaution of sending across twenty of his most loyal men to bolster its crew, including his boatswain, William Main, and John Walden – 'Miss Nanny'. He had no faith at all that, having taken the prize, the *Ranger* wouldn't simply desert. He'd also been careful to make sure it was carrying none of the crew's gold.

With the additional men aboard, the *Ranger* set off in pursuit of its prize. Seeing this Captain Ogle immediately realised the pirates' mistake. He continued out to sea, making sure he went slowly enough not to lose sight of the *Ranger.* Aboard the pirate ship there was wild excitement, the pirates brandishing their cutlasses and 'swearing every minute at the wind or sails to expedite so sweet a chase', according to Captain Johnson. One man was dancing manically around the deck. Its captain, the Welshman James Skyrm, 'in the hurry and warmth of his passion' slashed with his cutlass at a couple of the forced men whom he felt were showing less enthusiasm than the rest.

Amidst the mayhem one man aboard, peering closely at the prize, began to suspect its true identity. William Guinneys, who had been forced from the *Porcupine* in Whydah, mentioned his suspicion to a crewmate standing next to him. But the man 'bid him hold his tongue'. He too was a forced man and both knew HMS *Swallow* represented their best chance of being freed.

Around 10.30 a.m. Ogle judged they were out of earshot of the ships back at Cape Lopez and allowed the *Ranger* to come within gunshot. The pirates immediately opened fire with four chase guns, simultaneously hoisting their black flag and preparing to board. At this, Ogle swung HMS *Swallow* around, across the *Ranger*'s path, opened the lower gunports and delivered a broadside.

The effect was devastating. The *Ranger* was caught head on and the fire from HMS *Swallow* raked its decks from bow to stern, ripping through flesh and tearing off arms and legs. Stunned, the *Ranger* wheeled away. In the confusion, a young pirate, David Littlejohn, lowered the black flag, signalling surrender. But immediately William Main, the *Royal Fortune*'s boatswain, and another man rushed at him, pistols drawn, and forced him to raise it again. It was only with difficulty that other pirates persuaded them not to shoot him.

A chaotic pursuit now ensued, the two ships exchanging cannon fire at distance. Captain Skyrm, Main and other hard-liners were all for pulling alongside HMS *Swallow*, throwing out grappling hooks and making a desperate bid to board. But it was clear the bulk of the crew were reluctant. At 2 p.m. the poor steering of the pirates enabled *Swallow* to draw close again and deliver another devastating broadside. The *Ranger*'s main-mast came crashing down. On the deck men slithered around in their own blood. By now nine were dead and around fourteen wounded. Captain Skyrm's leg had been blown off, as had Miss Nanny's. Skyrm continued to hop back and forth across the deck, screaming dementedly at his men to continue fighting. But it was clear all was lost. At 3 p.m. the *Ranger* struck its colours and surrendered, the men throwing their black flags overboard so they could not be displayed in triumph over them on the gallows.

So often the hardened pirates among the crew had said they would blow themselves up and 'go all merrily to Hell together' rather than be captured. Now they were true to their word. Half a dozen of the most desperate gathered around the gunpowder they had left in the steerage, and fired a pistol into it. But it was too little to do anything other than leave them hideously burned.

HMS *Swallow*'s surgeon, John Atkins, heard the explosion as he was being rowed across to the *Ranger* to treat the wounded. Climbing aboard, he encountered a bizarre scene. The pirates were as dandily dressed as ever 'with white shirts, watches, and a deal of silk vests'. Those unhurt remained 'gay and brisk'. But the ship was awash with blood, and dead and hideously injured men lay all about, victims both of the battle and the explosion afterwards.

Captain Skyrm was still raging and refused to allow Atkins to dress the stump of his leg. Atkins turned instead to William Main, whom he identified as a boatswain by the silver whistle hanging at his waist. 'I presume you are the boatswain of this ship,' he said. 'Then you presume wrong,' replied Main, 'for I am the boatswain of the *Royal Fortune*, Captain Roberts commander.'

'Then Mr. Boatswain you will be hanged I believe,' Atkins retorted. 'That is as your honour pleases,' said Main. Main told him there were still 120 men (a figure which excluded slaves) aboard the *Royal Fortune* – 'as clever fellows as ever trod shoe leather: would I were with them!' But he denied responsibility for the explosion. The blast had blown him into the water and he complained he had 'lost a good hat by it'.

Atkins turned next to a pirate called Roger Ball, whom he could see from his hideous burns had been close to the seat of the explosion. Ball was sitting in a corner 'with a look as sullen as winter . . . bearing his pain without the least complaint'. He told him a pirate called John Morris had fired the pistol into the powder, but that 'if he had not done it, I would'. Like Skyrm, Ball refused to allow Atkins to dress him. As evening fell he entered 'a kind of delirium, and raved on the bravery of Roberts, saying, he should shortly be released, as soon as they should meet him'. Ogle's men strapped him down upon the forecastle and he screamed and strained at the ropes all night, despite his appalling injuries. He died the following day.

There were over a hundred men still alive on board, including twenty-three slaves and sixteen Frenchmen, taken when the new *Ranger* was seized at Whydah and still being held prisoner. It was decided to leave the wounded pirates aboard, along with the Frenchman and a skeleton crew from HMS *Swallow*, and to dispatch the *Ranger* to Princes Island. The remaining pirates, numbering around sixty, were stripped naked and shackled below decks on HMS *Swallow,* along with the slaves. Ogle's men spent a couple of days getting the *Ranger* in a fit state to sail. Then, on 7 February, the two ships parted company, *Swallow* heading back towards Cape Lopez where Ogle knew Roberts would be awaiting the return of his consort. Two days later, on 9 February, Captain Ogle caught sight of the *Royal Fortune* and the abandoned old *Ranger*, still riding at anchor just where he had left them.

Dusk was falling and Ogle, now confident of victory, decided to postpone his attack until the following day. The pirates had not spotted him. And he was delighted to note there were now three sails in the bay. This meant Roberts and his men had seized a prize, and would, at that moment, be plundering its liquor store.

In fact the vessel riding at anchor alongside the two pirate ships was the *Neptune* under Captain Thomas Hill – the same ship the pirates had encountered as they left Whydah, and onto which they had loaded the crew of the *Whydah* sloop. Its presence at Cape Lopez is suspicious. Hill was on his way to the port of Cabinda further south and later claimed he had simply put in to get water. But the pirates had not robbed Hill the first time they encountered him and it's likely they had reached an arrangement. Hill may have been bringing them supplies. Either way, as Ogle suspected, they were enjoying a party and when dawn broke on 10 February most of the pirates were either still drunk or nursing ferocious hangovers.

This was the scenario that Roberts had always dreaded – an encounter with a powerful naval vessel when his crew was the worse for drink. They were in such a state that they didn't see HMS *Swallow* initially as it began its approach that morning. They were 'very easy in the bay', recalled John Atkins, 'and stayed so long that we doubted whether they would stir for us'.

Roberts was in his cabin when the cry of 'Sail ahoy!' finally came. With him was Captain Hill from the *Neptune* and they were enjoying a breakfast of weak beer and salmagundi – a pirate speciality that included chunks of meat, pickled herrings, hard-boiled eggs and vegetables. In their befuddled state his men again failed to identify HMS *Swallow*. Some thought it was Portuguese, others a French slaver. But most believed it was the returning *Ranger*. Roberts, unconcerned, continued his breakfast. His men were debating how many guns they should fire as a salute to their returning consort when suddenly a look of horror passed across the face of David Armstrong, the deserter from HMS *Swallow* whom they had taken at Axim six months previously. Armstrong had recognised his old ship. He dashed down to Roberts' cabin.

It was probably at this moment, as Armstrong frantically gabbled the news, that Roberts realised he was going to die – if not that morning then on the gallows in the next few weeks. But if he felt fear he didn't show it. Perhaps to displace his own tension, he cursed the trembling Armstrong for cowardice and, taking leave of Captain Hill, went up on deck. Hill took the opportunity to slip back quietly to his own ship.

Looking through his telescope Roberts saw it was flying French colours, which was clearly a ruse. He ordered his men to battle stations. Many were terrified. At least one would spend the battle hiding in the 'heads' – the enclosed toilets at the front of the ship – and Roberts almost came to blows with others. But he himself kept his composure. If this was the end then he was determined to go out in style. He went below and dressed in 'a rich crimson damask waistcoat and breeches, a red feather in his hat, a gold chain round his neck, with a diamond cross hanging to it', according to Johnson. He put on his sword and slung four pistols over his shoulders on a silk sling, in 'the fashion of the pirates'. Then he went up on deck.

The strategy he devised was characteristically bold. Armstrong told him HMS *Swallow* sailed best 'upon a wind', that is, with the wind coming from the side. With the wind directly behind them the *Royal Fortune* might be able to outrun it. The wind at that moment was blowing from the south, in the face of the approaching man-of-war. Roberts decided to sail straight towards Ogle's ship, exchange broadsides, and then shoot out into open sea and try and make a run for it with the wind behind him. If badly damaged the ship would ground itself on the headland 'and everyone to shift for himself among the Negroes'. If the worst came to the worst they would come alongside and blow both ships up. Roberts knew it was a desperate gamble. And he knew most of his men were drunk and unfit for service – 'passively courageous', in Johnson's words. But he had little option.

By mid-morning a thunderstorm was breaking around them. In the wind and driving rain the pirate ship sped towards HMS *Swallow*. At 11 a.m. the two ships closed, raised their true colours, and exchanged broadsides. HMS *Swallow* was almost untouched. The *Royal Fortune* lost its mizzen-mast and suffered damage to its rigging. But it was still sailing and was soon half a gunshot beyond HMS *Swallow* and heading out into open sea. Just for a moment it looked as if Roberts might have got away with it. But then the crew's night of revelry took its toll. One man simply passed out on the deck having fired his gun. Many others were little better and the pirates' steering was erratic. By now the storm was gaining in strength. One clap of thunder 'seemed like the rattling of 10,000 small arms within three yards of our heads', John Atkins later recalled, and the simultaneous bolt of lightening split the top of HMS *Swallow*'s main-mast. But, with the wind swirling around unpredictably, the warship was soon gaining ground once more on the *Royal Fortune*. At half past one, it came close enough to deliver another broadside. As the smoke cleared the men on HMS *Swallow* saw the pirate's main-mast come crashing down. Shortly afterwards the pirates signalled surrender.

As on the *Ranger*, the crew of the *Royal Fortune* immediately divided between those who felt they might stand some chance of acquittal at trial and those who knew only the gallows awaited them. James Philips, one of the Old Standers, went down to the powder room with a lighted match, swearing 'let's all go to Hell together'. But there he encountered a sentry – Stephen Thomas – placed by Henry Glasby. Philips 'throwed [me] against the ladder at the hatchway, wounding [my] hand as [we] were struggling about the match,' Thomas later recalled. At that moment Glasby appeared and, together, they were able to subdue him.

Shortly afterwards HMS *Swallow*'s long boat arrived, com-manded by Lieutenant Isaac Sun. Recalling the attempt to blow up the *Ranger*, Ogle had opted to keep his ship at a distance. Working with Glasby, whose 'good character' he'd been informed of beforehand, Sun quickly secured control of the *Royal Fortune*. But there was one final moment of farce as crewman Joseph Mansfield, the former highwayman, suddenly burst from the hold, blind drunk. 'He came up vapouring with a cutlass to know who would go on board the prize,' Glasby later recalled. 'It was sometime before [we] could persuade him of the truth of [our] condition.'

By 7 p.m. the entire crew was secured below decks on HMS *Swallow*, side by side with their colleagues from the *Ranger*. The pirates had suffered three dead and ten injured in this second battle, while HMS *Swallow* hadn't suffered a single casualty in either engage/ ment. 'Discipline is an excellent path to victory,' Atkins commented in his memoir. 'The pirates, though singly fellows of courage', lacked 'a tie of order, some director to unite that force'. Defeat and capture would always 'be the fate of such rabble', he concluded. Naval discipline had won out over pirate bravado. But it was a harsh verdict on Roberts' leadership. This pirate crew, more than any other, had possessed a 'director' and 'a tie of order'. The problem was the pirates themselves, and their reluctance to submit themselves to his will.

But Roberts himself was the one man Atkins was never able to speak to. As the *Royal Fortune* had sailed towards HMS *Swallow* that morning Roberts had taken his place close to the wheel ready to direct operations. But as the smoke cleared after the first broadside the helmsman, John Stephenson, had noticed him apparently resting on the tackles of a gun. He ran over and swore at his captain to get up and fight like a man. But Roberts' throat had been ripped out by grapeshot. The greatest of all pirates, the 'Admiral of the Leeward Islands', the scourge of three continents, was dead.

At that moment they were within just a few miles of the spot where they had seized the *Expectation* back at the end of July 1719. Since then Roberts had taken around 400 ships – a figure which dwarfs that of any of his contemporaries. He had travelled around 35,000 miles. And he'd held together a larger crew for a longer period of time than any other pirate captain. But in the end he had lost his long battle with the anarchy of pirate life. For all the tensions within the crew Roberts was revered by his men and, although the battle raged on for three more hours, his death knocked the fight out of them. Ogle was in no doubt that, if he had been alive, Roberts would have blown up the *Royal Fortune* with everyone aboard rather than allow it to be taken.

Many times Roberts had sworn, 'Damnation to him who ever lived to wear a halter!' He, at least, had escaped hanging. He had left strict instructions that if he was killed at sea his body should be thrown overboard to prevent its being hung in chains. Stevenson wept over him for a time, as the pirates gathered round. And then they fulfilled their captain's last wish, heaving his body over the rail and consigning it to the deep, still dressed in all its finery.

12

COMMON ENEMIES OF MANKIND

WEST AFRICA
FEBRUARY–APRIL 1722

'HEAVEN, YOU FOOL . . . DID YOU EVER

HEAR OF ANY PIRATES GOING THITHER? GIVE

ME HELL, IT'S A MERRIER PLACE. I'LL GIVE

ROBERTS A SALUTE OF 13 GUNS AT THE

ENTRANCE'

THE JUDGE PLACED A black cap on his head, settled himself, and called on the prosecutor to begin proceedings.

'An't please your Lordship, and you Gentlemen of the Jury, here is a fellow before you that is a sad dog,' the prosecutor began. 'He has committed piracy upon the High Seas . . . robbing and ravishing man, woman and child, plundering ships' cargoes fore and aft, burning and sinking ship, bark and boat, as if the Devil had been in him.'

'What have you to say?' asked the judge, turning to the trembling prisoner. 'Are you guilty, or not guilty?'

'Not guilty, an't please your Worship,' he replied. 'I am as honest a poor fellow as ever went between stem and stern of a ship, and can hand, reef, steer and clap two ends of a rope together, as well as any that ever crossed salt water. But I was taken . . . and forced.'

'Is our dinner ready?' the judge suddenly barked, interrupting him.

'Yes, my lord,' replied the prosecutor. 'Then, hark'ee, you rascal,' the judge continued, addressing the prisoner once more. 'You must suffer for three reasons. First, because it is not fit I should sit here as Judge and nobody be hanged. Secondly, you must be hanged because you have a damned hanging look. And, thirdly, you must be hanged because I am hungry . . . Take him away gaolor.'

And with that judge, jury, prisoner and prosecutor all rolled about, howling with laughter. This was not an Admiralty courtroom, but a beach on a deserted Caribbean island. And these were not the men of Bartholomew Roberts, but of Thomas Anstis, who had deserted Roberts almost a year earlier. Still awaiting a response to their request for a pardon, they were whiling away the time on their hideaway off Cuba enacting a mockery of a trial, the judge sitting in a tree with a dirty tarpaulin wrapped around his shoulders as a robe.

How Roberts' men would have loved to be with them, lying on the sand, drinking rum in the shade of the palm trees one last time – poking fun at those who, for so long, had hunted them in vain. But at almost that very moment, thousands of miles away, they faced the dreadful reality of Admiralty justice. Manacled below decks in the hold of HMS *Swallow*, they were bound for Cape Coast Castle, where General Phipps awaited them in his laced suit.

The 1,000-mile journey back to the Gold Coast was a nightmarish one for Captain Ogle and his men. It rained incessantly and the ships were buffeted continuously by typhoons which swirled out of nowhere and turned the sea into a seething cauldron, before disappearing just as suddenly. And the pirates were by no means resigned to their fate.

Many were 'impudently merry', wrote Johnson, taking refuge in black humour. Still naked, and displaying a surprising knowledge of Greek mythology, they complained that Ogle's men 'had not left them a halfpenny to give old Charon, to ferry them over Styx'. Eyeing their meagre rations, they joked that they would not be heavy enough to hang once they got to Cape Coast Castle. Thomas Sutton, the gunner, was irritated to find himself chained to a man who prayed day and night. Eventually he exploded and asked him 'what he proposed by so much noise and devotion'. 'Heaven, I hope,' the man replied.

'Heaven, you fool,' scoffed Sutton. 'Did you ever hear of any pirates going thither? Give me Hell, it's a merrier place. I'll give Roberts a salute of 13 guns at the entrance.' Many of the more hardened pirates were soon plotting escape.

HMS *Swallow* made initially for Princes Island, with the *Royal Fortune* and the old *Ranger,* now manned by Ogle's own men, following in its wake. There it collected the new *Ranger,* with the Frenchmen and the wounded pirates from the first battle aboard. The vast bulk of the prisoners remained aboard HMS *Swallow,* which was grossly overcrowded with close to 400 men. But Captain Ogle placed a number of slaves aboard the *Royal Fortune,* along with 'three or four wounded' and Peter Scudamore, the surgeon taken by the pirates at Old Calabar, who was to tend them. It's a mark of the instant respect that was afforded to someone of Peter Scudamore's social position that he was not kept chained below. It was assumed he was a forced man and he ate with the officers on board the ship. But they had misjudged him.

Close to the island of St Thomas, HMS *Swallow* lost contact with the three former pirate ships in a typhoon. Aboard the *Royal Fortune* Scudamore saw his chance and immediately began plotting with the slaves, talking to them in 'a smattering he had in the Angolan language'. He proposed 'they demolish the white men, and afterwards go down to Angola and raise another company', a witness later said. 'Better venturing to do this,' he argued to the other pirates, 'than to proceed to Cape Coast, and be hanged like a dog, and sun dried.' Scudamore knew that, once back at Cape Coast Castle, there would be plenty of evidence against him. And he was now fantasising of becoming captain of an all-black crew. 'Having lived a long time in this piratical way', wrote Johnson, the slaves were 'as ripe for mischief as any', and quickly agreed. But Scudamore was betrayed by one of his fellow pirates, hoping to curry favour ahead of the trial. The plan was thwarted, Scudamore was stripped of his privileges and clapped in irons.

Aboard HMS *Swallow* there was also a conspiracy brewing. At its heart were a group of Old Standers, including Valentine Ashplant and William Magness, the quartermaster. They passed messages by means of a mulatto boy, who had been allowed to attend them, and proved sympathetic. But on the night of the planned rising Roberts' intimate friend, George Wilson, who was chained next to Ashplant, overheard them plotting. Also keen to ingratiate himself, he instantly betrayed the plot to Captain Ogle. Ogle ordered an inspection of the prisoners and found Ashplant, Magness and the others had managed to loosen their shackles. They were clapped back in irons and thereafter were kept under even closer guard, Ogle taking the precaution of keeping the gun room strongly barricaded.

It was with enormous relief that Captain Ogle finally pulled in to Cape Coast Castle on 15 March and with even greater relief that he saw his three prizes arrive a couple of weeks later, having got lost and initially hit the coast close to Sestos, almost 750 miles to the west. Ogle was greeted by an ecstatic General Phipps, whose letters to London were soon brimming with the 'joyful' news and gushing with praise for the 'gallant behaviour and good conduct' of Captain Ogle, whose bravery had destroyed 'the arch pirate Roberts' and his 'nest of villains'. When the three prizes arrived at the start of April, Phipps quickly went aboard and started scavenging for any goods he could find from the company ships they had plundered, salvaging some tallow, sails, water casks, three slaves and 'some cloths, which had suffered a little'.

Ogle immediately began transferring men from the hold of HMS *Swallow* to the cavernous, stone dungeons beneath the castle. The day after his arrival the *Hannibal*, the company ship the pirates had taken at Old Calabar five months earlier, finally limped home in a pitiful condition. As they were rowed across to the castle the chained pirates could see the face of John Wingfield, the company factor who John Philps had called a 'son of a bitch', glowering down at them over the ship's rail. There would be no shortage of witnesses against them. Captain Traherne from the *King Solomon* was also here, as was Captain Sharp of the *Elizabeth*, and the two Dutch captains of the *Flushingham* and the *Gertruycht*. There were passengers and crew too from all of these ships, and from the *Onslow*, including Captain Trengrove and his wife, Elizabeth, whose hooped petticoat William Mead had forced off back in August.

On 26 March HMS *Weymouth* arrived, having been patrolling the coast to the west, the crew still in a desperately sickly condition. Captain Herdman had learned of Ogle's success a couple of days before at Cape Three Points. It was agreed Herdman would be president of the court, Ogle obliged to take the role of prosecutor since the pirates' actions against HMS *Swallow* would form an important part of the case against them.

Admiralty Courts were regulated by the Act for the Most Successful Suppression of Piracy, passed in 1700. This had stripped pirates of the right to trial by jury, the government having found juries in the colonies were reluctant to convict them. Instead they were tried by a seven-man panel of officials and naval officers. Besides Herdman, the court at Cape Coast Castle would consist of Lt Barnsely and Lt Fanshaw from HMS *Weymouth,* Edward Hyde, the Royal African Company's secretary, Henry Dodson and Francis Boye, both merchants, and, of course, General Phipps, who wasn't going to miss his chance to exact revenge on the men who had so humiliated him over the previous eight months.

The castle buzzed with excitement, its normal population of fifty to a hundred men swollen by the arrival of the two men-of-war, the numerous witnesses, and curious onlookers who'd flocked from all along the coast. At least half a dozen ships bobbed in the road, their flags and pennants fluttering in the bright sunlight. The crew of HMS *Swallow* told and re-told the story of their double victory over the pirates, and men from other vessels swapped tales of their own suffering at the hands of Roberts and his men. Down in the African village the bemused fishermen went about their daily lives, perhaps stealing the occasional look at the curious Africans the pirates had brought with them, whose language they did not understand, but who had ranged thousands of miles over the oceans as slaves and as pirates and whose story would have been the most interesting of all – if only someone had troubled to write it down.

It took almost two weeks to get all the pirates ashore. By now they had finally given up all hope of escape. The mood among most of them had changed, wrote Johnson, 'and from vain insolent jesting they became serious and devout, begging for good books, and joining in public prayers and singing of psalms, twice at least every day'. Crowded together with slaves awaiting sale in the dungeons, their conditions were appalling. But preparations for the trial moved with brisk efficiency.

On 28 March 1722 the court assembled in the Great Hall of the castle, the sound of the waves crashing on the rocks audible through the high windows, the sea breeze doing little to dispel the intense, suffocating heat that left accusers and accused, along with those in the gallery, immediately drenched in sweat.

There was little discussion over the fate of the pirates' slaves. Ogle had taken seventy-five from the *Royal Fortune* and the new *Ranger*. The court took the view they were chattels rather than active agents in their own destiny and it was decided they would be sold. But the court agonised for some time over how to try the pirates themselves. Many of their crimes over the previous eight months had been committed against ships of the Royal African Company. This, technically, made General Phipps and the other company merchants ineligible to try them, since they were interested parties. Initially, therefore, it was decided to confine the evidence to the pirates' actions against HMS *Swallow*. But since both ships had resisted Ogle's ship this meant almost all the men would be found guilty. Many had only joined the pirates a month before and some were clearly forced. It was therefore decided to look at the behaviour of each man throughout their pirate careers. 'Such evidence, though it might want the form, still conveyed the reason of the law,' the court argued. In practice, General Phipps and his fellow merchants were trying the pirates for crimes committed against themselves.

Ogle had captured a total of 166 white pirates. Fifteen had died – many of their wounds – in the dreadful conditions in the hold of HMS *Swallow* en route to Cape Coast Castle and a further four died in the dungeons immediately after arriving. A total of 147 men therefore stood trial. Of these, eighty-seven had joined the pirates since they had returned to the coast of Africa the previous June. Twenty-three had joined in the year prior to that. Twenty-four had been taken off Newfoundland in the summer of 1720 and four during the first year of Roberts' captaincy. Just nine remained from the days of Howel Davis. All but five were British.

The pirates were summoned up from the dungeons one by one. Starved, emaciated and dressed in rags, they formed a pitiful procession. A number had hideous injuries from the final battles against HMS *Swallow*. Only a small handful retained their swagger. John Walden – 'Miss Nanny' – demanded a stool on which to rest the stump of the leg he'd lost when the *Ranger* was taken. He 'appeared undaunted though his wounds were great', according to the court record, and he was 'careless' of defending himself. Another Old Stander, John Coleman, defiantly admitted going aboard prizes, declaring 'if he must be hanged for it, God's will be done, 'twas not of his seeking'. But most pleaded for mercy, in almost all cases basing their defence on the argument that they had been forced.

The most obviously guilty and the most obviously innocent were among the first to be tried. On 31 March, the air cleared by a thunder- storm, the court rattled through sixteen of the Old Standers in one day. Fourteen were found guilty, six of whom were immediately sentenced to hang, the court anxious to remove any ringleaders who might yet attempt an uprising. These six can be viewed as the very core of the crew – William Magness, the quartermaster, Thomas Sutton, the gunner, Little David, Valentine Ashplant, and two other Old Standers called Christopher Moody and Richard Hardy. 'It is your aggravation, that ye have been the chiefs and rulers in these licentious and lawless practices,' said Captain Herdman, passing sentence. They were executed three days later. General Phipps ordered their bodies to be hung 'in gibbets on the most eminent hills around this place, very conspicuous to the shipping as it passes'. As the trial progressed in the sweltering heat over the next few weeks their rotting bodies were also visible to the pirates as they were dragged from the dungeons for trial and emerged blinking into the courtyard of the castle on their way to the Great Hall.

One of the men tried with them, John Dennis, attempted a plea bargain with the court. Dennis had been with the crew since Howel Davis's time. He knew the crew inside out and offered to distinguish the forced men from the real pirates. Herdman, Phipps and the others conferred, but eventually turned him down. They didn't trust him. More importantly, they didn't need him. They had Henry Glasby.

Glasby was brought up from the dungeons for trial on 2 April. At first glance he was in a dangerous situation. He had been with the pirates for more than eighteen months and, as sailing master aboard the *Royal Fortune*, was one of their most senior men. But Captain Traherne of the *King Solomon* made clear that he was master in name only. The pirates 'did as they would . . . never observing him', he said. Witness after witness testified that he was a prisoner, that he had striven to rein in the excesses of the pirates, and that, when he could, he had returned stolen goods to their owners. He was 'civil beyond any of them', said John Wingfield. Acquitted pirates testified Roberts had never required him to play any military role, his responsibilities being restricted to sailing the vessel. Speaking for himself, he told the story of his two escape attempts in the Caribbean, and said that 'Roberts after this was ever jealous of him and never committed his secrets or private designs to him'. Acquitting him, the court noted 'that his evidence would be of great use . . . for trying the remaining prisoners'.

For so long a prisoner among the pirates, Glasby was now the arbiter of their fate. Again and again he was called, and again and again it was his voice, above all, that decided whether a man lived or died. He strove to be fair. Twenty-four times he spoke in favour of men. Isaac Russell 'was forced out of the *Lloyd* Galley' and had 'feigned sickness' to avoid being made boatswain's mate, and had often told him 'it was a wicked life they all led', he said. George Ogle 'was a quiet fellow, not swearing or cursing like most of them, and rather melancholy'. Both escaped the hangman. Glasby identified all of those who had conspired with him to run away, and many of them too were acquitted. But he spoke against far more – forty-six in total. 'He was looked on as a brisk hand among them,' he said of Marcus Johnson, a description which was usually enough to send a man to the gallows. He ridiculed the defence of many that Roberts had forced them to take their turn aboard prizes. They went 'willingly, very willingly', he insisted, crowding aboard the boats 'sometimes as almost to sink them'. The pirates cast sour, bitter glances at him as they were hauled back down to the dungeons after sentencing.

The most hostile evidence came from the pirates' victims. Captain Traherne identified each of the men who had been in the boarding party that seized the *King Solomon*, and also helped secure guilty verdicts against five of his own crew – despite the fact they had been with the pirates only a month. Samuel Fletcher, he said, 'was always grumbling when ordered to any duty, and several times wished to God Almighty they might meet the pirates'. Fletcher pointed out this was true of most of the *King Solomon*'s crew, but to no avail.

John Wingfield from the *Hannibal* gave evidence against twenty-two men and spoke in favour of just four. William Davies 'was but ill charactered even among the worst of them', he said. The boatswain William Main 'very active on all piratical occasions'. Richard Hardy 'robbed his ship [and] broke the hinges of a box to get the gold out'. Elizabeth Trengrove took the stand and pointed an accusing figure at William Mead as the man who had forced her hooped petticoat off aboard the *Onslow*.

The surgeon, Peter Scudamore, was summoned on 5 April and found himself confronted with a battery of hostile witnesses, all ridiculing his claim to be a forced man. 'There was no force used to compel him,' said Glasby, contemptuously. Captain Traherne and Captain Sharp both accused him of stealing medicines and surgeon's tools from their ships. Most damningly, his fellow prisoners from the *Royal Fortune* described his attempt to incite an uprising among the slaves during the passage from Cape Lopez. Scudamore admitted he had spoken 'a few foolish words' during the voyage, but claimed they were hypothetical – he was merely pointing out that the slaves *could* have taken the ship *if* they had wanted to. In whispering to the slaves 'in the Angolan language', he was merely passing the time, 'trying his skill to tell twenty, he being incapable of further talk'. The court was unimpressed and sentenced him to hang.

Two days later George Wilson was brought from the dungeons. His case proved more complex than any other, Wilson demanding the right to cross examine witnesses at length. He claimed his supposed 'intimacy' with Roberts was merely a ruse. If he paid Roberts 'undue compliments and deference he did it with intention to ingratiate himself, and gain a good treatment from him . . . This was no more than what every prisoner endeavoured and practiced that had any regard to their own interest.' He urged also his youth in excuse for his 'rashness'. His case dragged on so long it was eventually adjourned until 17 April, enabling the court to get on with trying the other pirates. When he was recalled he was found guilty. But his betrayal of the proposed rising by the Old Standers aboard HMS *Swallow* saved him from immediate execution, the court granting him the right to return to England to plead for a royal pardon.

All the time John Atkins sat scribbling in a corner. He had been appointed court registrar on thirty shillings a day and the entire proceedings are recorded in his meticulous hand. Stretching to 184 pages, they provide us with a unique portrait of the inner workings and day-to-day life of a pirate crew. Not only are we given potted biographies of every man, but we learn of their different ranks, of how they organised the system of turns aboard prizes, of how booty was divided and how decisions were taken, of their punishments and rewards, and of how they spent their leisure time. It provides us with a mass of incidental detail, unavailable for any other pirate crew, freeing us from dependence on sensationalist and not always reliable secondary sources. From it, one fact emerges very clearly – this, the most prolific of all pirate crews, killed startlingly few people. Of their 400 prizes they had to fight for just two – the *Sagrada Familia* off Brazil in October 1719, and the *Puerto del Principe* off Dominica in January 1721. Other than in battle they never killed a single officer, crew member or passenger from any of the ships they captured – to their cost, since many went on to testify against them.

There were certainly thugs aboard, like Little David and Miss Nanny. Captives were beaten and 'drubbed' and some of the pirates took a sadistic pleasure in threatening and terrorising their victims. But the pressure from new recruits to punish their former captains was generally resisted. And, having heard hours of testimony, Phipps, Herdman and the rest of the judges were sceptical of many of the claims of mistreatment by 'forced' men. Usually this was a 'pretence' or 'complotment' for the benefit of witnesses, they concluded. And when men were genuinely reluctant, a beating was the worst they received. For all the tales of men having 'a pistol clapped to their breast', no one was ever executed for refusing to join Roberts' crew.

There was much wanton destruction of property, particularly aboard vessels belonging to the Royal African Company. But many of the ships taken by Roberts went on to complete a successful slaving voyage. The *Martha*, taken in August 1721, unloaded 114 slaves in Nevis five months later while the *King Solomon* sailed for Jamaica in June 1722 laden with 300 slaves. As often as not the cargo of trade goods was left intact and at times it feels almost as if Roberts was taxing the ships he captured as much as plundering them. At Whydah he took just eight pounds of gold from each ship, although some were carrying far larger amounts.

Roberts' men committed one truly barbaric act – the grotesque slaughter of the slaves at Whydah. To this might be added the attack on the African town at Old Calabar, and the use of Africans for target practice by Howel Davis's men immediately prior to Roberts' capture. For them, the lives of Africans were worth less than those of Europeans. But in this they were creatures of their time and no different from the law-abiding community of slave traders and plantation owners they preyed upon. The judges at Cape Coast Castle were not particularly concerned with the massacre at Whydah. For them it was just another crime against property, and it barely featured in the trial. Roberts' men stood accused of being 'traitors, robbers and pirates and common enemies of mankind'. Not one of them was on trial for murder.

But this was more than enough to send them to the gallows. When the trial concluded after little more than three weeks on 20 April a total of seventy-two men had been sentenced to hang. A further seventeen were referred to the Marshalsea prison in London for further examination. And George Wilson and one other were found guilty, but permitted to plead for a royal pardon. Of the seventy-two condemned men, twenty had their sentences commuted to seven years' service in the mines at Cape Coast Castle – an effective death sentence given the conditions there. This left just fifty-six men acquitted, most of them among the newer recruits. It was the greatest slaughter of pirates ever carried out by the Admiralty.

POSTSCRIPT

'THEY WERE POOR ROGUES, THEY SAID, AND SO HANGED WHILE OTHERS, NO LESS GUILTY IN ANOTHER WAY, ESCAPED'

OBERTS' MEN WERE HANGED in batches within days of being sentenced. Most were executed at Cape Coast Castle, but small groups were hanged in forts and stations up and down the West African coast. The bodies of eighteen were tarred and left hanging in gibbets. 'We hope the example that has been made of this gang will be a means to affright and deter all others from pursuing such vile practices on this coast,' wrote General Phipps, 'and that the trade thereby will be secured free and undisturbed from the depredations of such miscreants for some time to come.'

The versatile John Atkins now took the role of 'ordinary', or chaplain, accompanying the men to their deaths and trying to coax last-minute repentances from them. He gave Captain Johnson a detailed description of the executions. Atkins had little luck with the first six, the hard-core group hanged on 3 April while the trial was still in its early stages. According to Johnson, they continued to see themselves as rebels against an unjust social order. 'They all exclaimed against the severity of the court, and were so hardened as to curse, and wish the same justice might overtake all the members of it, as had been dealt to them . . . They were poor rogues, they said, and so hanged while others, no less guilty in another way, escaped.'

As with all Admiralty executions, the hangings were carried out at the water's edge within the tide marks. It was a grisly spectacle. The 'drop', which broke a prisoner's neck, was not perfected until the nineteenth century. In the 1720s prisoners were simply pushed from a ladder and died through slow strangulation, kicking and writhing, their faces swelling, their tongues protruding and their eyes popping. At Execution Dock in Wapping pirates' friends often came along and pulled on their legs to hasten the process. Without this assistance it could take as long as forty-five minutes and as death neared prisoners soiled themselves and their bodies entered into violent spasms. But these six men walked 'to the gallows without a tear . . . showing as much concern as a man would express at travelling a bad road'. Richard Hardy chided the inexperienced soldiers when they tied his hands behind his back rather than in front, as was standard practice. And Little David's last moments were taken up abusing a woman he had recognized in the crowd. He had slept with her three times and was indignant the 'bitch . . . was come to see him hanged'. 'The same abandoned and reprobate temper that had carried them through their rogueries, abided with them to the last,' Johnson commented.

But most of the others were contrite. David Armstrong, as a deserter from HMS *Swallow*, was hanged separately from the others aboard HMS *Weymouth* on 24 April. 'His last hour was spent in lamenting and bewailing his sins in general, exhorting the spectators to an honest and good life . . . In the end he desired they would join with him in singing two or three latter verses of the 140th psalm

['Thou art my Lord: hear the voice of my supplications']; and, that being concluded, he was, at the firing of a gun, triced up at the fore⁄ yard arm.'

Charles Bunce, who had joined the crew at the same time as Armstrong the previous August, 'declaimed against the gilded bates [temptations] of power, liberty and wealth, that had ensnared him among the pirates'. And the surgeon, Peter Scudamore, having finally seen 'the folly and wickedness' of his ways, persuaded the judges to grant him a couple of days reprieve, which he spent praying and reading the scriptures. He 'seemed to have a deep sense of his sins' and, on the gallows, sang the thirty⁄first psalm ('Into thine hand I commit my spirit; thou has redeemed me, O Lord God of truth') from beginning to end by himself before placing his head in the noose. Others were overwhelmed by their fate. Of William Williams, Atkins wrote only that he was 'speechless at execution'.

The men sent to the mines were forced to work in chains because Phipps didn't trust them not to make an escape. They were lacking tools to carry out their work, having thrown them overboard from the *Onslow*. And their overseer, Captain Trengrove, whose wife they had abused on the *Onslow*, was probably not a particularly tender master. They were almost all dead within three months.

The seventeen men referred to the Marshalsea in London were pressed into service on HMS *Weymouth*, on half rations, along with George Wilson and the other man granted the right to plead for a pardon. HMS *Weymouth*'s crew remained desperately sickly and Captain Herdman was also forced to buy fifty slaves from General Phipps to help man the ship. It left Cape Coast Castle on 1 May ('for my own part I hope till Domesday,' wrote Atkins), intending to return to Britain via the West Indies. But the pirates had brought with them 'a new malignant distemper' picked up in the dungeons. George Wilson died on 6 May, before they had even left the coast of Africa.

And by the time HMS *Weymouth* reached Port Royal in Jamaica on 23 August just nine of the nineteen pirates were still alive.

On 28 August Port Royal was hit by a powerful hurricane. More than forty ships sank in the harbour and a third of the town was destroyed, with considerable loss of life. HMS *Swallow* and HMS *Weymouth* just survived, the crews frantically cutting down their masts as the storm raged to lower their centre of gravity. The pirates' new *Ranger* was also still afloat when the wind finally eased. But the *Royal Fortune* and the old *Ranger* were dashed to pieces on the rocks, their skeleton crews – except for 'a negro or two', according to Lieutenant Sun – escaping at the last minute.

The disaster forced the two warships to stay longer than they'd planned and more men died as epidemics raged across Jamaica in the wake of the hurricane. By the time they finally returned to England in April 1723 – more than two years after they had left – HMS *Weymouth* had buried 280 men, most of the original crew of 240 having died, as well as many of the men pressed to replace them. Just eight of the pirate prisoners aboard made it home. All were eventually granted a pardon, the Admiralty unable to find any additional evidence against them.

Of Henry Glasby and the other fifty-five men acquitted we know nothing. It's possible some of them were also pressed aboard HMS *Swallow* and HMS *Weymouth*. They would certainly have had little option but to work their passage home and it's a fair bet that a number died of diseases contracted in the dungeons at Cape Coast Castle before they made it to Britain. Arriving back in London they discovered that justice had also caught up with Walter Kennedy, who'd been betrayed by one of the prostitutes at the brothel he ran and arrested in early 1721. To save himself he quickly handed the authorities a list of names and addresses of his former shipmates living in London. It provides an interesting insight into the lives of retired pirates. Like footballers of the

1960s and 1970s, most seem to have become publicans. But they had almost all fled by the time the authorities arrived and it did Kennedy little good. He was sentenced to death on 3 July 1721. He gave a lengthy confession to the Ordinary of Newgate on the eve of his execution and apparently showed repentance, asking 'to receive the Holy Sacrament in a private place, and not in the chapel, as he could there be more retired, and better lift up his Heart to God'. On 21 July 1721 he was taken to Execution Dock in Wapping, just a few yards from his birthplace. His courage failed him at the last moment. Standing on the gallows his knees buckled and he had to be revived with water before the execution could take place.

There was one distant echo of the havoc wrought on the African coast by Bartholomew Roberts. In October 1748, twenty-seven years later, the crew of a Royal Navy warship called the *Chesterfield* mutinied off Cape Coast Castle. One of the ringleaders was identified as 'John Place . . . a murderer and an ex-pirate who had sailed with Bartholomew Roberts'. There was no John Place among the men acquitted at the trial in 1722. But it's quite possible that he was known by a different name at that time, or had left the crew earlier. If he was one of Roberts' men then he met the same fate as so many of his former shipmates, hanged at Cape Coast Castle.

Roberts had taken piracy to a new level. His capture of the *Sagrada Familia* off Brazil was one of the most daring and audacious of the age. And he had shown extraordinary resilience and determination in rebuilding his crew following the disaster at Devil's Islands. In the period between June 1720 and January 1722 he wrought havoc on a scale unmatched by any other pirate of the period, covering extraordinary distances between Newfoundland, West Africa and the Caribbean. But his death in the thunderstorm off Cape Lopez on 10 February 1722 proved a turning point in the history of the Atlantic. Thereafter piracy went into rapid decline. The experiences of Thomas

Anstis and the men who had deserted Roberts aboard the *Good Fortune* in April 1721 were typical.

By August 1722, they had received no response to their request for a royal pardon and reluctantly put to sea again. They plundered shipping in the West Indies for several more months. But their numbers were dwindling and the crew was riven with factions. The one-handed Captain Fenn and a number of others were captured while on shore at Tobago in April 1723. Five – including Fenn – were hanged. Anstis managed to escape to sea with the remainder of the crew – around a dozen men – but they mutinied shortly afterwards and he was shot while lying in his hammock.

Anstis's death marked the final end of a crew which had existed continuously, in one form or another, since Howel Davis's mutiny aboard the *Buck* in September 1718, more than four and a half years before. This period marked the high point of the Golden Age of Piracy. It has been estimated that between 1716 and 1726 pirates seized 2,400 ships – a figure roughly equivalent to the total English losses in the War of the Spanish Succession between 1702 and 1714 – and that, in the peak years of 1719–22, there were consistently well over 2,000 pirates prowling the oceans. The crew led by Howel Davis, Bartholomew Roberts, Thomas Anstis and John Fenn took more than 500 of these ships and around 700 men served in it at one time or another.

But by 1723 the balance in the war on pirates was finally tipping in favour of the Royal Navy. Not only were there now warships patrolling the coast of West Africa, but the Admiralty had finally acceded to the desperate pleas of the Caribbean colonies for greater protection, dispatching a series of 40-gun ships. The pirates were running out of places to hide. And, as the risk–reward ratio tilted against life under the black flag, captains like Anstis and Fenn were increasingly dependent on unreliable, forced men. By 1724 the number of pirates roaming the Atlantic had dropped to 500. By 1725 it was 200 and after 1726 they disappeared altogether.

It had been Bartholomew Roberts' misfortune to live at the wrong time. Had he been born fifty or a hundred years earlier a man of his energy, drive and ability might have been a national hero. But by the 1720s such opportunities were closed to a man of his class and – like the outlaws of the Wild West 150 years later – the pirates of the Caribbean were being hemmed in by the slowly encroaching forces of civilisation.

It was pressure from slave-trading and plantation-owning interests that finally brought the Golden Age of Piracy to an end. They had provided both the bulk of pirates' prey and the bulk of their crews, and they were the main beneficiaries from their suppression.

The activities of Roberts and others had helped depress the number of slaves exported from Africa between 1720 and 1722. But following his death the number leapt from 24,780 in 1720 to 47,030 in 1725. The average number of slaves carried across the Atlantic increased from 33,000 a year in the first quarter of the eighteenth century to 45,000 in the second quarter, to 66,000 in the third quarter. Slave imports to mainland North America more than tripled in this period. The destruction of piracy was just one factor among many behind this dramatic increase. But piracy had been the grit in the oyster of the fabulously lucrative triangular trade between Britain, Africa and the New World. With its destruction the last major obstacle was removed. The defeat of men like Roberts had achieved one thing above all – it created a world safe for slavery.

At a distance of three hundred years Roberts is a morally ambiguous figure – a thief, certainly, a killer, occasionally, but never the ruthless cut-throat of pirate myth. Even the massacre at Whydah was committed against his orders. If we remove the lens of eighteenth century disapproval and view him dispassionately, he was no more brutal than many of his law-abiding contemporaries. And his crimes pale into insignificance besides those of seventeenth-century Buccaneers like Henry Morgan, whose brutality was given a sharper edge by the national and religious antagonisms of his day. Roberts and other pirates of the Golden Age owe their bloodthirsty reputation to one fact, and one fact alone – unlike their predecessors, they stole from Englishmen. There can be no doubt Bartholomew Roberts was responsible for a greater quantity of human suffering during his career as a slaver than his career as a pirate.

In the decades following his death Roberts was quietly forgotten. The more theatrical Blackbeard lived on much longer in the popular imagination, as did Captain Kidd, whose highly political trial in 1701 was much publicised. But in a more oblique way Roberts' memory survived to influence our perception of pirates. Roberts was by far the most important character in Captain Johnson's *General History of the Pirates*. Johnson admitted his description of pirate culture in general was largely based on Roberts, since he knew so much more about him than any of his contemporaries. And the *General History* was the bible for later novelists. They took Johnson's description, stripped it of the subtleties of democracy and egalitarianism, and added their own liberal dose of brutality and bravado, and created the pantomime stereotype that we live with today. If we doubt the hidden influence of Roberts, just look at the names of the pirates in Walter Scott's *The Pirate* – Fletcher, Goffe, Bunce, Harry Glasby. They are all taken from Roberts' crew. In *Treasure Island* Roberts even gets a direct mention in Long John Silver's description of the surgeon that took his leg off, who must surely be Peter Scudamore:

> It was a master surgeon him that ampytated me – out of college and all – Latin by the bucket, and what not; but he was hanged like a dog, and sun-dried like the rest, at Corso Castle. That was Roberts'

men, that was, and comed of changing names to their ships – Royal Fortune and so on. Now, what a ship was christened, so let her stay, I says.

There remains one final mystery to resolve – that of Roberts' missing treasure. Although the period since Kennedy's desertion at Devil's Islands two years before had yielded no spectacular prizes, the sheer number of ships Roberts had captured led many to assume that he and his men had accumulated huge quantities of gold and money. As soon as HMS *Swallow* and HMS *Weymouth* arrived in the West Indies in August 1722 wild rumours began to circulate that they were carrying a fortune in captured booty aboard. Captain Ogle had 'barred up all the hatches . . . intending it for a secret until his arrival in England', the *Boston Gazette* reported. The speculation was that Ogle's share alone amounted to £100,000. In fact, the figure was far, far smaller than this – at least according to the official Admiralty figures. Ogle informed the Admiralty that he found just £3,000 worth of gold aboard the *Royal Fortune*. Combined with money from the sale of the new *Ranger* and various recovered goods, this yielded total prize money of £5,364.

This did not account for all of Roberts' treasure. After the final battle the pirates on the *Royal Fortune* informed Ogle that there was a further '£4,000 or £5,000' on board the old *Ranger*, still back at Cape Lopez. Roberts had not permitted the men in the new *Ranger* to take it with them when they set off in pursuit of HMS *Swallow* on 5 February. And he hadn't had time to take it himself that morning. Ogle returned to Cape Lopez a few days later to recover the gold and receive the thanks of Captain Hill of the *Neptune*, the ship that had been with the pirates when he'd arrived on 9 February, for his liberation. But he found the old *Ranger* riding alone at anchor, deserted, 'all the men's chests . . . broke open and rifled', and Captain Hill and the *Neptune* nowhere to be seen. Ogle ordered a thorough search of the ship but it yielded just ten ounces of gold – around £40.

The tale of the old *Ranger's* treasure is puzzling. If there was £4,000 to £5,000 on the consort, how is it there was only £3,000 on the *Royal Fortune,* Roberts' the main ship? When John Atkins wrote his memoirs some years later he recalled that the buzz on HMS *Swallow* following the search of the *Royal Fortune* was that the quantity of gold found was not £3,000 – but £8,000 to £10,000. This would make a lot more sense, since the pirates had taken £5,600 worth of gold at Whydah alone. Was Ogle cooking the books?

He was certainly ruthless in his efforts to maximise his personal profit. By law he was obliged to share the prize money with his men. In addition, the government was obliged to pay a bounty – or 'head money' – to every man aboard out of public funds. In this instance it came to £1,940. In practice the government often reneged on its obligation to pay head money, and captains often cheated their crews of their share of the prize money – and this was precisely what happened in the case of HMS *Swallow*. The government granted the whole prize to Ogle himself, and asked him to pay the head money to his crew from it. Ogle's response was to quietly ignore them, and keep everything for himself.

It was only with the publication of Captain Johnson's *General History of the Pirates* in May 1724, with its vivid description of HMS *Swallow*'s destruction of Roberts and his crew, that Ogle's men became aware that they were entitled to a reward. They instantly petitioned the Treasury for the head money. The Treasury chased up Ogle to hand the money over, which he finally did, with great reluctance, in April 1725 – a full three years after the battle. The crew then petitioned for a share of the prize money itself. This time Ogle dug his heels in. The King, he pointed out, had burdened him with a knighthood – 'which must necessarily have increased my expense'. He therefore needed all of the remaining £3,147 to live in a manner befitting his 'new rank in the world'. This argument can't have cut much ice with his former crew. But it did with the Admiralty and the case was quietly dropped.

It's likely Roberts' crew was carrying £10,000 to £15,000 on the eve of its capture. This is still surprisingly small. The figure is a testimony to the pirates' ability to squander money during stopovers at places like St Bartholomew and Sierra Leone. But it also reveals a profound truth about pirates of the Golden Age. They loved gold and they loved jewels. But it was the pirate existence – 'drink and a lazy life' in Joseph Mansfield's words – that drew them above all. Prizes like the *Sagrada Familia*, which yielded around £100,000, were rare. Most pirates lived hand to mouth. Roberts himself gave the most accurate and, via the pen of Captain Johnson, most eloquent, description that we have of the lure of piracy:

> In an honest service there is thin commons, low wages, and hard labour; in this, plenty and satiety, pleasure and ease, liberty and power; and who would not balance creditor on this side, when all the hazard that is run for it, at worst is only a sour look or two at choking. No, a merry life and a short one shall be my motto.

'A merry life and a short one' was a formula often placed in the mouths of pirates, and sailors generally, by writers of the age. Roberts himself had certainly hoped for more and, with no interest in wine and women, he had probably been rather more careful to save his money than many others. But the passage captures perfectly the attitude of his men. It was the promise of freedom that drew them. It was their great strength and, as Roberts knew to his cost, their great weakness.

There was one final twist to the saga of Roberts' treasure. After leaving Cape Lopez with the money from the old *Ranger* Captain Hill and the *Neptune* did not disappear. They continued south and picked up 400 slaves at the port of Cabinda. They then headed across the Atlantic and, on 23 August, pulled in to Port Royal in Jamaica, where they were probably alarmed to see HMS *Swallow* already at anchor. Captain Hill and his slaves survived the hurricane a few days later and he spent several weeks at the port, selling his cargo. Port Royal was a tiny place. It's inconceivable Captain Ogle and Captain Hill did not meet. And it's inconceivable that the subject of the missing treasure was not raised. But there is no record of Hill ever being asked to account for it. Doubtless the two men reached a mutually beneficial arrangement, one they didn't feel the need to inform the authorities of, or their own crews. When he died twenty-nine years later Captain Ogle was Admiral of the Fleet, and the money he'd acquired one way and another following the defeat of Roberts doubtless greased his path.

It is a fitting image on which to finish; the slaver and the rising Royal Navy captain enjoying a conspiratorial drink together in a Port Royal tavern, dividing the legacy of the pirates between them. This was where power now lay in the Atlantic world.

APPENDIX 1: ROBERTS' SHIPS, CREW AND PRIZES

SHIPS

Bartholomew Roberts initially commanded just one ship, the Royal Rover. *But from June 1720 onwards he always operated with two ships. In all he commanded nine vessels — the* Royal Rover, *three* Royal Fortunes, *two* Good Fortunes, *two* Rangers *and one vessel whose name was not recorded.*

	Main Vessel	Second Vessel
July 1719	*Royal Rover*	—
	(formerly *Marquis del Campo*, inherited from Davis; 32 guns)	
Nov. 1719		*Good Fortune* (1)
		(formerly *Princess*, taken at Cayenne, French Guiana; 6–12 guns)
Dec. 1719	*Royal Rover* deserts	
June 1720	**Un-named vessel**	
	(Bristol galley, taken at Trepassey, Newfoundland; 18 guns)	
July 1720	*Royal Fortune* (1)	
	(French fishing vessel, taken on Newfoundland Banks; 26–28 guns)	
Oct. 1720	*Royal Fortune* (2)	
	(French ship, taken in West Indies; 34–42 guns)	

Jan. 1721	**Good Fortune** (2)
	(brigantine from Rhode Island, taken at St Lucia, West Indies; 18 guns)
April 1721	**Good Fortune** deserts
May 1721	**Ranger** (1)
	(formerly French cruiser, *Count de Toulouse*, taken off River Senegal; 24–36 guns)
Aug. 1721	**Royal Fortune** (3)
	(formerly *Onslow*, taken off River Sestos, West Africa; 40 guns)
Jan. 1722	**Ranger** (2)
	(formerly French slaver, *St Agnes*, taken at Whydah, West Africa; 32 guns)

PRIZES

The following are documented captures by Roberts and his men. Excluding the 150 to 250 fishing shallops taken at Newfoundland, and the six vessels taken during the brief period Thomas Anstis was captain, they come to between 136 and 141. Of these 78–82 were either from Britain or British colonies, 36–37 were from France or French colonies, 9 were Portuguese, 7 were Dutch, 1 was an indigenous fishing vessel, and 5 were of unknown nationality. Captain Johnson's figure of 400 for the total number of prizes taken by Roberts presumably includes the shallops taken at Newfoundland.

Date	Ship	Captain	Location

1719

West Africa

25 July	Dutch ship	?	off Princes Island
27 July	*Experiment*, of London	Grant	off Cape Lopez

South America

Oct.	small indigenous fishing boat	–	off Bahia, Brazil
Oct.	small Portuguese ship	?	off Pernambuco, Brazil
Oct.	*Sagrada Familia*, Portugal	?	off Pernambuco, Brazil
19 Nov.	*Princess* sloop, of Rhode Island	Cane	off Cayenne, Fr. Guyana

(Roberts replaced as captain by Anstis)

c. Dec.	fly boat (Dutch?)	?	Surinam

West Indies

25 Dec.	*Essex* schooner, of Salem, New England	Putnam	off Barbados

1720

10 Jan.	*Phillipa* sloop, of Barbados	Graves	Tobago
12 Feb.	*Benjamin*, of Liverpool	Hayes	off Barbados
c. 13 Feb.	*Joseph* sloop	Jelfs	off Barbados
c. 20 Feb.	sloop, from Virginia	?	off Windward Isles
c. 22 Feb.	French pink	Grant	off Windward Isles

(Roberts re-instated as captain)

Newfoundland

June	2 fishing boats	–	Ferryland
June	brigantine, of Teignmouth, Devon	?	off Western Newfoundland
June	pink, from St Johns, Newfoundland	Lucas	off Western Newfoundland
June	fishing boat from Bristol	Thomas	off Western Newfoundland
June	*Expectation*, of Topsham, Devon	?	off Western Newfoundland
June	2–3 other fishing boats	–	off Western Newfoundland
21 June	galley from Bristol	?	Trepassey
21 June	*Bideford Merchant*, British	Babidge	Trepassey

21 June	*Sudbury* sloop (Devon?)	Thomas	Trepassey
21 June	19 large British fishing boats	—	Trepassey
21 June	150–250 fishing shallops	—	Trepassey
July	5–6 large French fishing boats	—	Grand Banks
July	*Willing Mind*, of Poole, Dorset	?	south-east of Grand Banks
13 July	*Samuel*, of London	Cary	south-east of Grand Banks
14 July	snow from Bristol	Bowles	south-east of Grand Banks
c. 15 July	? (bound for New England, from Ireland)	Marston	south-east of Grand Banks
16 July	*Richard* pink, of Bideford, Devon	Whitfield	south-east of Grand Banks
c. 16 July	*Little York*, of Virginia	Phillips	south-east of Grand Banks
17 July	*Phoenix* snow, of Bristol	Richards	south-east of Grand Banks
17 July	*Essex* brigantine, of Salem, New England	Peate	south-east of Grand Banks
18 July	*Love*, of Lancaster	?	south-east of Grand Banks
July	*Blessing*, of Lymington, Hants	?	south-east of Grand Banks
Atlantic			
July	small Portuguese ship	?	mid-Atlantic
July–Aug.	French ship?	?	off Cape Verde Islands
West Indies			
4 Sep.	*Relief* sloop, Bermuda	Dunne	Carriacou
19 Sep.	French sloop	?	off Dominica
20 Sep.	snow (from Rhode Island?)	Cane	off Dominica
27 Sep.	*Mary and Martha*, of Bristol	Wilcox	St Christophers
27 Sep.	?	Hingston	St Christophers
27 Sep.	*Mary*, of Boston	Fowle	St Christophers
Oct.	*Greyhound* sloop, of St Christophers	?	?
c. Oct.	*Happy Return* sloop	Taylor	?
Oct.	*Success* sloop, British	Fensilon	north of Leeward Isles
Oct.	French ship, from Martinique	?	north of Leeward Isles
30 Oct.	*Thomas* brigantine, of Newton Abbot, Devon	Long	off Bermuda

1721

13 Jan.	brigantine, of Rhode Island	Norton	St Lucia
13 Jan.	*Fisher* sloop, of Barbados	Simes	St Lucia
14 Jan.	*St Anthony* sloop, of Bordeaux	Royée	St Lucia
c. 15 Jan.	*Poly* sloop, of Bordeaux	?	St Lucia
c. 15 Jan.	*Mary* sloop, French	?	St Lucia
c. 15 Jan.	French sloop	?	St Lucia
c. 18 Jan.	15 French sloops	–	Dominica
c. 18 Jan.	'several' English vessels	–	Dominica
18 Jan.	*Puerto del Principe*, of Flushing, Holland	Gibson	Dominica
c. 21 Jan	French fly-boat	?	Guadeloupe
c. 21 Jan	sloop	?	Guadeloupe
c. Mar.	*Mayflower* sloop, British	?	?
26 Mar.	*Lloyd* galley, of London	Hingston	off Guadeloupe
9 Apr.	*Jeremiah and Anne*, of London	Turner	off Bermuda

Atlantic

17 Apr.	*Prince Eugene*, Dutch	Meake	mid-Atlantic
c. May	*Christopher* snow	Hardwick	mid-Atlantic
c. May	sloop	?	St Nicholas, Cape Verde Islands
c. May	*Norman* galley, British	Norman	Cape Verde Islands

West Africa

c. May	*Count de Toulouze*, French cruiser	?	off River Senegal
c. May	French cruiser	?	off River Senegal
Aug.	*Martha* snow, of Liverpool	Lady	off Cape Mount
c. 6 Aug.	*Robinson*, of Liverpool	Canning	off Cape Mesurado
c. 6 Aug.	*Stanwich* galley, of Liverpool	Tarlton	off River Senegal
8 Aug.	*Onslow*, British	Gee	River Sestos
Aug.	*Empress* galley, of La Rochelle, France	Corril	Windward or Gold Coast
Aug.	*Africa*, Dutch	?	Windward or Gold Coast
Aug.–Sep.	*Semm* galley, Dutch	?	off Axim
c. 10 Sep.	Portuguese sloop	De Torres	Gold Coast
Sep.–Oct.	*Joceline* brigantine, British	Loan	Old Calabar

1 Oct.	*Hannibal* brigantine, British	Ousley	Old Calabar
Oct.	*Mercy* galley, of Bristol	Harrison	Old Calabar
c. 5 Oct.	*Cornwall*, of Bristol	Rowles	Old Calabar
14 Dec.	*Gertruycht*, of Rotterdam	Keft	off River Gabon

1722

1 Jan.	*Tarlton*, of Liverpool	Tarlton	off Cape Lahou
2 Jan.	*Elizabeth*, of London	Sharp	off Jacques a Jacques
5 Jan.	*Diligence*, British	Thomas	off Assinie
6 Jan.	*King Solomon*, British	Traherne	off Cape Apollonia
c. 6 Jan.	*Flushingham*, Dutch	De Haen	off Axim
early Jan	3 ships	–	Windward and Gold Coasts
11–13 Jan.	*Porcupine*, British	Fletcher	Whydah
11–13 Jan.	*Carlton*, British	Alwright	Whydah
11–13 Jan.	British ship	?	Whydah
11–13 Jan.	*St Agnes*, French	?	Whydah
11–13 Jan.	2 French ships	–	Whydah
11–13 Jan.	5 Portuguese ships	–	Whydah
13 Jan.	*Whydah* sloop, British	Stokes	off Whydah
9 Feb.	*Neptune*, British	Hill	Cape Lopez

CREW

A total of 147 men stood trial at Cape Coast Castle. We have the ages of 56. They ranged from 17 to 45 and the average was 28. Of the 73 men for whom we have a clearly identifiable place of origin, 30 came from the West Country, 12 from London, 8 from elsewhere in England, 9 from Scotland, 5 from Wales, 4 from Holland, 1 from Greece, 1 from Antigua, 1 from Jersey, 1 from the Isle of Man, and — despite the ban imposed in the wake of Kennedy's desertion — 1 from Ireland.

NAME	AGE	'HABITATION'	WHEN CAPTURED
Hanged in chains (18)			
Valentine Ashplant	32	Minories, London	pirate with Davis
Thomas Sutton	23	Berwick, Scotland	pirate with Davis
David Simpson (Little David)	36	North Berwick, Scotland	pirate with Davis
Christopher Moody	28	?	pirate with Davis
Richard Hardy	25	Wales	pirate with Davis
Agge Jacobson	30	Holland	Surinam, c. Dec. 1719
James Philips	35	Antigua	Dominica, c Apr. 1720
William Fernon	22	Somerset	*Sudbury*, June 1720
John Philips	28	Alloway, Scotland	*Richard*, July 1720
John Walden (Miss Nanny)	24	Somerset	*Blessing*, July 1720
James Skrym	44	Wales	*Greyhound*, Oct. 1720
John Coleman	24	Wales	Hispaniola, Mar. 1721
William Magness	35	Minehead, Somerset	*Mayflower*, c. Mar. 1721
William Davies	23	Wales	Sierra Leone, July 1721
William Watts	23	Ireland	Sierra Leone, July 1721
Edward Watts	22	Dunmore (Ireland?)	*Onslow*, Aug. 1721
Israel Hynde	30	Aberdeen	*Mercy*, Oct. 1721
Peter Scudamore	35	Bristol	*Cornwall*, Oct. 1721

Hanged (34)

Michael Mare	41	Ghent, Holland	pirate with Davis*
Marcus Johnson	21	Smyrna, Greece	pirate with Davis
Joseph Mansfield	30	Bristol	Dominica, c. Apr. 1720
Robert Birdson	30	Other St Mary's, Devon	Dominica, c. Apr. 1720
Joseph Nossiter	26	Sudbury, Devon	*Expectation*, June 1720
William Williams (1)	40	near Plymouth	*Sudbury*, June 1720
William Williams (2)	c. 27	near Falmouth	*Sudbury*, June 1720
John Parker	22	Winfreth, Dorset	*Willing Mind*, July 1720
William Mackintosh	21	Canterbury	*Richard*, July 1720
Richard Harris	45	Cornwall	*Phoenix*, July 1720
William Main	28	?	*Essex*, July 1720
John Jaynson	22	Lancaster	*Love*, July 1720
George Smith	25	Wales	*Mary and Martha*, Sep. 1720
Robert Crow	44	Isle of Man	*Happy Return*, c. Oct. 1720
James Clement	20	Jersey	*Success*, Oct. 1720
Daniel Harding	26	Croomsbury, Somerset	*Puerto del Principe*, Jan. 1721
Joseph More	19	Mere, Wiltshire	*Mayflower*, c. Mar. 1721
Robert Johnson	32	?	*Jeremiah and Anne*, Apr. 1721
Benjamin Jeffreys	21	Bristol	*Norman*, May 1721
Robert Hays	20	Liverpool	*Stanwich*, Aug. 1721
Philip Bill	27	St Thomas's	*Onslow*, Aug. 1721
Abraham Harper	23	Bristol	*Onslow*, Aug. 1721
William Wood	27	York	*Onslow*, Aug. 1721
William Petty	30	Deptford, London	*Onslow*, Aug. 1721
John Stephenson	40	Whitby	*Onslow*, Aug. 1721
Peter Lesley	21	Aberdeen	*Onslow*, Aug. 1721
John Jessup (1)	20	Plymouth	*Onslow*, Aug. 1721
Charles Bunce	26	Exeter	*Semm*, Aug.–Sep. 1721
Robert Armstrong	34	?	*Semm*, Aug.–Sep. 1721
Robert Harris	31	Yarmouth	*Joceline*, Sep.–Oct. 1721
Cuthbert Goss	21	Topsham, Devon	*Mercy*, Oct. 1721
Thomas Giles	26	Minehead, Somerset	*Mercy*, Oct. 1721
Peter Divine	42	Stepney, London	*King Solomon*, Jan. 1722
William Phillips	29	Lower Shadwell, London	*King Solomon*, Jan. 1722

*Deserted at Devil's Islands. Re-joined at Martinique, Jan. 1721

Guilty, but sentence commuted to labour in mines (20)

John Dennis	?	Bideford, Devon	pirate with Davis
John Jessup (2)	?	?	pirate with Davis*
Roger Scot	?	?	*Sudbury*, June 1720
Thomas How	?	Barnstaple, Devon	Trepassey, June 1720
Hugh Harris	?	Corfe Castle, Dorset	*Willing Mind*, July 1720
James Greenham	?	Marshfield, Glos	*Little York*, July 1720
Thomas Owen	?	Bristol	*Little York*, July 1720
William Taylor	?	Bristol	*Little York*, July 1720
David Littlejohn	?	Bristol	*Phoenix*, July 1720
William Shuren	?	Wapping, London	*Jeremiah and Anne*, Apr. 1721
John Mitchel	?	Shadwell, London	*Norman*, c. May 1721
Joshua Lee	?	Liverpool	*Martha*, Aug. 1721
Robert Hartley (1)	?	Liverpool	*Stanwich*, Aug. 1721
James Cromby	?	Wapping, London	*Onslow*, Aug. 1721
John Horn	?	St James's, London	*Onslow*, Aug. 1721
John Griffin	?	Blackwall, Middx	*Mercy*, Oct. 1721
David Rice	?	Bristol	*Cornwall*, Oct. 1721
John King	?	Shadwell, London	*King Solomon*, Jan. 1722
Samuel Fletcher	?	East Smithfield, London	*King Solomon*, Jan. 1722
John Lane	?	Lambert St, London	*King Solomon*, Jan. 1722

Guilty, but granted right to plead for pardon (2)

Died aboard Weymouth *before reaching England*

George Wilson	?	?	*Stanwich*, Aug. 1721†

Pardoned

Thomas Oughterlaney	?	Scotland	*Cornwall*, Oct. 1721

Referred to Marshalsea for further examination (17)

Died aboard Weymouth *before reaching England*

James Harris	c. 28	Bideford, Devon	*Richard*, July 1720
John Du Frock	?	?	*Lloyd*, Mar. 1721
Isaac Russell	?	?	*Lloyd*, Mar. 1721
John Wilden	?	?	*Martha*, Aug. 1721
James Barrow	?	?	*Martha*, Aug. 1721

*Left pirates after 2 days. Captured for 2nd time aboard *Elizabeth*, Jan. 1722.

†Deserted at Cape Lopez at end of 1721. Made his way to Princes Island, where he was seized by the authorities and handed to Captain Ogle for trial

James Crane	?	?	Robinson, Aug. 1721
John Rimer	?	?	Stanwich, Aug. 1721
Robert Bevan	?	?	Cornwall, Oct. 1721
Andrew Rance	?	Scotland	Semm, Aug.–Sep. 1721
James Couzens	?	?	Porcupine, Jan. 1722

Pardoned

Christopher Long	?	?	Newfoundland, June–July 1720
Hercules Hankins	?	?	Success, Oct. 1720
William Mead	?	?	Jeremiah and Anne, Apr. 1721
Thomas Withstandyenot	?	?	Norman, c. May 1721
Robert Fletcher	?	?	Stanwich, Aug. 1721
Henry Graves	?	?	Stanwich, Aug. 1721
George Ogle	?	?	Onslow, Aug. 1721

Acquitted (56)

Henry Glasby	?	Scotland	Samuel, July 1720
Hugh Menzies	?	Scotland	Samuel, July 1720
Thomas Wills	c. 27	Bideford, Devon	Richard, July 1720
John Francia	17	?	Cape Verde Islands, Aug. 1720
William Champnies	?	?	Lloyd, Mar. 1721
George Danson	?	?	Lloyd, Mar. 1721
Robert Lillburn	?	?	Jeremiah and Anne, Apr. 1721
William Darling	?	?	Jeremiah and Anne, Apr. 1721
Peter La Fever	?	?	Jeremiah and Anne, Apr. 1721
Thomas Diggles	?	?	Christopher, c. May 1721
John Watson	?	?	Martha, Aug. 1721
Roger Gorsuch	?	?	Martha, Aug. 1721
Robert Hartley (2)	?	?	Robinson, Aug. 1721
Benjamin Parr	?	?	Robinson, Aug. 1721
George Smithson	?	?	Stanwich, Aug. 1721
Roger Pye	?	?	Stanwich, Aug. 1721
Thomas Stretton	c. 18	?	Onslow, Aug. 1721
Michael Lemmon	?	?	Onslow, Aug. 1721
Thomas Watkins	?	?	Onslow, Aug. 1721
Thomas Garrat	30+	?	Onslow, Aug. 1721
William Child	?	?	Mercy, Oct. 1721
James White	?	?	Cornwall, Oct. 1721
Nicholas Brattle	?	?	Cornwall, Oct. 1721
Christopher Granger	?	?	Cornwall, Oct. 1721

James Morris	?	?	*Cornwall*, Oct. 1721
Thomas Davies	?	?	*Cornwall*, Oct. 1721
Thomas Lever	?	?	*Cornwall*, Oct. 1721
William Church	?	?	*Gertruycht*, Dec. 1721
Edward Tarlton	?	Liverpool	*Tarlton*, Jan. 1722
John Arnott	?	?	*Tarlton*, Jan. 1722
Isiah Robinson	?	?	*Tarlton*, Jan. 1722
John Davies	?	?	*Tarlton*, Jan. 1722
Thomas Clephen	?	?	*Tarlton*, Jan. 1722
Thomas Howard	?	?	*Tarlton*, Jan. 1722
William Smith	?	?	*Elizabeth*, Jan. 1722
Edward Thornden	?	?	*Elizabeth*, Jan. 1722
William May	?	?	*Elizabeth*, Jan. 1722
Adam Comrie	?	?	*Elizabeth*, Jan. 1722
Stephen Thomas	?	?	*Diligence*, Jan. 1722
Hugh Ridley	30+	?	*Diligence*, Jan. 1722
John Stodgill	?	?	*King Solomon*, Jan. 1722
Jacob Johnson	?	Holland	*King Solomon*, Jan. 1722
John Johnson	?	?	*King Solomon*, Jan. 1722
William Graves	?	?	*King Solomon*, Jan. 1722
Philip Haak	?	Holland	*Flushingham*, Jan. 1722
William Guinneys	?	?	*Porcupine*, Jan. 1722
Richard Scott	?	?	*Porcupine*, Jan. 1722
Richard Wood	?	?	*Porcupine*, Jan. 1722
Edward Evans	?	?	*Porcupine*, Jan. 1722
William Davison	?	?	*Porcupine*, Jan. 1722
Samuel Morwell	?	?	*Porcupine*, Jan. 1722
Thomas Roberts	?	?	*Carlton*, Jan. 1722
John Richards	?	?	*Carlton*, Jan. 1722
John Cane	?	?	*Carlton*, Jan. 1722
Henry Dawson	?	?	*Whydah*, Jan. 1722
William Glass	?	?	*Whydah*, Jan. 1722

APPENDIX 2
THOMAS ANSTIS'S ARTICLES

Thomas Anstis deserted Roberts in the brigantine Good Fortune *in April 1721. His crew immediately agreed a new set of articles.*

ARTICLE I – That the Captain shall have one full share as the rest of the Company the Master Gunner, Carpenter and Boatswain the same.

ARTICLE II – If any man should disobey any lawful command of the commanding officers, shall suffer punishment the company and captain shall think fit.

ARTICLE III – If any person or persons should go on board of any prize and should break open any chest without the knowledge of the quartermaster, shall suffer what punishment the company and captain shall think fit.

ARTICLE IV – If any person or persons shall be found guilty of thievery from one another to the value of one piece of eight, shall be marooned on an island with one bottle of powder, one bottle of water and shott equivalent.

ARTICLE V – If any person or person should be found negligent in keeping their arms clean and fitting for an engagement, shall lose his share or shares.

ARTICLE VI – If any person or persons should be found to snap their arms [pull the trigger of their musket or pistol] on cleaning in the hold, shall suffer Moses Law, that is forty [lashes] lacking one.

ARTICLE VII – If any person or persons should be found back-ward in the time of an engagement, should be marooned.

ARTICLE VIII – If any person or persons shall be found to game on board this privateer of the value of one Rial plate [a small silver coin, worth around sixpence] shall suffer Moses law.

ARTICLE IX – If any person or persons shall go on board of a prize and meet with any Gentlewoman or Lady of Honour and should force them against their will to lye with them, shall suffer death.

ARTICLE X – If any person or persons should loose a leg or a limb or a joint, shall for a limb have eight hundred pieces of eight and for one joint 200 ditto.

ARTICLE XI – If any time we shall come in company with any other marooner [pirate] [he that] shall offer to sign their articles without the consent of the company shall be marooned. [Any] runaway shall receive the same.

ARTICLE XII – But if at any time we shall hear from England and have an account of an act of grace [pardon] they that are minded to receive it shall go with their money and goods and the rest have the privateer [i.e. keep the ship].

SELECTED SOURCES

PRIMARY SOURCES

BRITISH LIBRARY

The Lives of the Most Remarkable Criminals, London, 1735

A New General Collection of Voyages, vols 1 and 3, Thomas Astley, London 1745–7

A Select and Impartial Account of the Lives, Behaviour and Dying Words of the Most Remarkable Convicts, vol. 1, Charles March, London, 1745

Anonymous (manuscript), *Voyage to Guinea, Bay of Campeachy, Cuba, Barbados & co. 1714–23*

Atkins, John, *The Navy Surgeon,* C. Ward and R. Chandler, London, 1734

——, *A Voyage to Guinea, Brazil and the West Indies in His Majesty's Ships,* C. Ward and R. Chandler, London, 1735

Bosman, Willem. *A New and Accurate Description of the Coast of Guinea,* J. Knapton, London, 1704

Boyer, Abel, *The Political State of Great Britain,* vols 21 and 28, T. Cooper, London, 1733

Calendar of State Papers, Colonial Series, America and West Indies, 1716–1725

Charlevoix, Pierre Francois Xavier, *Histoire de L'Isle Espagnole,* Francois Barois, 1731

Churchill (ed.), *Collection of Voyages and Travels,* vols 5–6, Henry Lintot and John Osborn, London, 1744–6

Downing, Clement, *A Compendious History of the Indian Wars*, London, 1737

Executive Journals of the Council of Colonial Virginia, Richmond, Virginia, 1925

Exquemelin, Alexander, *The Buccaneers of America*, William Crooke, London, 1684

Falconbridge, Alexander, *An Account of the Slave Trade on the Coast of Africa*, James Phillips, London, 1788

Fenton, Richard, *A Historical Tour Through Pembrokeshire*, Longman, London, 1811

Frezier, Amadée Francois, *A Voyage to the South Sea, and Along the Coasts of Chile and Peru in 1712, 1713 and 1714*, London, 1717

Houston, James, *Some New and Accurate Observations of the Coast of Guinea*, London, 1725

Johnson, Charles, *A General History of the Robberies and Murders of the Most Notorious Pirates*, Rivington, London, 1724

Labat, Jean Baptiste, *The Memoirs of Pere Labat, 1693–1705*, Constable & Co., London, 1931

Owen, George. *Description of Pembrokeshire*, Cymmrodorion Society, London, 1892

Smith, William, *A New Voyage to Guinea*, J. Nourse, London, 1744

Snelgrave, William, *A New Account of Some Parts of Guinea and the Slave Trade*, Knapton, London, 1734

Spotswood, Alexander. *The Official Letters of Alexander Spotswood*, vol. 2, Virginia Historical and Philosophical Society, 1882

du Tertre, Jean Baptiste, *Histoire Generale des Antilles Habites par Les Français*, Paris, 1667

Voyage des Chevaliers des Marchais en Guinee etc., Saugrain, Paris, 1730

NEWSPAPERS

Applebee's Original Weekly Journal, The Boston Gazette, The Boston Newsletter, The Post Boy, The Weekly Journal or British Gazetteer, The Weekly Journal or Saturday Post

THE NATIONAL ARCHIVES

Admiralty Series (ADM): 1/1472/11, 1/1597/1, 1/1694/9, 1/1880/3, 1/2242/5, 1/2242/6, 1/2282/2, 1/2378, 1/2452, 1/2649, 1/2650/10, 1/4102-4, 2/50, 8/14+15, 51/954/6+7, 51/1057/5, 51/4394/2, 52/296, 52/316

Chancellery Series (C): 113/165, 113/274+5

Colonial Office Series (CO): 5/1319, 28/17, 31/15, 31/16, 37/10, 137/14, 152/13+14, 194/6, 323/8, 324/34, 388/25

High Court of the Admiralty Series (HCA): 1/17+18, 1/32 1/54+55, 1/99

State Papers Series (SP): 42/17, 89/28

Treasury Series (T): 52/32, 70/ 4, 70/7, 70/27, 70/922, 70/1225

NATIONAL LIBRARY OF WALES

SP/CPD/5, SD/1744/44

NATIONAL ARCHIVES OF SCOTLAND

AC 16/1

NATIONAL MARITIME MUSEUM

ADM/L/S/563+4, 341.362.1:094

SECONDARY SOURCES

Bolster, W. Jeffery, *Black Jacks: African American Seamen in the Age of Sail*, Harvard University Press, London, 1997

Boxer, C.R., *The Golden Age of Brazil, 1695–1750*, Carcanet, Manchester, 1995

Burg, B.R., *Sodomy and the Pirate Tradition*, New York University Press, New York, 1984

Carr Laughton, L.G., 'Shantying and Shanties', in *Mariner's Mirror*, vol. 9, 1923

Clifford, Barry, *The Black Ship: The Quest to Recover an English Pirate Ship and Its Lost Treasure*, Headline, London, 1999

Cordingly, David, *Life Among the Pirates: The Romance and the Reality*, Little Brown, London, 1995

Craton, Michael, *A History of the Bahamas*, 2nd edn, Collins, London, 1968

Dictionary of National Biography, vols 2 and 42, 1885

Dunn, Richard S., *Sugar and Slaves: The Rise of the Planter Class in the English West Indies*, University of North Carolina Press, London, 1972

Earle, Peter, *Sailors; English Merchant Seamen 1650–1775*, Methuen, London, 1998

——, *The Pirate Wars*, Methuen, London, 2003

Edwards, Rev. Richard, *Hanes Llangloffan (The History of Llangloffan)*, W.H. John and Son, Solva, Pembrokeshire, 1932

Eltis, David, 'Volume and Structure of the Slave Trade', in *William and Mary Quarterly*, vol. 58, No. 1, January 2001

Eltis, D., S.D. Behrendt, D. Richardson, and H.S. Klein, *The Transatlantic Slave Trade*, database on CD-Rom

Engerman, Stanley L. and Eugene D. Genovese (eds), *Race and Slavery in the Western Hemisphere: Quantitative Studies*, Princeton University Press, Princeton, 1974

Fuller, Basil and Alexander Ronald Leslie-Melville, *Pirate Harbours and Their Secrets*, Stanley Paul & Co., London, 1935

Gilkerson, William, *Boarders Away*, vols I & II, A. Mowbray Inc., Providence, RI, 1991

Hornsby, Stephen, *British Atlantic, American Frontier*, University of New Hampshire, Hanover, NH, 2004

Hughes, B.H.J., *More Names in the History of Pembrokeshire, Hearth Tax, 1670*, B.H.J. Hughes, Pennar, 1999

Innis, Harold A., *The Cod Fisheries*, Yale University Press, New Haven, 1940

Jameson, John Franklin, *Privateering and Piracy in the Colonial Period: Illustrated Documents*, Macmillan, New York, 1923

Kelly, James, *'That Damn'd Thing Called Honour': Duelling in Ireland, 1570–1860*, Cork University Press, Cork, 1995

Lang, James, *Portuguese Brazil: The King's Plantation*, Academic Press, London, 1979

Lucie-Smith, Edward, *Outcasts of the Sea: Pirates and Piracy*, Paddington Press, London, 1978

Mannix, Daniel Pratt, *Black Cargoes: A History of the Atlantic Slave Trade, 1518–1865*, Longmans, London, 1963

May, Commander W.E., 'The Mutiny of the Chesterfield', in *Mariner's Mirror*, vol. 47, 1961

Preston, Diana and Michael, *A Pirate of Exquisite Mind: The Life of William Dampier: Explorer, Naturalist and Buccaneer*, Corgi, London, 2004

Rediker, Marcus, *Between The Devil and the Deep Blue Sea: Merchant Seamen, Pirates and the Anglo-American Maritime World, 1700–1750*, Cambridge University Press, Cambridge, 1987

——, *Villains of All Nations,* Verso, London, 2004

Roberts, Walter Adolphe, *The French in the West Indies*, Bobbs-Merrill Co, New York, 1942

Sheridan, Richard, *Sugar and Slavery: An Economic History of the British West Indies*, University Microfilms, Ann Arbor, 1986

Thomas, Hugh, *The Slave Trade*, Picador, London, 1997

Williams, Eric, *From Columbus to Castro: The History of the Caribbean, 1492–1969*, Andre Deutsch, London, 1970

INDEX